SEX OFFENDER REGISTRATION AND COMMUNITY NOTIFICATION LAWS: AN EMPIRICAL EVALUATION

Despite being in existence for over a quarter of a century, costing multiple millions of dollars, and affecting the lives of hundreds of thousands of individuals, sex offender registration and notification (SORN) laws have yet to be subject to a book-length assessment of their empirical dimensions, examining their premises, coverage, and impact on public safety. This volume, edited by Professors Wayne A. Logan and J.J. Prescott, assembles the leading researchers in the field to provide an in-depth look at what have come to be known as "Megan's Laws," offering a social science-based analysis of one of the most important and controversial criminal justice system initiatives undertaken in modern times.

Wayne A. Logan is Steven M. Goldstein Professor of Law, Florida State University. He is the author of *Knowledge as Power: Criminal Registration and Community Notification Laws in America* (2009), cited by the US Supreme Court in *United States v. Kebodeaux* (2013), and has published several dozen book chapters and articles, with work appearing in publications such as the *Georgetown Law Journal*, the *Michigan Law Review*, and the *Pennsylvania Law Review*. Logan is an elected member of the American Law Institute and a past chair of the Criminal Justice Section of the Association of American Law Schools.

J.J. Prescott is Henry King Ransom Professor of Law, University of Michigan. He is the author of peer-reviewed economics and legal articles on the effects of SORN laws, and his work has been cited in several important legal decisions, including *Does v. Snyder* (6th Cir. 2016). Prescott publishes broadly on criminal justice issues, employment law, and civil litigation, often using empirical tools and data to inform controversial policy debates. Prescott is also Editor-in-Chief of the *American Law and Economics Review*, and he codirects the Empirical Legal Studies Center and the Program in Law and Economics at the University of Michigan.

Sex Offender Registration and Community Notification Laws

AN EMPIRICAL EVALUATION

Edited by

WAYNE A. LOGAN

Florida State University College of Law

J.J. PRESCOTT

University of Michigan Law School

CAMBRIDGE
UNIVERSITY PRESS

CAMBRIDGE
UNIVERSITY PRESS

University Printing House, Cambridge CB2 8BS, United Kingdom

One Liberty Plaza, 20th Floor, New York, NY 10006, USA

477 Williamstown Road, Port Melbourne, VIC 3207, Australia

314-321, 3rd Floor, Plot 3, Splendor Forum, Jasola District Centre, New Delhi - 110025, India

103 Penang Road, #05-06/07, Visioncrest Commercial, Singapore 238467

Cambridge University Press is part of the University of Cambridge.

It furthers the University's mission by disseminating knowledge in the pursuit of
education, learning and research at the highest international levels of excellence.

www.cambridge.org
Information on this title: www.cambridge.org/9781108411356
DOI: 10.1017/9781108328425

© Cambridge University Press 2021

First published 2021
First paperback edition 2022

A catalogue record for this publication is available from the British Library

Library of Congress Cataloging in Publication data
NAMES: Logan, Wayne A., 1960- author. | Prescott, J.J., author.
TITLE: Sex offender registration and community notification laws : an empirical evaluation /
edited by Professor Wayne A. Logan, Florida State University School of Law; J.J. Prescott,
University of Michigan Law School.
DESCRIPTION: Cambridge, United Kingdom ; New York, NY : Cambridge University Press,
2021. | Includes bibliographical references and index.
IDENTIFIERS: LCCN 2020047022 (print) | LCCN 2020047023 (ebook) | ISBN 9781108420020
(hardback) | ISBN 9781108328425 (epub)
SUBJECTS: LCSH: Sex offenders – United States – Registers. | Sex offenders – Legal status,
laws, etc. – United States. | Publicity (Law) – United States. | Recording and registration –
United States.
CLASSIFICATION: LCC KF9751 .L647 2021 (print) | LCC KF9751 (ebook) | DDC 345.73/0253–dc23
LC record available at https://lccn.loc.gov/2020047022
LC ebook record available at https://lccn.loc.gov/2020047023

ISBN 978-1-108-42002-0 Hardback
ISBN 978-1-108-41135-6 Paperback

Contents

Contributors

Alissa R. Ackerman
California State University-Fullerton
Division of Politics, Administration, and Justice
Fullerton, CA

Amanda Agan
Rutgers University
Department of Economics
New Brunswick, NJ

Andrew J. Harris
University of Massachusetts-Lowell
School of Criminology and Justice Studies
Lowell, MA

Elizabeth J. Letourneau
Johns Hopkins University
Bloomberg School of Public Health
Baltimore, MD

Jill S. Levenson
Barry University
Ellen Whiteside McDonnell School of Social Work
Miami Shores, FL

Wayne A. Logan
Florida State University
College of Law
Tallahassee, FL

J.J. Prescott
University of Michigan
Law School and Department of Economics
Ann Arbor, MI

Lisa L. Sample
University of Nebraska–Omaha
School of Criminology and Criminal Justice
Omaha, NE

Kelly Socia
University of Massachusetts-Lowell
School of Criminology and Justice Studies
Lowell, MA

Richard Tewksbury
University of Louisville (Retired)
Department of Criminal Justice
Louisville, KY

Scott M. Walfield
East Carolina University
Department of Criminal Justice
Greenville, NC

Kristen M. Zgoba
Florida International University
Department of Criminology and Criminal Justice
Miami, FL

Preface

In the early 1990s, a handful of US jurisdictions embarked on what would soon become an unprecedented nationwide experiment in social control. The idea was straightforward: require convicted sex offenders to provide identifying information to law enforcement, so that they could be monitored and more readily apprehended if they committed a sexual offense in their community. Imposing this "registration" requirement might, moreover, instill in targeted individuals the sense that they were being monitored, reducing the likelihood that they would re-offend.

The idea of requiring individuals convicted of crimes to apprise police of their whereabouts was not in itself an innovation, as several states and many localities had done so in various ways since the early 1930s. In the 1990s, however, registration was combined with a new strategy: "community notification," which shared identifying information of registrants with the public at large. No longer was registry information monopolized by police. It was now made available to individual community members, in the name of allowing them to both assist police in monitoring registrants and take safety measures to guard themselves or their family members against sexual victimization.

Initially, registrant information was provided to the public by police at community meetings, by flyers and newspaper postings, by making records available for inspection at police stations, and the like. Early on, police focused on a select group of registrants, those thought to pose a particularly serious risk of sexual recidivism. Over time, however, the number and intensity of notification methods grew, including use of the internet to disseminate the information via websites. At the same time, the scope of registration laws grew, covering new offenses, and notification evolved in many places to target all registrants, not a select few, often for their lifetimes.

Today, over twenty-five years after their modest origin, sex offender registration and notification (SORN) laws are in effect in all fifty states, the District of Columbia, Indian tribes, and US territories. SORN directly affects the lives of hundreds of thousands of registrants (closing in on, if not past, one million as of this writing), and indirectly impacts untold millions of individuals with whom they associate, especially family members. Meanwhile, governments – at the federal, state, and local level – have spent and continue to spend many millions of dollars to create and sustain the vast legal and technological apparatus SORN requires, often contracting out work to private companies (which now have a business stake in the status quo).

SORN laws represent a remarkable political episode in our nation's history. Very often enacted in rapid-fire fashion by enormous legislative majorities, the laws have mushroomed over time, with political leaders fearful of being labeled "soft" on crime or "pro-sex offender," or being condemned for opposing or limiting a law named after a particular child victim (e.g., "Megan's Law," "Zachary's Law"). Rounding out the political dynamic, the federal government since 1994 has required that jurisdictions adopt SORN laws and amend them in accord with increasingly demanding federal policy preferences, threatening the loss of criminal justice funds if they do not comply. Moreover, SORN has figured in other social control measures targeting sex offenders, such as state and local laws prohibiting registrants from living near (e.g., within 2,000 feet of) places where children might congregate, such as community centers or schools. Emblematic of its appeal and adaptability as a social control strategy, governments have now applied registration and notification to other subpopulations (e.g., convicted drug offenders, individuals convicted of animal abuse).

The foregoing history, while interesting and important in its own right, ignores an important part of the story: the assumptions that advocates and politicians have used – for decades – to support the enactment and growth of SORN laws. From the outset, SORN has been predicated on several key empirical beliefs: (1) that convicted sex offenders recidivate at alarmingly higher rates compared to other criminal subpopulations, justifying the need for SORN; (2) that communities need identifying and locational information on registered sex offenders because most child and adult sexual victimization is by strangers; and (3) that SORN laws "work" – that is, they reduce sexual offending and promote public safety.

Research has shown, however, that the first two empirical premises are incorrect: Sex offenders, as a group, do not recidivate at significantly higher rates than other offender populations (Hanson et al., 2018) and most sex offenses are committed by first-time offenders (Sandler et al., 2008) (who, by definition, are not registrants). Furthermore, the vast majority of sex offenses targeting adults and children alike are committed not by strangers but rather by individuals familiar to victims (Bureau of Justice Statistics, 2010). The third premise – that SORN "works" in achieving its public safety goals – has always been accepted as an article of faith by proponents. As several of the chapters here attest, however, a growing body of research casts doubt on whether SORN actually does promote public safety; worse yet, concern exists that the negative life impacts of SORN significantly hinder the challenging reentry prospects of an already reviled subpopulation.

Viewed in a broader context, the sustained willingness of law and policy makers to blithely assume the effectiveness of SORN, or to not care, is striking. One would be hard-pressed to identify a governmental policy having similar human and fiscal costs and consequences that has, for such a long time, rested on untested foundational empirical assumptions. Year after year since the early 1990s, SORN laws have eluded critical scrutiny in legislative chambers and governors' offices, not only enduring but flourishing in scope. And they have done so despite widely reported system failures, such as the discovery of California registrant Philip Garrido, who, while compliant with SORN, kidnapped and sexually abused a young woman for almost two decades (Farrell, 2009).

This volume seeks to remedy the basic knowledge deficit that for too long has marked SORN, assembling in one place the research and insights of the nation's leading SORN researchers.

The first chapters of the book provide important background on how SORN laws came about and their current nature and coverage. Chapter 1 provides a brief history of SORN laws, which, as noted earlier, have their origins in registration laws enacted in the 1930s, complemented in the early 1990s by the important innovation of community notification. Chapter 2 describes modern SORN laws in the United States, identifying their shared features and variations, especially vis-à-vis federal SORN requirements, recognizing as well the far less ambitious SORN-like laws adopted in a handful of other countries. Chapter 3 provides an in-depth examination and analysis of the populations on the nation's registries, painting a demographic picture (age, race, sex) of registries and the criminal histories of the individuals on registries, and discusses the research challenges regarding the collection of reliable data.

Focus then shifts to the measurable consequences of SORN laws. Chapter 4 examines the effects of SORN laws and their enforcement on the beliefs and behavior of law enforcement–critically important participants in SORN systems–as well as the fiscal consequences of SORN enforcement. Chapter 5 assesses the impact of SORN on the beliefs and behaviors of community members, the intended beneficiaries of notification in particular. Chapter 6 evaluates the many ancillary consequences of SORN, including its impact on the ability of registrants to secure and maintain work and housing, the negative reactions of community members (such as harassment), the spatial ghettoization of registrants, and the influence of SORN on sex offense reporting rates and the charging and judicial processing of sex offenders.

Chapter 7 sits at the center of the empirical policy debate on SORN; it explores existing research on the effects of SORN laws on registrant criminal behavior, especially with regard to the key policy question of whether SORN reduces sexual offending recidivism, as well as its potential for deterring first-time offenders. Chapter 8 focuses on research regarding the etiology of sexual offending and examines whether this knowledge base aligns with the assumptions underlying SORN, addressing as well whether SORN laws may, as some evidence suggests, contribute to sex offense recidivism. The chapter also includes recommendations for SORN policy and management practices based on what we know about offender risks, needs, and patterns. Chapter 9 addresses the controversial but quite common practice of subjecting juveniles to SORN, examining the impact of SORN on juveniles and surveying research on whether SORN actually reduces juvenile sexual offending.

The volume concludes with a call for evidence-based action with regard to SORN. With sex offender policy in particular, one often hears that a policy or practice is justified if "even one child is saved," regardless of broader public safety efficacy. Even less constructive, there is the view that, if nothing else, public shaming of convicted sex offenders is valuable in itself. Of late, however, there appears to be emerging a willingness to critically examine SORN and an openness to testing its basic suppositions and public safety impact.

For instance, courts, which typically have rejected constitutional challenges to SORN out of deference to legislative assumptions concerning the need for and efficacy of SORN, are now exhibiting a greater degree of critical scrutiny (see, e.g., *Does #1–5 v. Snyder*, 2016; *In re* J. B., 2014). Also, governmental bodies have recently urged changes to SORN (see, e.g., Connecticut Sentencing Commission, 2017; Washington State Sex Offender Policy Board, 2016), as have entities such as the Council of State Governments (2010) and the highly respected American Law Institute (ALI, 2019). The State of California, faced with criticism of its lifetime, one-size-fits-all SORN system (Calif. Sex Offender Mgmt. Bd., 2014), recently adopted a slate of major reforms, shifting from a one-tiered, purely offense-based scheme, requiring lifetime registration, to a three-tiered scheme of lesser durations based in part on individual risk assessments (Calif. Dept. of Justice, 2020).

Together, these developments, and others still likely to come, highlight a modest yet important shift, providing a potential window of opportunity for evidence-based reevaluation of SORN laws. Given the popularity of SORN among political leaders and the public alike, it is unlikely that these laws will disappear in their entirety anytime soon. We hope, however, that the insights provided in this volume, a single-source compilation of the latest empirical understandings of SORN, will advance the cause of evidence-based policy and guide the way toward adoption of SORN laws and policies that best promote public safety.

REFERENCES

American Law Institute, *Model Penal Code: Sexual Assault and Related Offenses* § 213.11A et seq. (Prelim. Draft No. 11, October 16, 2020), https://www.ali.org/smedia/filer_private/31/38/3138e339-a68f-4bac-9616-5e308904c827/mpc_sa_pd_11_-_online.pdf

Bureau of Justice Statistics, National Crime Victimization Survey 2010, Washington, www.bjs.gov/content/pub/pdf/cv10.pdf

Calif. Dept. of Justice, *Frequently Asked Questions-California Tiered Sex Offender Registration* (Last Updated January 1, 2020), https://oag.ca.gov/sites/all/files/agweb/pdfs/csor/registrant-faqs.pdf

Calif. Sex Offender Mgmt. Bd., *A Better Path to Community Safety: Sex Offender Registration in California* 5 (2014), www.casomb.org/docs/Tiering%20Background%20Paper%20FINAL%20FINAL%204-2-14.pdf

Connecticut Sentencing Commission, *A Study of the Sex Offender Sentencing, Registration, and Management System* (December 2017), http://ctsentencingcommission.org/wp-content/uploads/2018/05/Sex_Offender_Report_December_2017.pdf

Council of State Governments, *Sex Offender Management Policy in the States: Strengthening Policy & Practice, Final Report* 6 (2010), www.csg.org/policy/documents/SOMFinalReport-FINAL.pdf

Does #1–5 v. Snyder, 834 F.3d 696, 706 (6th Cir. 2016), *cert denied*, 138 S. Ct. 55 (2017)

Farrell, M. B. (November 6, 2009), *Report: GPS Parole Monitoring of Phillip Garrido Failed*, Christian Science Monitor, www.csmonitor.com/USA/2009/1106/po2so4-usgn.html

In re J. B., 107 A.3d 1, 20 (Pa. 2014)

Hanson, R. K., Harris, A. J., Letourneau, E., Helmus, L. M., & Thornton, D. (2018). Reductions in Risk Based on Time Offense-free in the Community: Once a Sexual Offender, Not Always a Sexual Offender, *Psychology, Public Policy, & Law*, 24(1), 48–63

Sandler, J., Freeman, N., & Socia, K. (2008). Does a Watched Pot Boil? A Time-Series Analysis of New York State's Sex Offender Registration and Notification Law, *Psychology, Public Policy & Law*, 14, 284–302

Washington State Sex Offender Policy Board, *General Recommendations for Sex Offender Management* 10 (2016), https://sgc.wa.gov/sites/default/files/public/sopb/documents/general_recommendations.pdf

Acknowledgments

The editors wish to express their gratitude to their fellow contributing authors, who generously dedicated their time and effort, and without whom this volume would not have been possible. Also, thanks to research assistants Alex Lenk (FSU Law, 2020), Genevieve Lemley (FSU Law, 2021), and German Marquez Alcala (UM, Empirical Legal Studies); administrative assistants Derinda Kirkland and Kathleen Meell; research librarians at FSU Law and Michigan Law; and Michigan Law for hosting the volume's authors one beautiful fall weekend in Ann Arbor to meet, discuss, and critique draft versions of chapters.

Origins and Evolution

Wayne A. Logan

Chapter 1 recounts the historical evolution of sex offender registration and notification (SORN) laws in the US. Registration laws originated in the 1930s, first in municipalities in the Los Angeles area, and later several states, typically targeting individuals with criminal convictions more generally. Over time, interest in registration flagged, but experienced a major resurgence in the early 1990s, when states, acting in the wake of high-profile sexual victimizations of children, quickly enacted new laws, this time targeting convicted sex offenders in particular. The new-era laws were not only more expansive and onerous than their antecedents, they differed in a critically important respect: For the first time, the information they contained concerning individuals was made publicly available, in the name of community self-protection. SORN laws have since continued to expand, in significant part due to pressure from the federal government, and today are in effect nationwide affecting the lives of hundreds of thousands of individuals.

For most Americans, sex offender registration and notification (SORN), which today directly affects the lives of hundreds of thousands of convicted sex offenders, is likely viewed as a long-standing pillar of the criminal justice system. In actuality, however, SORN has been in use only since the early 1990s. Its rapid embrace by US jurisdictions since then marks a critically important social, political, and legal shift in the national zeitgeist. No longer does "doing one's time" mean that post-prison an individual is entitled to re-enter society free of social stigma and correctional surveillance. Rather, a conviction triggers potentially lifelong notoriety and monitoring by community members – not only police – who are expected to be "co-producers" of public safety.

This chapter surveys the origins and evolution of SORN laws, which have grown increasingly expansive and onerous over time.

1.1 EARLY ERA (1930S–1990)

1.1.1 *Historical Antecedents*

Human societies have long sought to amass information on individuals thought to pose potential criminal risk. With the eventual passing in acceptability of physical branding and mutilation, efforts were undertaken to collect and maintain information on particular individuals.

In the mid-to-late 1800s, England, for instance, required that all felons and certain misdemeanants register with police, for inclusion in a "Register of Distinctive Marks."[1] German authorities, for their part, maintained a nationwide ledger of citizens (the *Meldewesen*), recording individuals with criminal convictions.[2] France, starting in the early 1900s, required that "Gypsies" (thought to engage in such barbarities as child theft) register with authorities, permitting them to be monitored by newly organized mobile police squads.[3] Later, Nazis utilized the *Meldewesen* as a basis to monitor and round up Jews and others targeted by the Third Reich.[4]

Americans felt this same need to de-anonymize their populations, reflecting anxiety over the reality expressed in Alexis de Tocqueville's assessment that in America "[n]othing is easier than to pass from one state to another, and [it is in] the criminal's interest to do so."[5] With advances in photography, police created "rogues galleries" containing images of arrestees and suspicious persons, and borrowing a technique from the French, they assembled massive file cabinets containing photos, bodily measurements, and notations of "peculiar marks" (e.g., a scar or birthmark) of convicted individuals (a technique known as anthropometry).

At the turn of the twentieth century, fingerprinting became a prime method of recording individual identity, promising greater reliability and easier storage and retrieval capacity. As the Boston Police Department asserted in 1910, "as the digits record themselves there are no inaccuracies."[6] Chicago officials, in urging universal fingerprinting in the wake of a reported record-breaking increase in crime the year before, attributed the increase to "ignorance of who the criminals are."[7]

1.1.2 *Local Registries*

Against this backdrop, in the first decades of the twentieth century, a time when national concern regarding crime was at a fever pitch and Americans had greater

[1] Leon Radzinowicz & Roger Hood, "Incapacitating the Habitual Criminal: The English Experience," 78 *Michigan Law Review* 1305, 1340–43, 1349 (1980).

[2] Raymond B. Fosdick, *European Police Systems* 354–55 (New York, NY: The Century Company, 1915).

[3] Martine Kaluszynski, "Republican Identity: Bertillonage as Government Technique," in *Documenting Individual Identity: The Development of State Practices in the Modern World*, 131–37 (Jane Kaplan & John Torpey, eds.) (Princeton, NJ: Princeton University Press, 2001).

[4] Ian Hacking, *The Taming of Chance: Ideas in Context* 383 (Cambridge: Cambridge University Press, 1900).

[5] Gustave de Beaumont & Alexis de Tocqueville, *The Penitentiary System in the United States and Its Application in France* 101 (Carbondale, IL: Southern Illinois University Press, 1964). Tocqueville's observation no doubt stemmed in significant part from the differences between the highly migratory US population and the sedentary French population, as well as the fact that French prisoners were required to return to their village of origin until allowed by police to relocate. Ibid., at 131.

[6] Simon A. Cole, *Suspect Identities: A History of Fingerprinting and Criminal Identification* 165 (Cambridge, MA: Harvard University Press, 2001).

[7] United News, "May Check Crime by Registration: Chicago Proposes Trying Police System Used in European Cities," *Dallas Morning News*, January 3, 1921.

access to transport than ever before, criminal registration was born. In 1925, August Vollmer, Police Chief of Berkeley, California, and part-time professor at the University, urged registration of "all known criminals coming to California so that police can check their movements."[8] Doing so, Vollmer asserted, would have manifold benefits, including "keeping track of migratory criminals"; "locating persons wanted for crime"; "tracing family deserters"; "cataloging sex inverts and perverts"; and "preventing criminals from roaming about and concealing their identity."[9] Echoing Vollmer's enthusiasm, another police chief asserted in 1930 that registration would permit "police officers throughout the cities and throughout the rural districts ... to say to a suspected person, 'Who are you? Where do you belong? Where is your card?'"[10] The official predicted that the strategy "would cut down crime by fifty percent or more, because [criminal actors would] know they must have an identification card with them."[11]

Los Angeles, California, concerned about "striking at the steady flow of gangsters and their followers" from Chicago and eastern cities,[12] enacted the nation's first criminal registration law, which focused on persons convicted of an array of criminal offenses (not including those of a sexual nature). In late September 1931, Los Angeles District Attorney Burton Fitts presented for consideration to the County Board of Supervisors a registration provision. A statement accompanying the proposed ordinance provided as follows:

> While the registration system is in vogue generally throughout the world outside the United States and has proved a great deterrent to criminals changing their location with facility to avoid detection or to carry on their operations, such registration has not been initiated in the United States.
>
> The class of persons whose criminal convictions are the basis for the requirement of their reporting to the Sheriff are the type who are moving from one large center to another and enjoying the immunity that their residence in new locations affords them. They are able to become installed in this community under aliases, and to operate directly or through their associates with comparative freedom.[13]

While chiefly targeting "culprits en route to Los Angeles or harboring expectancy of visiting the area," the Los Angeles Times reported, the proposed law also provided "means for the indexing of all persons convicted" of the crimes specified who already resided in the area.[14]

---

[8] "Life Terms to End Crime Advocated," Oakland Tribune, September 28, 1925.
[9] Current Note, "Universal Registration," 25 Journal of the American Institute of Criminal Law and Criminology 650 (1934–1935).
[10] Donald Dilworth, ed., Identification Wanted: Development of the American Criminal Identification System, 1893–1943, at 214 (Gaithersburg, MD: International Association of Chiefs of Police, 1977).
[11] Ibid., at 215.
[12] "Gangsters to Be Fought with Registration Law," Los Angeles Times, September 23, 1931, at A1.
[13] Ibid.
[14] Ibid.

Despite initial optimism over its quick passage, public resistance soon surfaced. In one account, the *Times* reported that a local attorney, representing a "delegation of citizens," appeared before the Board in opposition to the proposed ordinance, arguing:

> Not only is the measure vicious but it places in the hands of ignorant police officers too much power. It will create a tremendous amount of suffering for ex-convicts who are trying to rehabilitate themselves, especially those who are in good positions of trust. It appears to be a harmless law, but we have too many harmless laws that appeared to be harmless until adopted, when they became dangerous weapons in the hands of certain interests.[15]

Some, the *Times* reported, worried that registration would "work a hardship on the man at one time convicted but who is now attempting to go straight." Such hardships, a local reverend contended, would include loss of work, and the reverend cited several instances of men he personally knew who would lose jobs if their pasts were disclosed. A representative of the State Department of Welfare worried about the effects on dependent members of households who "had never committed a crime but who would have to suffer if the man in the house had to expose his past."[16]

Practical concerns over the law's implementation were also expressed. A probation supervisor worried that individuals trying to remain law abiding would be penalized by the law, while "the man who is breaking the law now will keep on breaking it and will evade registering." A spokesperson for the Los Angeles County sheriff similarly offered that "the criminal not intending to live right will evade the law. It will be a law that will be very difficult to enforce."[17]

Despite these concerns, in 1933 the nation's first criminal registration law was enacted in Los Angeles County, California, in what the *New York Times* called a "quick move" to rid the area "of organized crime and a possible reign of gangsterism,"[18] and an "ace card" in the campaign to rid itself of organized crime.[19] Offenses triggering registration included counterfeiting, grand theft, grand larceny, embezzlement, forgery, burglary, felonious assault, robbery, arson, murder, kidnapping, and possession, sale, or transportation of narcotics.[20] Individuals subject to registration had to do so within forty-eight hours of arrival or, if already a resident, within forty-eight hours of the law's enactment. In addition to being fingerprinted and photographed, registrants were required to provide information such as their name and any aliases, a physical description, their

[15] "Board Delays Gang Check," *Los Angeles Times*, September 29, 1931.
[16] "Gangster Law Threshed Out," *Los Angeles Times*, October 28, 1931.
[17] Ibid.
[18] Associated Press, "Los Angeles County Registers Felons in a Drastic Move to Wipe Out Gangs," *New York Times*, September 13, 1933.
[19] Ibid.
[20] Los Angeles County Ordinance No. 73013, adopted September 12, 1933.

criminal history, and where they resided.[21] Although not required to verify the information at specified intervals, registrants were obliged to notify authorities of any change of address or living location within twenty-four hours of making the change.[22] Violation of the ordinance was punishable by a maximum $500 fine, imprisonment of up to six months, or both.[23]

In the ensuing decades, registration caught on with dozens of local governments in other parts of the nation. By 1969, fifty-two US localities had registration laws.[24] They apparently did not, however, figure very prominently in local criminal justice systems. In Philadelphia, for instance, "registration data [were] rarely used by the police,"[25] and police expressed concern over the constitutionality of registration, considering it indistinguishable from New Jersey's anti-"gangster" law, recently invalidated by the US Supreme Court.[26] An officer in an unspecified jurisdiction believed "this was not the kind of control that the police should have" and that individuals should not be subject to continued police scrutiny after they served their time in prison or jail.[27]

1.1.3 *State Registries*

State legislatures gravitated to registration somewhat later. Florida, in 1937, became the first state to require registration, but did so sparingly, only targeting individuals convicted of felonies involving "moral turpitude" who resided in counties with a population over 150,000 (Dade, Duval, and Hillsborough).[28] In 1947, California enacted the nation's first statewide registration law, targeting convicted sex offenders in particular; by 1967, eight states had registration laws; and by 1989, twelve states at some point had criminal registration laws on the books.[29]

Unlike local governments, which often focused on broad categories of crimes, early state laws, such as in California, were more prone to focus on particular offender subgroups. With the exception of Florida, which as noted initially required that persons convicted of felonies involving "moral turpitude" register, and later targeted felons more generally, other states targeted specific subgroups with registration. Sex offenders

---

[21] Ibid.
[22] Ibid.
[23] Ibid.
[24] Robert H. Dreher & Linda Kammler, *Criminal Registration Statutes and Ordinances in the United States; a Compilation* 32 (Carbondale, IL: Center for the Study of Crime, Delinquency, and Corrections, Southern Illinois University, 1969). The number was based on a national survey of 384 localities and excluded 10 California localities where local laws were invalidated on preemption grounds by the California Supreme Court in 1960.
[25] Note, "Criminal Registration Ordinances: Police Control Over Potential Recidivists," 103 *University of Pennsylvania Law Review* 60, 86 (1954).
[26] Ibid.
[27] Ibid.
[28] Ch. 18107, Laws of Fla. 1937, § 2.
[29] Wayne A. Logan, *Knowledge as Power: Criminal Registration and Community Notification Laws in America* 30–31 (Stanford, CA: Stanford University Press, 2009).

were a main target of state government concern. Of the state laws all except two targeted sex offenders (New Jersey and Illinois had "drug addict" registration laws). Altogether, as of 1989, every state with at least one registration law targeted sex offenders.[30]

States as a whole, however, showed only comparatively modest interest in registration. No new state registration laws were enacted between 1968 and 1984,[31] and thereafter only Illinois (1985)[32] and Arkansas (1987)[33] adopted laws. Arizona repealed its law (enacted in 1951) in 1978 but reinstated it in 1983.[34]

1.1.4 *Critical Scrutiny*

As noted earlier, registration had its critics. Indeed, when the first statewide registration law (targeting convicted sex offenders) was being considered in California, Director of Corrections Richard McGee outlined his concerns to Governor Earl Warren in a memorandum.[35] McGee wrote that while sex offenses were "revolting," there was a "principle involved which should not be disregarded. It has never been the practice in America to require citizens to register with the police, except while actually serving a sentence under the Probation or Parole Laws." McGee also worried that subjecting sex offenders to registration would establish a problematic precedent, warning that "[b]efore embarking upon this new practice with a particularly offensive group of individuals, we should not overlook the fact that we may be opening the door to similar practices for other groups as time goes on."

McGee predicted that individuals would likely fail to comply with the registration requirement and not update their registry information, undercutting the knowledge-based premise of registration itself. To McGee, it was

> questionable whether those cases most in need of careful supervision would continue to register and hence submit to questioning every time a sex crime is committed in the community. It is probable that a large percentage of these individuals would change their residence without registering and run the risk of being convicted of a misdemeanor for failing to do so.

McGee closed his memo by stating that while he was "entirely in sympathy" with the purposes of the bill, he felt "the problem was far too complex to attempt to control it by such a simple expedient as registration with the police."

---

[30]   Ibid., at 31.

[31]   Scott Matson & Roxanne Lieb, *Sex Offender Registration: A Review of State Laws* 5 (Olympia, WA: Washington Institute for Public Policy, 1995).

[32]   730 Ill. Comp. Stat. Ann. § 150/1–150/10 (West 1983) (citing 1986 Ill. Laws 84–1279).

[33]   Ark. Code Ann. § 12–12-901 to 909 (1993) (citing 1987 Ark. Acts 585).

[34]   Ariz. Code Ann. § 13–3821 to 3824 (1983).

[35]   Memorandum from State of California Director of Corrections Richard A. McGee to Governor Earl Warren, July 2, 1947 (on file with author).

Similar concern was expressed by the Utah Attorney General in 1956. With the state embroiled in public debate over whether Utah should enact a registration law, the state's chief law enforcement officer expressed uncertainty over the constitutionality of registration:

> The imposition of the registration requirements upon persons merely because they have been convicted of a single crime, the fact that persons in some cases are subject to the registration requirement for the rest of their lives, and especially the manner in which these laws are often used, leads to the conclusion that these ordinances are of questionable constitutionality.[36]

Corrections personnel voiced similar concerns. For instance, in 1958 a nationwide survey of administrators charged with overseeing the interstate transfer of probationers and parolees reflected that 63 percent of respondents opposed registration.[37] One anonymous respondent related that registration "would be evaded by the very ones we would like to have recorded" and believed that "the philosophy is wrong and smacks of a Communistic or Nazi police state."[38]

Later, in 1983, the Los Angeles City Attorney branded the state registry "dysfunctional," because it included many nonserious sex offenders and was of no use in the effort to locate the "Hillside Strangler" who terrorized the community.[39] And in 1986, the *Los Angeles Times* published a lengthy exposé on problems with the state registry, focusing on the widespread failure of eligible individuals to register and the many data inaccuracies in the registry.[40] A spokesperson for the attorney general had "no idea" of the extent of wrong address information in the registry, adding that the fundamental problem was that "we have a people-tracking system of people that don't want to be tracked."[41]

The *Times* also reported that some authorities felt that any effort to construct and maintain a comprehensive and accurate registry was impossible due to resource and personnel limits. The captain in charge of records for the Los Angeles County Sheriff's Office offered that "[i]t's totally impractical to follow up to the degree that we'd be able to know where they are. It's a matter of workload and numbers." In light of this, the Sheriff's Office had ceased mailing notices to newly released offenders who did not voluntarily present themselves for registration because the Office was receiving a less than 1 percent response rate.[42]

---

[36] W. Keith Wilson et al., "Are Criminal Registration Laws Sound?," 4 *National Probation and Parole Journal* 272 (1958) (citing Opinion of the Utah State Attorney General to W. Keith Wilson, Compact Administrator, Utah Department of Probation and Parole, December 6, 1956).

[37] Ibid., at 271–74.

[38] Ibid., at 274.

[39] *In re* Reed, 663 P.2d 216, 219 n.7 (Cal. 1983).

[40] Kenneth Reich, "Many Simply Ignore Law: Sex Offender Registration Not Working, Experts Say," *Los Angeles Times*, August 8, 1986.

[41] Ibid.

[42] Ibid.

Finally, the *Times* noted that uncertainty remained over whether registration achieved its public safety goal. The Sacramento County Sheriff stated:

> And the question is, how much is gained? Suppose we had a file that was 100% accurate. What use is that file? How effective is that file in combating the sex crime problem? I'm not sure that anyone has really done that kind of analysis. We don't know how many crimes we would solve, or prevent.[43]

A few years later, a California Department of Justice study concluded that "address compliance is quite poor. Sex offenders, like other types of offenders[,] are a mobile group and, given the inconsistent approach to offender registration, it is unlikely that offenders more likely to offend are those keeping their residence address information up-to-date with law enforcement."[44]

1.2 MODERN ERA (1990–PRESENT)

The relative disinterest in registration, and qualms regarding its public safety effectiveness, evaporated in the 1990s. Whereas in 1990 only a handful of states had registration laws, by the mid-1990s such laws were in effect nationwide. Moreover, no longer would registry information be monopolized by police; it would be provided to community members.

The dramatic shift was triggered by several widely publicized child victimizations. In May, 1989, in Tacoma, Washington, a seven-year-old boy was kidnapped, raped, sexually mutilated, and left to die in the woods, but was able to identify his assailant, Earl Shriner. Shriner, recently released from prison, had a long record of convictions involving physical and sexual victimization of children, and was well known to authorities, who had unsuccessfully sought to have him involuntarily committed out of concern that he would re-offend.

Upon learning that authorities knew of Shriner's background, a group of outraged citizens demanded that the governor initiate a special session to revamp Washington's sex offender laws.[45] Three weeks after the assault, the governor ordered the creation of a task force to conduct a comprehensive reexamination of the state's efforts to combat sexual violence.[46] In late November 1989, the task force issued its report, which

---

43   Ibid.
44   Roy Lewis, *Effectiveness of Statutory Requirements for the Registration of Sex Offenders* 6 (Sacramento, CA: California Dept. of Justice, 1988).
45   David Boerner, "Confronting Violence: In the Act and in the Word," 15 *University of Puget Sound Law Review* 525 (1992).
46   Shriner's crime was the latest in a series of child and adult sexual victimizations by released sex offenders. *See* Barry Siegel, "Locking Up 'Sexual Predators': A Public Outcry in Washington State Targeted Repeat Violent Sex Criminals," *Los Angeles Times*, May 10, 1990 (noting September 1988 rape and murder of Diane Ballasiotes and history of Gary Minnix, who had been found incompetent to stand trial for four rape charges and in December 1988 raped and stabbed another adult female victim while in the community on furlough).

contained an expansive array of suggested reforms, which the legislature unanimously adopted as the Community Protection Act of 1990.

The new law, in addition to containing a controversial provision designed to broaden involuntary civil commitment of "sexual psychopaths," a strategy first used in the 1930s,[47] not only contained the state's first registration requirement, but it also authorized the nation's (indeed the world's) first community notification system. While notification had been considered by California in the mid-1980s,[48] Washington became the first jurisdiction to officially authorize public dissemination of registrants' identifying information.

The Washington Legislature backed its new regime with legislative findings. With respect to registration, the Act provided:

> The legislature finds that sex offenders often pose a high risk of reoffense, and that law enforcement's efforts to protect their communities, conduct investigations, and quickly apprehend offenders who commit sex offenses, are impaired by the lack of information available to law enforcement agencies about convicted sex offenders who live within the law enforcement agency's jurisdiction. Therefore, this state's policy is to assist local law enforcement agencies' efforts to protect their communities by regulating sex offenders by requiring sex offenders to register with local law enforcement agencies ... .[49]

With respect to community notification, the legislature reiterated that persons convicted of sex offenses posed a "high risk" of recidivism and concluded that

> [p]ersons found to have committed a sex offense have a reduced expectation of privacy because of the public's interest in public safety and in the effective operation of government. Release of information about sexual predators to public agencies and under limited circumstances, the general public, will further the governmental interests of public safety and public scrutiny of the criminal and mental health systems so long as the information released is rationally related to the furtherance of those goals. Therefore, this state's policy ... is to require the exchange of relevant information about sexual predators among public agencies and officials and to authorize the release of necessary and relevant information about sexual predators to members of the general public.[50]

The law was sex offender-specific yet targeted a relatively narrow scope of sexual offenders. Local law enforcement was responsible for handling community

---

[47] *See generally* Deborah W. Denno, "Life before the Modern Sex Offender Statutes," 92 *Northwestern University Law Review* 1317 (1998). In contrast to prior commitment laws, Washington's new law did not commit individuals in lieu of criminal confinement. Rather, it permitted potentially indefinite institutionalization in addition to – and after – prison terms served by individuals deemed "sexual predators," a new phrase destined to be a staple of the American lexicon. *See* Eric S. Janus & Wayne A. Logan, "Substantive Due Process and the Involuntary Confinement of Sexually Violent Predators," 35 *Connecticut Law Review* 319, 325 (2003).

[48] Joe Cantlupe, "Sex Offender Registration is Questioned," *San Diego Union-Tribune*, June 7, 1987.

[49] Wash. Rev. Code § 71.05.440.

[50] Ibid., § 71.05.670.

notification, and was authorized to "release relevant and necessary information" on registrants when "necessary for public protection." Such necessity was determined in part on the basis of information provided by an entity that evaluated individuals prior to release from prison, yet notification decisions were primarily made by local police. Risk level determined the scope of notification: for level I offenders, only local police; for level II, community groups, school districts, and registrants' neighbors; for level III, registrants posing most serious risk, all of these mentioned as well as members of the media.[51] Other departments opted for a more liberal policy and made information on all registrants (including photographs, and home and work addresses) available to the public upon request. Still others made case-by-case decisions on notification in a less category-specific manner.[52]

Washington's 1990 SORN regime was hugely significant. With it, the nation's attention was drawn to registration, and the legislation opened the door to notification. It was not, however, the sole catalyst behind the resurgence of registration and the advent of notification. Events elsewhere also played a key role. Chief among them was the October 1989 disappearance of an eleven-year-old boy, Jacob Wetterling, who while riding his bike in rural Minnesota was abducted by a masked man brandishing a gun. His mother, Patty Wetterling, in February 1990 created the Jacob Wetterling Foundation, which soon became a highly influential national force on matters relating to child victims of violence and sexual abuse. The group's influence was felt in Minnesota with the creation of the Task Force on Missing Children, the findings of which resulted in the state's June 1991 adoption of a registration law.[53]

In June 1992, Louisiana, after the murder of a six-year-old boy by a recidivist sex offender living in the community,[54] became the second state to adopt a registration law with a community notification feature, adopting in almost verbatim form legislative findings contained in Washington's law.[55] While Louisiana limited community notification to probationers and parolees,[56] it was more demanding than Washington's seminal law because it required registrants themselves to notify

[51] Washington State Institute for Public Policy, "Washington State's Community Notification Law: 15 Years of Change," 1 (February 2006); Jolayne Houtz, "When Do You Unmask a Sexual Predator?," *Seattle Times*, August 30, 1990.

[52] *See* Mary Anne Kircher, "Registration of Sexual Offenders: Would Washington's Scarlet Letter Approach Benefit Minnesota?," 13 *Hamline Journal of Public Law & Policy* 171 (1992). Local departments also varied in terms of the kinds of information they publicly disclosed, e.g., actual versus approximate registrant addresses, work addresses, and vehicle identification information. *See* Sheila Donnelly & Roxanne Lieb, *Washington's Community Notification Law: A Survey of Law Enforcement* 5 (Olympia, WA: Washington State Institute for Public Policy, 1993).

[53] *See* Wayne A. Logan, "Jacob's Legacy: Sex Offender Registration and Community Notification Laws, Practice, and Procedure in Minnesota," 29 *William Mitchell Law Review* 1287 (2003).

[54] "Girl's Slaying Adds Momentum to Plans to Track Sex Offenders," *San Francisco Chronicle*, August 8, 1994.

[55] 1991 La. Sess. L. Act No. 338, S.B. No. 1111 (June 18, 1992).

[56] Margaret Litvin, "Metairie Parents Alarmed by Paroled Sex Offender," *Times Picayune* (New Orleans), October 19, 1995.

community members by means of mailings and newspaper advertisements (at their own expense).[57]

In 1993, a series of highly publicized child victimizations by recidivist sex offenders propelled legislative interest in other states, including Indiana, Texas, and California. Of even greater national influence, in July 1994, seven-year-old Megan Kanka was abducted, sexually assaulted, and murdered in New Jersey. Police soon arrested Jesse Timmendequas, a twice-convicted sex offender who lived on the same street as the Kankas, along with two other convicted sex offenders he had met in a correctional facility. Although local police were aware of Timmendequas's history, his neighbors reputedly were not. Voicing a sentiment that would come to define modern registration and notification laws, Megan's outraged and grieving mother, Maureen Kanka, asserted that if she and her family "had known there was a paedophile living on our street, [Megan] would be alive today."[58] The sentiment had immediate resonance with the public. As a story in the *Philadelphia Inquirer* noted, "the public outcry last week said: let us know. Tell us when dangerous sex criminals are living next door."[59]

After Timmendequas' arrest, a petition drive was initiated to urge the adoption of community notification, gathering more than 200,000 signatures.[60] The Speaker of the New Jersey Assembly declared a legislative emergency, and a registration and notification law was unanimously adopted. On October 31, 1994, three months after Megan Kanka was murdered, Governor Christine Todd Whitman (with Maureen Kanka at her side) signed *Megan's Law*.[61] With its passage, New Jersey joined a handful of states allowing for some form of community notification (Tennessee and Alaska adopted notification laws earlier in 1994).[62]

Unlike laws in Washington and other states, New Jersey required, rather than only permitted, that information on particular registrants (those deemed most likely to re-offend) be disseminated to community members.[63] The goal, as the New Jersey Supreme Court observed in a 1995 constitutional challenge to the law, was "to give people a chance to protect themselves and their children."[64]

---

[57] Ed Anderson, "'Scarlet Letter' Bill Signed by Edwards," *Times Picayune* (New Orleans), July 14, 1992.

[58] Michelle Reuss, "A Mother's Plea: Pass Megan's Bill – Panel Oks Compromise," *Record* (N.J.), September 27, 1994, at A1.

[59] Douglas A. Campbell, "'Megan's Law': Is There Really a Right to Know?," *Philadelphia Inquirer*, August 7, 1994.

[60] Jan Hoffman, "New Law Is Urged on Freed Sex Offenders," *New York Times*, August 4, 1994.

[61] As with Earl Shriner in Washington State, Timmendequas's brutal act was not the sole catalyst for change. Roughly four months before Megan Kanka's murder, six-year-old Amanda Wengert of Manalapan Township was abducted and murdered by a neighbor with a history of sexual offenses against children. Ivette Mendez, "Megan's Law: 10 Sex Offender Bills Clear the Senate," *Star-Ledger* (Newark, NJ), October 4, 1994.

[62] For discussion of the law's particular provisions, along with details of its swift legislative adoption, see Robert J. Martin, "Pursuing Public Protection Through Mandatory Community Notification of Convicted Sex Offenders: The Trials and Tribulations of Megan's Law," 6 *Boston University Public Interest Law Journal* 6, 33–36 (1996).

[63] Doe v. Poritz, 662 A.2d 367, 422 (N.J. 1995) (noting same).

[64] Ibid., at 372–73.

The year 1994 also marked a key turning point because it was then that the federal government first enacted laws pressuring states to expand their efforts. After several false starts, in 1994 Congress enacted what came to be known as the *Jacob Wetterling Crimes Against Children and Sexually Violent Offender Registration Act*, which contained an array of requirements for states to adopt, backed by the threat of losing ten percent of their federal criminal justice funding if they failed to comply. Although twenty-four states at the time had registration laws, a federal "stick"[65] was thought to be needed "to prod all States to enact similar laws and to provide for a national registration system to handle offenders who move from one State to another."[66] President Bill Clinton[67] signed the legislation into law on September 13, 1994 (with Maureen Kanka at his side)[68] as part of a massive $30-billion omnibus anti-crime bill.[69]

Wetterling was not the federal government's last word on registration and notification. Two years later, in 1996, Congress, concerned that states were "reluctant" to release information on registrants,[70] unanimously required that they adopt community notification laws, again under the threat of loss of federal grant money.[71] In May 1996, President Clinton signed the federal *Megan's Law*.[72] With Richard and Maureen Kanka, Patty Wetterling, and Marc Klaas (father of child murder victim Polly Klaas) at his side at the White House Rose Garden signing ceremony, Clinton remarked:

> From now on, every State in the country will be required by law to tell a community when a dangerous sexual predator enters its midst. We respect people's rights, but today America proclaims there is no greater right than a parent's right to raise a child in safety and love.
>
> Today, America warns, if you dare prey on our children, the law will follow you wherever you go, state to state, town to town. Today, America circles the wagon[s] around our children.[73]

---

[65] *Cong. Rec.* 139 (November 20, 1993): H 10320 (statement of Rep. Sensenbrenner).

[66] *Cong. Rec.* 139 (November 20, 1993): H 10321 (statement of Rep. Ramstad).

[67] See Philip Jenkins, *Moral Panic: Changing Concepts of the Child Molester in Modern America* 198–99 (New Haven, CT: Yale University Press, 1998) (noting Clinton's concern over being vulnerable to Republican assertions of being soft on crime and being politically outflanked by Republicans' "family values" mantra).

[68] Jennifer Bucksbaum, "NJ Victims' Parents See Crime Bill Signed," *New Jersey Record*, September 14, 1994.

[69] *Violent Crime Control and Law Enforcement Act of 1994*, Public Law 103–322, § 17010(b)(3), *Stat.* (1994): 1796, 2038 (codified at 42 U.S.C. § 17010).

[70] House Committee on the Judiciary, *House Report No. 104-555*, 104th Cong., 2d sess., May 6, 1996, 2.

[71] The unanimous vote was specifically sought by floor leaders and occurred after a handful of initially dissenting House members changed their votes. For fuller discussion of this evolution see Lord Windlesham, *Politics, Punishment, and Populism* 179–80 (Oxford: Oxford University Press, 1998).

[72] *Megan's Law*, Public Law 104–145, *Stat.* 110 (1996): 1345 (amending 42 U.S.C. § 14071(d) (1994)).

[73] Bill Clinton, "Remarks on Signing Megan's Law and an Exchange with Reporters," in *Public Papers of the Presidents of the United States, William J. Clinton* (Washington, DC: Government Printing Office, 1996), 763–764.

With *Megan's Law*, federal law did not merely permit community notification, it required it, providing that states "shall release relevant information that is necessary to protect the public concerning a specific person required to register."[74] States could not comply by affording "purely permissive or discretionary authority" to officials to conduct notification. Rather, "[i]nformation must be released to members of the public as necessary to protect the public from registered offenders."[75]

Federal conditional funding pressure achieved its goal. By 1996, all states had registration laws (when Massachusetts passed its law),[76] and by 1999, all states required notification to some extent (when New Mexico passed its law).[77] Over time, state laws have significantly expanded, affecting the scope of registerable offenses (both in terms of specified offenses and retroactive reach), length of registration and penalties for noncompliance, verification and updating requirements, the inclusion of adjudicated (not only convicted) juvenile offenders, and methods of notification (including, most notably, nationwide use of website registries, which proved enormously popular[78]).

Many changes in state laws came about as a result of another round of federal conditional spending pressure, this time with the Adam Walsh Act (AWA), enacted in 2006, which among other things expanded the range of registerable offenses, required in-person verification, increased the penalty for noncompliance (to a felony), and was retroactive in scope. In addition, for the first time Indian tribes were expected to commence registration on their lands (or delegate a state to do so), as were US territories.

The centerpiece of the AWA is its tier classification system. Whereas in the past, federal law left to states how individuals were to be distinguished for the purposes of registration requirements and notification, the AWA specifies that an offense-based regime must be employed. Unlike the individual risk-based tier systems, such as those employed in Washington State and New Jersey, the AWA expressly eschews individualized risk assessments. Registrants are relegated to Tier I–III (the latter being the most serious),[79] with the tier driving duration of registration and the intervals at which registration information must be verified. Tier I offenders must register for a minimum of fifteen years and verify their registration on an annual basis; Tier II

---

[74] 42 U.S.C. § 14071(d) (1996).

[75] *Final Guidelines for Megan's Law and the Jacob Wetterling Crimes Against Children and Sexually Violent Offender Registration Act*, 62 Federal Register 39019 (July 21, 1997).

[76] Doris Sue Wong, "Weld Signs Bill Creating Sex-Offender Registry – Those Convicted Have to Register," *Boston Globe*, August 15, 1996.

[77] "Roundhouse Roundup," *Albuquerque Tribune*, March 13, 1999, D5.

[78] During 2005 alone, for instance, California's website (available in thirteen languages) had sixteen million visitors. California, Office of the Attorney General, *Megan's Law: California Sex Offender Information: Report to the California Legislature, July 2002*, at 5 (Sacramento, CA: Violent Crime Information Center, 2002).

[79] 42 U.S.C. § 16911(1)-(4).

must register for 25 years and verify information twice a year; and Tier III offenders must register for their lifetimes and verify information on a quarterly basis.[80]

The AWA also imposed federal (not state) criminal liability when an individual required to register knowingly fails to satisfy registration requirements and "travels in inter state or foreign commerce, or enters or leaves, or resides, in Indian country." Violators are subject to a $250,000 fine and a maximum 10 years in federal prison.[81] Furthermore, the AWA specified that federal law enforcement, including the US Marshals Service, shall "assist jurisdictions in locating and apprehending sex offenders who violate sex offender registration requirements."[82]

Finally, the AWA enlarged the federal bureaucratic role in registration and notification. It authorized a grant program to help jurisdictions implement and satisfy new requirements,[83] and created a Sex Offender Sentencing, Monitoring, Apprehending, Registering and Tracking (SMART) Office within the Department of Justice to administer and enforce standards and issue grants.[84] Furthermore, the attorney general was required to maintain the Dru Sjodin National Sex Offender Public Website, which makes jurisdictions' registries collectively available.

Motivated by concern over the diversity of state registration provisions, which advocates asserted created "loopholes" and "deficiencies," allowing thousands of registrants to become "lost,"[85] the AWA sought to establish a "comprehensive national system for the registration [of] sex offenders and offenders against children."[86] The AWA and the state legislative responses to it are discussed further in Chapter 2.

1.2.1 *Ancillary Strategies Generated*

Over time, states and local governments have used SORN as the foundation for a cluster of ancillary social control strategies.

For instance, some states tie registrant status to the requirement that registrants carry special identification, such as drivers' licenses or identification cards indicating their registrant status. In Louisiana, the cards, which must be renewed annually and

---

[80] 42 U.S.C. § 16915 (duration), 16916 (verification intervals). The AWA specifies, however, that certain individuals can have their designated registration periods reduced: (i) Tier I registrants, reduced by five years if they have a "clean record" for 10 years (i.e., 10-year total duration) and (ii) Tier III registrants who are juveniles, reduced to 25 years if "clean" for 25 years (e.g., 25-year total duration). Ibid., § 16915(b)(2),(3). For a definition of "clean record" see ibid., § 16915(b)(1).

[81] 18 U.S.C. § 2250.

[82] 42 U.S.C. § 16941(a).

[83] 42 U.S.C. § 16926(c).

[84] 42 U.S.C. § 16926.

[85] *See, e.g.*, House Committee on the Judiciary, *Report on Children's Safety Act of 2005*, 109th Cong., 1st sess., September 9, 2005, 23–24; *Cong. Rec.* 151 (September 14, 2005): H 7889 (statement of Rep. Green); *Cong. Rec.* 152 (July 20, 2006): S 8018 (statement of Sen. George Allen), S 8022 (Sen. DeWine), S 8030 (statement of Sen. Frist).

[86] 42 U.S.C. §. 16901 ("Declaration of Purpose").

carried "on the person at all times," must have in orange emblazoned capital lettering the term "sexual offender."[87] States have also considered requiring registrants to affix special color-coded license plates to their vehicles.[88] Being a registrant also means that one's passport will be marked with a "unique identifier that indicates they were convicted of a sexual offense," and requires that authorities be provided notice of intended international travel plans.[89]

Registration can also affect where individuals can live. Many states and localities prohibit registrants from living within specified distances (e.g., 2000') of schools, day care centers, and other places where minors congregate.[90] The laws can apply even though registrants lack offending history relating to minors and even if they established residence within the area prior to the provision taking effect. In addition, private homeowner associations have banned registrants,[91] and jurisdictions have enacted laws requiring separate housing of registrants in the event of natural disasters such as hurricanes.[92] Laws also curtail the capacity of registrants to visit and work in certain areas, such as parks and playgrounds.[93]

Other ancillary effects are more personal. For example, states often prohibit or severely restrict the ability of registrants to change their legal names[94] and require that they inform authorities when they change their facial features (e.g., grow a beard) or borrow a car.[95] Moreover, in keeping with a federal directive, states are now collecting information on registrants' email addresses and internet identifiers.[96]

1.3 CONCLUSION

As the preceding discussion suggests, SORN laws have swept the nation over the past quarter century, marking a historic change in American criminal justice. Although generated by a "moral panic" over a series of widely reported sex crimes against children, in the late 1980s and early 1990s, the laws have not only endured, they have proliferated in number and expansiveness. In short, the term "panic,"

[87] La. Rev. Stat. § 40:1321(J). *See also* John Hill, "Bill Would Mark Licenses of Sex Offenders," *The Times* (Shreveport, La.), May 19, 2006 (noting that the law passed the State Senate unanimously and would generate an estimated $116,000 in annual renewal fees).

[88] *See, e.g.,* Dave Wedge, "IMAPERV Plate Proposed," *Boston Herald,* May 3, 2005; "Lawmakers Want Pink Plates Put on Cars of Sex Offenders," *Columbus Dispatch,* May 3, 2005.

[89] 42 U.S.C. § 16914.

[90] *See* Wayne A. Logan, "Constitutional Collectivism and Ex-Offender Residence Exclusion Laws," 92 *Iowa Law Review* 1 (2006).

[91] Ibid., at 9.

[92] *See, e.g.,* La. Rev. Stat. § 29:726.

[93] Logan, "Constitutional Collectivism," *supra,* at 7.

[94] *See, e.g.,* Cal. Civ. Proc. Code § 1279.5 (e) (no change unless "it is in the best interest of justice to grant [the change] and that doing so will not adversely affect the public safety"); 735 Ill. Comp. Stat. § 5/21–101 (registrants not allowed to change names unless pardoned); N.H. Rev. Stat. § 547:3-I (allowed only if registrant "makes a compelling show that a name change is necessary").

[95] *See* Smith v. Doe, 538 U.S. 84, 101–02 (2003) (discussing requirement in Alaska).

[96] *See, e.g.,* Fla. Stat. § 943.0435.

suggestive of a resulting short-term spasm of policy overreaction, fails to accurately capture the history and evolution of SORN laws.

In this respect, they differ from predecessor laws, which originated in the 1930s, yet fell into disuse by the 1980s. Yet, commonalities exist between modern SORN and early generation registration laws. Both seek to empower police by providing them with information regarding individuals and discourage recidivism by instilling among registrants a sense that they are being watched. In the early 1930s, "gangsters" were the subject of concern but soon thereafter broad swaths of specified criminal subgroups received attention. Starting in the 1990s, sex offenders and child kidnappers became the dominant focus of concern, and failure to update and verify registry information was punished more severely, obliging that individuals be complicit in their own ongoing surveillance.

Another key difference is that registration today, unlike in the past, is in effect nationwide. Whereas before the late 1990s individuals could lawfully travel-evade registration, such a possibility has been largely foreclosed today. The goal, as President Clinton intoned when signing federal legislation authorizing a national registry, has been an all encompassing surveillance: "if you dare prey on our children, the law will follow you wherever you go, state to state, town to town."[97]

Another hugely important difference is that modern registration is complemented by community notification. Although early registration laws had some informational "leakage," modern laws affirmatively require that registry information be provided to communities, in the name of allowing them to take self-protective measures and surveil registrants.

Finally, SORN laws have spawned other social control strategies, including most notably laws that prohibit registrants from living in or visiting particular geographic areas, such as near churches, schools, or playgrounds.

---

[97]   Ron Fournier, "Clinton Signs Law on Sex Offenders," *Chicago Sun-Times*, May 18, 1996.

2

Variations in the Structure and Operation of SORN Systems

Andrew J. Harris and Scott M. Walfield

Chapter 2 explores the structure and evolution of federal, state, and international SORN policies. The chapter first outlines the history of federal legislation in the United States that has shaped the current SORN environment, beginning with the 1994 Jacob Wetterling Act and continuing through the 2006 Sex Offender Registration and Notification Act (SORNA) and its subsequent amendments. The chapter then explores the key points of variation in state SORN policies, underscoring the elusive nature of fulfilling SORNA's vision of a uniform national system. This analysis examines two particularly prominent points of interstate variation: provisions for the registration of juveniles and mechanisms for registrant classification. The chapter concludes with a brief examination of SORN systems outside the United States, indicating that, although many countries have adopted provisions for requiring registration with law enforcement, the provision of public access to registrant information is far less common.

2.1 INTRODUCTION

In recent decades, sex offender registration and notification (SORN) laws and policies have emerged as central elements in federal and state efforts to manage the risk presented by individuals living in the community with histories of sex offense convictions. Their general nature and evolution were summarized in Chapter 1 of this volume. This chapter provides an overview of current SORN laws and policies, which exist in all fifty states, four US territories, the District of Columbia, and over one hundred tribal jurisdictions. As will be seen, SORN systems exhibit a fair amount of variation, reflecting among other things each jurisdiction's particular mix of constitutional demands, bureaucratic structures, political preferences, and legislative and executive balances of power.[1]

The chapter has four sections. It begins with a review of the statutory initiatives informing SORN policy, with an emphasis on the federal parameters that have influenced them. Particular focus will be on the requirements prescribed in the 2006 Sex Offender Registration and Notification Act (SORNA). Next, the chapter examines state-level implementation of federal SORNA guidelines, offering a window

---

[1] For discussion of laws and policies concerning registration of college and university students in particular see Custer (2019).

into the extent and nature of variation among state SORN systems. The chapter then surveys key areas of interstate variation, with specific focus on a pair of particularly challenging and contentious areas of SORN policy: state provisions governing juvenile registration and the offender classification methods used to establish registry requirements. The section will also highlight some of the key points of operational variation across jurisdictions that are not directly addressed by SORNA, including factors related to registry management and enforcement. The chapter concludes with an examination of sex offender registration in an international comparative context, including a general review of global sex offender registry practices and a comparison of these practices to those in the United States.

2.2 GENERAL POLICY BACKGROUND

To understand the current scope and structure of SORN systems in the United States, one must first have a sense of the broader policy context in which they have evolved. Initially designed as localized tools for law enforcement, usually targeting a wide variety of convicted individuals, in the early 1990s state legislatures embraced registration, with particular emphasis on convicted sex offenders. In the early to mid-1990s, as well, states enacted laws allowing for community notification, which provides registry information to the public by various means (today, primarily via websites). Since then, SORN systems have become centerpieces in the effort to manage and control perceived risk posed by individuals previously convicted of sexual offenses who live in communities.

The federal government has played a key role in the expansion and nature of SORN throughout the US. Federal involvement was set in motion with the Jacob Wetterling Crimes Against Children and Sexually Violent Offender Registration Act (the Wetterling Act), passed as Title XVII of the Violent Crime Control and Law Enforcement Act of 1994. The Wetterling Act included a range of provisions that were intended to protect children from sexual victimization, including a requirement that states establish registries to enable law enforcement to monitor targeted individuals. The law set forth certain baseline standards for registration systems, including a requirement that registered sex offenders (RSOs) remain on the registry for at least ten years, and that RSOs convicted of certain offenses be subject to lifetime registration. The law also established a fiscal mechanism to promote state compliance with the Act's provisions, stipulating that states that did not comply would receive a 10 percent reduction on their federal justice block grant funding.

The Wetterling Act was amended several times over the ensuing five years, including as a result of the passage of Megan's Law (1996), which required that states implement policies that provide for public disclosure of registry information; the Pam Lychner Sex Offender Tracking and Identification Act (Lychner Act), which required the FBI to establish a national database (the National Sex Offender Registry) and broadened the Department of Justice's jurisdictional authority over SORN compliance; and the Jacob Wetterling Improvements Act (1998),

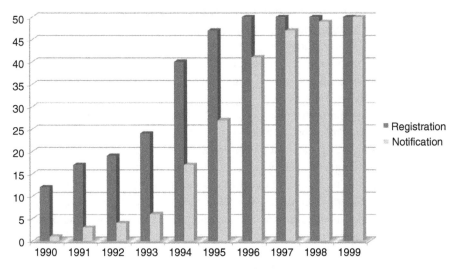

FIGURE 2.1 Expansion of state sex offender registries, 1990–1999

which expanded the requirements imposed on state courts associated with making sexually violent offender determinations, addressed a range of interjurisdictional issues, and required that states participate in the National Sex Offender Registry.

Although the emergence of SORN systems among the states was underway prior to passage of the initial Wetterling Act in 1994, it is apparent that federal action played a significant role in promoting their expansion. As noted in Figure 2.1, state adoption of sex offender registration systems accelerated in the wake of the Wetterling Act, with registries in place within all fifty states by the end of 1996. Similarly, state adoption of community notification provisions witnessed a similar expansion following the 1996 passage of the federal Megan's Law, which also contained a federal threat of funding loss in the event of noncompliance. By the end of the 1990s, all states had established registration and notification systems.

Significantly, these developments converged in the late 1990s with a substantial growth in the use of personal computers and the rise of the internet – factors that facilitated the expansion of online public registries and other electronic means of sharing information about registrants.

2.2.1 *2006 Sex Offender Registration and Notification Act*

Although the Wetterling Act and its subsequent amendments prescribed a range of requirements that guided and promoted the expansion of state registries, the laws generally offered states significant latitude regarding how registry requirements and notification systems were to be designed and implemented. As the regimes evolved, states adopted distinct rules and guidelines pertaining to a range of operational details, including who was required to register; the extent of information made available to the public; methods of classifying RSO populations for purposes of establishing registrant requirements; duration of required registration; frequency of required updates; and mechanisms for relief from registry requirements.

The state-level variation, coupled with growing congressional concern that the variations might be exploited by RSOs to avoid coverage, prompted congressional efforts to achieve greater uniformity in the nation's SORN systems (Harris, 2011). In 2006, the Adam Walsh Child Protection and Safety Act (AWA) was enacted in response, laying the groundwork for an even greater federal role in the nation's SORN systems. The AWA, in addition to expanding federal crimes and penalties for various crimes against children, repealed many of the registration provisions contained in the Wetterling Act and set forth a new and significantly more prescriptive set of parameters related to the operation of SORN systems (for instance, an offense-based tiering system for RSOs and in-person verification of registry information). These changes are embodied within the Sex Offender Registration and Notification Act (SORNA). Moreover, in addition to addressing states and territories, federal SORN policy for the first time covered tribal jurisdictions and established a new office within the Department of Justice, the Office of Sex Offender Sentencing, Monitoring, Apprehending, Registering, and Tracking (SMART), charged with developing and managing guidelines for SORNA implementation. The AWA set a compliance deadline of July 2009, providing jurisdictions with the possibility of a two-year extension to satisfy its requirements.

2.2.1.1 State Variation in Implementing SORNA Standards

Examining adherence to the SORNA standards represents an important initial step in understanding the contours of current state registry systems. In the years immediately following SORNA's passage in 2006 and the 2008 release of the initial SORNA guidelines (US Department of Justice, 2008), state-level compliance with SORNA mandates has proved an elusive goal (Government Accountability Office, 2013). Despite significant state legislative activity aimed at reforming registries (National Conference of State Legislatures, 2009), states initially struggled to bring their systems in line with SORNA requirements, citing an array of operational, legal, and fiscal challenges (Harris & Lobanov-Rostovsky, 2010). Several states cited the additional costs associated with changing their systems, which they maintained exceeded the funding that would be lost, and concerns related to particular SORNA requirements, including those related to the registration of juveniles and retroactive application of registry requirements (Harris & Lobanov-Rostovsky, 2010; Logan, 2010). By the initial SORNA compliance deadline in July 2009, only one state (Ohio) had been designated by the SMART Office to have met the requirements, and even those states that had passed SORNA-enabling legislation (e.g., Ohio and Nevada) found themselves fighting legal challenges related to the laws' implementation (Harris, 2011).

Since 2011, however, states have made progress toward SORNA implementation, amid some key shifts in federal policy. The first such shift involved revisions to the SORNA guidelines in 2011, which included modification of certain requirements, including those related to public websites, international travel, and registration of adjudicated juveniles (US Department of Justice, 2011). SORNA's juvenile registration requirements were further modified in a subsequent series of policy revisions in 2016 (US Department of Justice, 2016a).

Concurrent with these changes, the Department of Justice established a mechanism for noncompliant jurisdictions to avoid loss of the 10 percent Byrne Justice Assistance Grant "penalty," applicable if the funds are invested in registry improvements linked to SORNA. The SMART Office also modified its processes for working with states to facilitate implementation and adjusted its standards for evaluating adherence to SORNA criteria and requirements. Recognizing each jurisdiction's distinct legal and operational landscape, the SMART Office shifted from a fairly literal standard (termed "substantial compliance") to a more flexible standard ("substantial implementation") (US Department of Justice SMART Office, 2016). Whereas the "substantial compliance" threshold required states to adhere to the letter of the law regarding SORNA guidelines, "substantial implementation" recognized that many states had adopted policies that did not substantially disserve (DNSD) the purpose of each SORNA's fourteen standard-based areas.[2] This more flexible DNSD designation also offered a mechanism for the Department of Justice to grant waivers for particular standards in cases where implementation was precluded by a state supreme court constitutional ruling requiring an approach inconsistent with SORNA directives (e.g., use of an individualized risk-based, as opposed to an offense-based, approach to classifying RSOs). Utilizing these more flexible standards, the Department deemed 18 states (and 135 tribes and 4 territories) as achieving "substantial implementation" of SORNA as of March 2020 (SMART Newsroom, 2020).

On the surface, the fact that barely one-third of the states received SORNA "substantial implementation" designation over a decade following SORNA's passage might be interpreted as evidence that perhaps Congress and the SMART office failed in their effort to render the nation's SORN systems more uniform. Yet closer scrutiny suggests that SORNA implementation is more complex and multifaceted than such a blanket binary assessment allows. In this context, Harris et al. undertook a multidimensional view of state-level SORNA implementation, based

---

[2] The fourteen areas were identified by the SMART Office as a way of conceptualizing substantial implementation through clustering similar SORNA requirements into broad categories: immediate transfer of information; offenses that must be included in the registry; tiering of offenses; required registration information; where registration is required; initial registration: generally; initial registration: retroactive classes of offenders; keeping the registration current; verification/appearance/duration requirements; public registry website requirements; community notification; failure to register as a sex offender; when a sex offender fails to appear for registration; and when a jurisdiction has information that a sex offender may have absconded.

TABLE 2.1 *Extent of state SORNA implementation as of July 2017*

	Not substantially implemented (n = 31)		All states (n = 49)	
Standards Met or DNSD	%	Cumulative (%)	%	Cumulative (%)
14	0	0	36.7	36.7
13	9.7	9.7	6.1	42.9
12	6.5	16.1	4.1	46.9
11	16.1	32.3	10.2	57.1
10	12.9	45.2	8.2	65.3
9	3.2	48.4	2.0	67.3
8	12.9	61.3	8.2	75.5
7	19.4	80.6	12.2	87.8
6	3.2	83.9	2.0	89.8
5	3.2	87.1	2.0	91.8
4	9.7	96.8	6.1	98.0
3	3.2	100.0	2.0	100.0
2	0.0	100.0	0.0	100.0
1	0.0	100.0	0.0	100.0

Source: Adapted from Harris, Walfield, Lobanov-Rostovsky, and Cubellis, 2017

on analysis of SMART Office and state-level documentation (Harris, Walfield, Lobanov-Rostovsky, & Cubellis, 2017).

The study's first finding of note was that full implementation of SORNA standards is the exception rather than the rule. Other than Kansas, all states (whether deemed "substantially implemented" or not) were found to deviate in some respect from SORNA standards, albeit most commonly in ways that were found to not substantially disserve (DNSD) the law's purpose. Among the substantially implemented states, half (9 of 18) had five or more SORNA standards in which they received DNSD designations.

Conversely, the study found that most states, including not substantially implemented (NSI) states, had been found by SMART to meet thresholds for substantially implemented for a majority of standards. As indicated in Table 2.1, more than two-thirds (67.3 percent) of all states and nearly half (48.4 percent) of NSI states were found to meet or not substantially disserve nine or more of SORNA's fourteen standards. All but four states (Kentucky, New York, Rhode Island, and West Virginia) were found to either meet or not disserve at least half of the standard areas, and three NSI states (Iowa, Nebraska, and Virginia) were deemed as failing to meet only one standard.

Regarding the specific areas of nonadherence to SORNA standards, the study identified five "problem areas" that accounted for nearly two-thirds (65 percent) of the instances in which states failed to meet SORNA standards: registry verification and appearance requirements (n = 26; 53 percent), public registry website requirements (n = 23; 47 percent), offenses that must be included in the registry (n = 21; 44 percent), keeping the registration information current (n = 18;

TABLE 2.2 *SORNA standards not met (rank ordered) as of July 2017*

Standard	N	%	Cumulative (%)
9: Verification/Appearance requirements	26	16.4	16.4
10: Registry website requirements	23	14.5	30.8
2: Offenses that must be included in the registry	21	13.2	44.0
8: Keeping the registration current	18	11.3	55.3
3: Tiering of offenses	15	9.4	64.8
11: Community notification	12	7.5	72.3
4: Required registration information	12	7.5	79.9
1: Immediate transfer of information	11	6.9	86.8
6: Initial registration: Generally	8	5.0	91.8
14: When a jurisdiction has information that a sex offender may have absconded	5	3.1	95.0
13: When a sex offender fails to appear for registration	4	2.5	97.5
5: Where registration is required	2	1.3	98.7
7: Initial registration: Retroactive classes of offenders	1	0.6	99.4
12: Failure to register as a sex offender: State penalty	1	0.6	100.0
Total Standards Not Met	159		

Source: Adapted from Harris, Walfield, Lobanov-Rostovsky, and Cubellis, 2017

38 percent), and tiering of offenses ($n = 15$; 31 percent). These data are summarized in Table 2.2.

With more than half of states not meeting the verification and in-person appearance requirements, this standard represents the biggest impediment toward full implementation. The vast majority of state SORN systems (92 percent) did not meet the requirements to the frequency of in-person appearances, a result largely stemming from under-classifying offenses and/or utilizing mail-in verification forms. Furthermore, a number of states had established guidelines for registrants to petition for removal from the registry that did not meet the duration required by SORNA.

SORNA requires each state to maintain a public registry website, which is comprised of, at minimum, ten core items,[3] supplemented by other requirements such as links to safety and sexual offending-related educational resources. Whereas every state had information posted regarding the registration-triggering offense(s), name(s) and alias(es), current photograph, and physical description, numerous states did not provide employer address, school address, vehicle information, or required criminal history information. The posting of a registrant's school and employer information continues to be controversial and was cited as a barrier when the initial guidelines were released (National Consortium for Justice Information and Statistics, 2009).

[3] These ten items are: absconder status, criminal history of convictions, current offense, employer address, name and aliases, current photograph, physical description, resident address, school address, and vehicle information.

The failure of states to meet the standard governing covered offenses has largely stemmed from their failure to include juveniles adjudicated delinquent for sexual offenses in a manner specified by SORNA. The matter of state adherence to SORNA's juvenile registration requirements is explored in greater detail in the next section.

In order to keep the registration current, the duties of jurisdictions vary depending on if they are the residence jurisdiction, employment jurisdiction, or school juris-diction. The failure of states to meet this standard was largely driven by the information required by the residence jurisdiction. Specifically, of the eighteen states that did not meet this standard, a vast majority ($n = 16$) did not require registrants to notify the authorities in their residence jurisdiction twenty-one days in advance of travel outside the United States. Additionally, some states did not require in-person updates or the occurrence of updates within the required time frame of three business days. Of the states that failed to meet the employer and school jurisdiction information requirement, this was largely attributed to not requiring offenders to update all of their information and/or allowing for mail or online changes rather than in person.

The last barrier to implementation concerns the tiering of offenses. Of the fifteen states found to not meet this requirement, the vast majority (87 percent) had a large number of offenses that were under-classified, relative to SORNA classifications, resulting in a shorter duration for registration and fewer in-person verifications for RSOs. This issue is addressed in greater detail later.

2.2.1.2 Key Issues and Points of Variation in State Systems

Building on the systematic quantitative analysis described above, Harris and col-leagues conducted a series of in-depth case studies of ten states with varied "substan-tial implementation" profiles, producing a more refined understanding of state SORNA implementation experiences (Harris, Kras, & Lobanov-Rostovsky, 2020; Harris, Kras, Lobanov-Rostovsky, & Ann, 2020). In tandem with the quantitative data, these findings suggest that, although states diverge from SORNA in varying degrees and in various ways, two areas in particular account – either directly or indirectly – for a substantial proportion of states' failure to meet SORNA standards. Perhaps not coincidentally, these two areas have each engendered significant policy debate and account for much of the inter-state variation in the structure and operation of SORN systems. The first such area involves state provisions regarding the registration of juveniles who have been adjudicated delinquent (as opposed to convicted in adult court) for sexual offenses; the second involves the systems and criteria used by states to classify RSOs for the purposes of establishing registry requirements and eligibility for community notification. Below, we address each of these issues in turn.

2.2.2 *Registration of Juveniles*

Prior to SORNA's passage, thirty-six states already had provisions requiring certain juveniles who are adjudicated delinquent and/or convicted in adult criminal court to be subject to some form of registration and notification (US Department of Justice, 2015). Although states before SORNA often subjected juveniles convicted in adult court to SORN, SORNA required that juveniles adjudicated delinquent for certain types of sexual offenses also be targeted. In the wake of SORNA, five states (Florida, Louisiana, Maryland, Tennessee, and Wyoming) amended their laws to permit registration of juveniles in general accordance with federal standards (US Department of Justice, 2015).

The initial SORNA guidelines issued by the SMART Office in 2008 adopted a fairly "hard line" surrounding the law's adjudicated juvenile provisions, despite substantial concerns raised by states, juvenile justice experts, and others during the guidelines' public comment period (Harris & Lobanov-Rostovsky, 2010). These concerns were further reflected in the results of surveys conducted in the years following the release of the 2008 guidelines, indicating that state officials perceived SORNA's requirements surrounding juvenile registration to be among the most significant impediments to SORNA implementation (US Department of Justice, 2016a). The concerns were also a prominent focus of congressional hearings surrounding the AWA's reauthorization (and hence SORNA) in 2009 (Sex Offender Registration and Notification Act (SORNA): Barriers to Timely Compliance by States, 2009).

Partially in response to these concerns, the SMART Office issued revised guidelines in 2011 and 2016, modifying aspects of SORNA, and granted states a measure of flexibility, especially regarding the implementation of SORNA's juvenile registration requirements (US Department of Justice, 2011; US Department of Justice, 2016a). Among the key changes, the guideline revisions served to narrow the universe of adjudicated juveniles who would be required to register and afforded states the ability to exempt juveniles from public notification requirements. Despite these changes, state failure to include juvenile adjudications within the range of covered offenses remained a SORNA implementation barrier for nineteen states as of 2017 (Harris, Walfield, Lobanov-Rostovsky & Cubellis, 2017).

Although many states have failed to meet SORNA thresholds surrounding juvenile registration, it should be noted that many states actually exceed the federal requirements. As noted earlier, most states that require the registration of juveniles did so prior to SORNA's passage. Many utilize more expansive criteria for including juveniles on the registry, require greater registration durations for juveniles, allow judges and prosecutors more discretion in making registration eligibility decisions, and allow for more juvenile registration information to be released to the public (Harris, Walfield, Shields, & Letourneau, 2015).

Based on a 2015 Department of Justice review, as indicated in Table 2.3, forty states in some manner register adjudicated juveniles. Of these, twenty-six states (52 percent) mandate registration of juveniles who have been adjudicated delinquent for

TABLE 2.3 *Summary of juvenile registration requirements*

	n	%	Cumulative (%)
Juvenile registration			
Mandatory	26	52	52
Discretionary	11	22	74
Hybrid	3	6	80
None	10	20	100
Public registry inclusion			
Mandatory	16	32	32
Discretionary	9	18	50
None	25	50	100

serious sexual offenses based solely on the offense. Eleven states (22 percent) allow such registration subject to judicial discretion and three others (6 percent) provide for a "hybrid" system under which registration may be warranted based on both the nature of the offense and certain other criteria. Compared to states with discretionary systems, states with mandatory registration tend to have longer periods of registration and more stringent rules regarding removal from the registry.

Of the forty states that provide for juvenile registration, sixteen require that this information be posted on the public website, nine allow for such posting based on some form of discretion, and fifteen prohibit such posting. Coupled with the ten states that do not provide for registration of adjudicated juveniles, twenty-five states in total include them on their public websites, and twenty-five do not. Among the ten states that do not provide for registration of adjudicated juveniles, most allow for registration of youth who are criminally convicted in adult court, although states vary considerably in specifying the minimum age and qualifying offenses (US Department of Justice, 2015).

2.2.3 *Registrant Classification Systems*

Another significant point of variation across state SORN systems involves the methods and criteria used to distinguish RSOs from one another. Along with the issue of juvenile registration, the means of classifying RSOs has emerged as perhaps the most significant source of debate surrounding the implementation of state SORN systems, particularly when viewed in the context of SORNA implementation. This is attributable in large part to the fact that RSO classification is central to determining a broad range of SORN parameters, including length of registration, frequency of annual verification of registry information, and the means and extent to which RSO information is made publicly available. Additionally, RSO classification designations can affect provisions contained in state or local law, including mandatory lifetime supervision and restrictions on residence, loitering, or employment.

Over time, states have developed varied methods of classifying RSOs. The methods vary on three general dimensions: (1) the extent to which classes of registrants are distinguished from one another; (2) the criteria used in the classification process; and (3) the systems by which classification decisions are made.

Regarding the first dimension, states vary considerably in the extent to which they differentiate among the populations that they require to register. The majority of states operate some form of a multi-tier system, typically involving two or three categories that are ostensibly tied to the levels of risk to the community. As discussed shortly, these states vary in the standards and methods used to determine tiers or levels. At the other end of the spectrum are states operating single-tier systems that make none or few classificatory distinctions among registrants for purposes of reporting, registration duration, notification, and related factors. Such systems, which as of mid-2017, were operative in seven states, are generally coupled with universal lifetime registration requirements.[4] In most cases, these states also include special designations and provisions for populations such as juveniles or those deemed "sexual predators" based on certain standards (Gotch, Ann, & Harris, 2017). Florida, for instance, distinguishes between "sexual offenders" (designated on the basis of registerable offense) and "sexual predators" (designated on the basis of registerable offense and a judicial finding), with both categories requiring lifetime registration and notification, but the latter requiring more frequent verification requirements (Florida Department of Law Enforcement, 2017).

The second dimension of variation in state SORN classification practices relates to the criteria employed in classification decisions. A majority of states operate "offense-based" systems that utilize the nature and severity of the conviction offense and/or the number of prior offenses as the sole criteria for classifying individuals. Others operate systems (sometimes referred to as "risk-based" systems) that require classification of individuals based on consideration of factors that have been empirically linked to sexual recidivism risk, such as age, number of prior sex offense convictions or adjudications, victim gender, relationship to the victim, and indicators of psychopathy and deviant sexual arousal. As of mid-2017, thirteen states operated SORN systems that utilized such risk-based systems in some shape or form (Gotch, Ann, & Harris, 2017).[5]

Third and finally, states distinguishing among registrants vary in terms of the systems and processes employed in establishing tier designations. In general, offense-based classification systems are marked by their relative simplicity and uniformity, and they permit most classification decisions to be made via standardized administrative processes that require minimal professional judgment. Risk-based systems, which generally employ the use of actuarial risk assessment

---

[4] As of 2017, these states are Alabama, California, Colorado, Florida, Missouri, South Carolina, and Wyoming. In October 2017, the California governor signed into law a provision that will transition the state to a three-tiered system as of 2021.

[5] These states, which vary significantly in the extent and nature of their risk evaluation systems and protocols, were Arizona, Arkansas, Georgia, Massachusetts, Minnesota, Montana, New Jersey, New York, North Dakota, Oregon, Rhode Island, Texas, and Washington.

instruments and in some cases clinical assessments, are generally more resource-intensive and require higher levels of personnel involvement in the classification process. For example, some states rely predominantly on professional clinical assessments conducted under the auspices of correctional or law enforcement agencies, while others utilize multidisciplinary review boards or judicial discretion to establish registrant tiers and/or sexual predator status.

In its effort to foster uniformity among state systems, SORNA predicated its standards on a uniform offense-based classification scheme, benchmarked to the federal criminal code and based on the presumptive severity of the conviction offense. Tier 1 registrants, for whom SORNA mandated 15-year registration and annual in-person registration updates, includes those convicted of misdemeanors or sexual-related offenses that carry a penalty of less than 1 year in prison. Tier 2, which requires 25-year registration and semiannual in-person updates, includes those convicted of offenses involving sexual abuse or exploitation involving minors. Tier 3, mandating lifetime registration and quarterly in-person updates, applies to individuals convicted of aggravated sexual assault, contact offenses against children younger than 13 years, kidnapping of minors (unless committed by a parent or guardian), and attempts or conspiracies associated with any of these crimes (US Department of Justice, 2008).

SORNA requirements have presented a particular challenge to states utilizing individual risk-based systems. Although SORNA guidelines do not preclude consideration of supplemental risk factors for certain limited purposes (e.g., identifying those in lower offense tiers who might be candidates for more stringent or higher tier requirements), SORNA requires jurisdictions with risk-based models to make substantial modifications to their classification systems by supplanting their existing registrant categories with offense-based tiers.

A study by Harris et al. (2010) evaluated the impact of transitioning to the SORNA offense-based classification system, drawing on the experiences of Ohio and Oklahoma, two of the first states to undertake a reclassification of their registrant populations under the SORNA guidelines. The study found that the transition to SORNA tiers in those states produced a redistribution of registrants from lower SORN levels to higher ones and found statistically significant differences between newly reclassified "high-risk" individuals and those designated as high risk under prior registration classification systems (Harris, Lobanov-Rostovsky, & Levenson, 2010). In practical terms, these findings indicate that the transition to SORNA-based tiers, at least for some states, may produce a fundamental recalibration of what is considered "high risk."

Research regarding the SORNA offense-based tier system has called into question the reliability of the SORNA tiers as predictors of recidivism risk. A study in New York State, which uses a risk-based classification system, concluded that the SORNA tiers were less effective at predicting re-offense than that state's existing risk-based system (Freeman & Sandler, 2009). Another study applied SORNA offense-based tiers to approximately 1,700 convicted adult sex offenders released from prison in Minnesota, New Jersey, Florida, and South Carolina, and determined that they did a poor job of identifying actual high-risk offenders and recidivists. Indeed, in one state, Florida, individuals who would be placed in Tier 2 under SORNA had higher actual recidivism rates than those whose prior convictions would place them in Tier 3 (the highest SORNA risk category) (Zgoba et al., 2016).

2.2.3.1 International Systems

In the wake of its nationwide adoption in the United States, SORN has attracted the attention of other countries. A 2016 review conducted by the SMART Office indicated that about twenty-five countries have established some form of registry at either the national and/or local level, with several others considering doing so. Some, such as Poland's legislation introduced in 2016, resemble US policy (US Department of Justice, 2016b).[6] In general terms, English-speaking countries have taken a more ambitious approach to registration, especially compared to other nations in continental Europe (Jones & Newburn, 2013; Petrunik & Deutschmann, 2008).

Registration requirements concerning the scope of registerable offenses, duration, frequency, timeliness when updating information, and information demanded vary significantly among countries; most countries do not require notice of international travel, in stark contrast to US policy. Furthermore, some countries limit their registry exclusively to individuals convicted of a sex offense against a minor (US Department of Justice, 2016b).

International resort to community notification is much less common. Compared to the United States, other countries not only have much smaller registry populations, they most often prohibit general public access to registries and refrain from broad dissemination of registry information (US Department of Justice, 2016b). South Korea is the only nation that allows the public access to and the display of a registry website, which features only high-risk offenders convicted of offenses against minors based on a risk assessment. Registered sex offenders there, moreover, are subject to registration for five or ten years, shorter than is common in the United States (Logan, 2011; Shin & Lee, 2005). Public registries, targeting comparatively small populations, also exist in Alberta and Manitoba, Canada; Western Australia, Australia; and Lagos, Nigeria (US Department of Justice, 2016b; Victorian Law Reform Commission, 2017). A few countries allow for public disclosure by request pursuant to specific circumstances, which vary widely (US Department of Justice, 2016b).

---

[6] Argentina, Australia, Bahamas, Canada, Chile, Cyprus, France, Germany, India, the Republic of Ireland, Jamaica, Kenya, Maldives, Malta, New Zealand, Nigeria, Portugal, South Africa, South Korea, Spain, Taiwan, Trinidad and Tobago, and the United Kingdom in addition to six United Kingdom Commonwealth Nations.

Of the international systems, those in the United Kingdom and Australia have been the most extensively studied and documented. While their registries were inspired by those established in the United States, the two jurisdictions have taken a more conservative approach to public notification, limiting who can obtain registry information and the circumstances under which such information can be released.

Following the passage in the United States of Megan's Law by Congress in 1996, the United Kingdom passed the Sex Offenders Act 1997, which directed agencies to create local registries, requiring any individual convicted of a sex crime against adults or juveniles to register with law enforcement (Edwards, 2003; Jones & Newburn, 2013). However, as a result of a high-profile child sexual victimization that was blamed on the system's purported failure to manage risk appropriately, in part due to the lack of a nationwide registry, the Act was later modified. In particular, the Sexual Offences Act 2003 established the Violent and Sex Offender Register, which made registry information accessible to law enforcement, probation, and prison officials throughout the United Kingdom (Bichard Inquiry, 2004; Edwards, 2003; Harper & Harris, 2017).

Under the amended regime, individuals (including juveniles), who receive a caution, community order, or prison sentence, for certain sexual offenses are required to register and placed in one of four tiers based on the length of their sentence and the circumstances of the offense committed. For adults, this ranges from two years to indefinitely; juveniles typically are targeted for half the duration, though they may be placed on the register indefinitely as well (O'Sullivan, Hoggett, Kemshall, & McCartan, 2016). Once released into the community, individuals must register within three days and henceforth verify their information annually; all verifications are done in person. Information requirements are similar to the United States and include things such as DNA samples, fingerprints, address(es), social media identifiers, with any changes also reported in person within three days (Jones & Newburn, 2013).

While the United Kingdom initially resisted community notification, following another high-profile case, the Child Sex Offender Disclosure Scheme, commonly known as "Sarah's Law," was piloted in four police English districts in 2008, and based on its reported success, a second pilot program was undertaken in Tayside, Scotland, 2009–2010 (Zgoba, 2017). The regime is quite narrow, compared to SORN laws currently operable in the United States. As described by Zgoba:

> The law allows parents, care givers, guardians and even third parties (when appropriate) to apply with the police concerning whether a specific individual who has contact with a child has a criminal conviction for child sex offenses. The applicant will have to agree to sign a confidentiality agreement. If the police consider the named individual a risk, they will disclose this information to the applicant,

otherwise no information will be provided; a "risk" means they have a previous conviction for sexual abuse and/or other acts regarding the safeguarding children. . . . Information will only be provided to the person best suited to protect the child and may only be used for the purpose it was requested (i.e., child protection) (Zgoba, 2017).

In 2015, Northern Ireland implemented its own provision, referred to as the Child Protection Disclosure Scheme (Police Service of Northern Ireland, 2017). Disclosure in England, Northern Ireland, Scotland, and Wales generally follows the same multistage process described previously, but at times differs in law, policy, and practice (O'Sullivan, Hoggett, Kemshall, & McCartan, 2016; Zgoba, 2017). Requests for registrant information and approvals for access have been low (Manson, 2015; O'Sullivan et al., 2016).

Australia's system was established first at the state level, beginning with New South Wales in 2000, and was modeled after the UK's Sex Offenders Act 1997 (Vess, Langskaill, Day, Powell, & Graffam, 2011). By 2006, each of the Commonwealth's six states and two mainland territories had their own registry. A national registry was created in 2004, now known as the National Child Offender System, which runs concurrently with the registries operated by the states and territories (US Department of Justice, 2016b). These jurisdictions have some autonomy, including setting requirements for registrants, registrable offenses, duration of reporting periods, and penalties for failure to register (Vess et al., 2011; Australian Institute of Family Studies, 2013). Access to these registries remains restricted to law enforcement personnel and contains only offenders who have committed sexual offenses against children, though some states and territories now include other serious, nonsexual offenses against children (Australian Criminal Intelligence Commission, 2017; Vess et al., 2011). Although states and territories introduced bills for community notification and a public registry, only the State of Western Australia passed legislation to do so, in 2012. Western Australia employs a three-tiered approach similar to many US jurisdictions, a publicly accessible registry that is limited to less than 5 percent of registrants (high risk, missing, and noncompliant registrants), and a disclosure scheme based on the system in the United Kingdom (Whitting, Day, & Powell, 2017).

Most Australian jurisdictions, however, utilize a two-tier, offense-based system (Vess et al., 2011). Class 1 offenses require adult offenders to register for 8 years and class 2 offenses 15 years, though jurisdictions vary in how they handle repeat offenders. While each state and territory allows for lifetime registration (with the exception for juveniles whose maximum reporting period can only be 7.5 years), requirements are not uniform. There is further variation in offense classifications, with some jurisdictions including nonsexual violent crimes against children. The Australian Capital Territory, Tasmania, Victoria, and Western Australia additionally register individuals who have committed sex offenses against adults

(Victorian Law Reform Commission, 2017). Annual in-person reporting is required regardless of classification across all states and territories; failure to comply typically results in a fine (referred to as penalty units) and/or a two-year prison term though two states have a maximum sentence of five years (Australian Institute of Family Studies, 2013; Vess et al., 2011; Victorian Law Reform Commission, 2017). The information required when registering is uniform across the country and mirrors that required in the United States (Vess et al., 2011; Victorian Law Reform Commission, 2017).

2.3 SUMMARY AND CONCLUSION

Over the past quarter century, SORN has emerged as a prominent fixture in sex offender community management policies within the United States, and while federal efforts to create a uniform system have achieved some success, true uniformity among states is likely to remain an elusive goal. State SORN systems have been and remain idiosyncratic, reflecting political, bureaucratic, and historical forces operative within individual jurisdictions. Furthermore, relative to the international community, US policy regarding SORN has been the most ambitious, including inter alia the scope of registerable offenses, registration requirements and, most especially, resort to community notification. Recognizing and accounting for this diversity is an important first step for anyone engaged in evaluating the impact of SORN or advocating for the reform of SORN policies.

REFERENCES

Adam Walsh Child Protection and Safety Act, Pub. L. No. 109–248.
Australian Criminal Intelligence Commission (2017). National Child Offender System. www
.acic.gov.au/our-services/child-protection/national-child-offender-system.
Australian Institute of Family Studies (2013). Offender Registration Legislation in Each Australian State and Territory. https://aifs.gov.au/cfca/offender-registration-legislation-each-australian-state-and-territory.
Bichard Inquiry (2004). *The Bichard Inquiry Report*. London, UK: The Stationery Office.
Custer, B. (2019). Variations in State Sex Offender Statutes: Implications for U.S. Higher Education. *Criminal Justice Policy Review*, 30(6), 906–924.
Edwards, D. (2003). ViSOR – Violent and Sex Offender Register. *Criminal Justice Matters*, 51(1), 28.
Florida Department of Law Enforcement (2017). *Florida Sexual Offenders and Predators, Frequently Asked Questions*. http://offender.fdle.state.fl.us/offender/FAQ.jsp.
Freeman, N. & Sandler, J. (2009). The Adam Walsh Act: A False Sense of Security or an Effective Public Policy Initiative? *Criminal Justice Policy Review*, 21(1), 31–49.
Gotch, K., Ann, Q., & Harris, A. J. (2017). Sex Offender Registration and Notification Systems in the United States: A Review of System Characteristics. *Working manuscript under development*.

Government Accountability Office. (2013). *Sex Offender Registration and Notification Act: Jurisdictions Face Challenges to Implementing the Act, and Stakeholders Report Positive and Negative Effects* (Publication No. GAO-13-211). Reported to the Subcommittee on Crime, Terrorism, and Homeland Security, Committee on the Judiciary, House of Representatives, Washington, DC: www.gao.gov/assets/660/652032.pdf.

Harper, C. A. & Harris, A. J. (2017). Applying Moral Foundations Theory to Understanding Public Views of Sexual Offending. *Journal of Sexual Aggression*, 23(2), 111–123. DOI: 10.1080/13552600.2016.1217086.

Harris, A. J. (2011). SORNA in the Post-Deadline Era: What's the Next Move. *Sex Offender Law Report*, 12(6), 81–86.

Harris, A. J. & Lobanov-Rostovsky, C. (2010). Implementing the Adam Walsh Act's sex offender registration and notification provisions: A survey of the states. *Criminal Justice Policy Review*, 21(2), 202–222. DOI: 10.1177/0887403409346118.

Harris, A. J., Lobanov-Rostovsky, C., & Levenson, J. S. (2010). Widening the Net: The Effects of Transitioning to the Adam Walsh Act's Federally Mandated Sex Offender Classification System. *Criminal Justice and Behavior*, 37(5), 503–519.

Harris, A. J., Kras, K., & Lobanov-Rostovsky, C. (2020). Information sharing and the role of sex offender registration and notification: Final technical report submitted to National Institute of Justice (Award # 2014-AW-BX-K003).

Harris, A. J., Kras, K. R., Lobanov-Rostovsky, C., & Ann, Q. (2020). States' SORNA Implementation Journeys: Lessons Learned And Policy Implications. *New Criminal Law Review*, 23(3), 315–365. doi:https://doi.org/10.1525/nclr.2020.23.3.315.

Harris, A. J., Walfield, S. M., Lobanov-Rostovsky, C., & Cubellis, M. (2017). State Implementation of the Sex Offender Registration and Notification Act: A Multi-Dimensional Analysis. *Justice Research and Policy*, 18(1), 24–47. DOI: 10.1177/1525107117745645.

Harris, A. J., Walfield, S. M., Shields, R. T., & Letourneau, E. J. (2015). Collateral Consequences of Juvenile Sex Offender Registration and Notification: Results from a Survey of Treatment Providers. *Sexual Abuse: A Journal of Research and Treatment*, 28(8), 770–790. DOI: 10.1177/1079063215574004.

Home Office. (2010). *The Child Sex Offender (CSO) Disclosure Scheme Guidance Document*. London, UK: Home Office. www.gov.uk/government/publications/child-sex-offender-disclosure-scheme-guidance.

Jacob Wetterling Crimes Against Children and Sexually Violent Offender Registration Act, 42 U.S.C. 14071 (1994).

Jones, T. & Newburn, T. (2013). Policy Convergence, Politics and Comparative Penal Reform: Sex Offender Notification Schemes in the USA and UK. *Punishment & Society*, 15(5), 439–467. DOI: 10.1177/1462474513504801.

Justice Act (Northern Ireland) 2015 (c.9).

Logan, W. A. (2010). The Adam Walsh Act and the Failed Promise of Administrative Federalism. *George Washington Law Review*, 78, 993–1013.

Logan, W. A. (2011). Prospects for the International Migration of U.S. Sex Offender Registration and Community Notification Laws. *International Journal of Law and Psychiatry*, 34(3), 233–238. DOI: 10.1016/j.ijlp.2011.04.007.

Manson, W. (2015). "Keeping Children Safe": The Child Sex Offender Disclosure Scheme in Scotland. *Journal of Sexual Aggression*, 21(1), 43–55. DOI: 10.1080/13552600.2014.950352.

National Conference of State Legislatures. (2009). *NCSL's Top 10 Issues of 2010*. www.ncsl.org/default.aspx?tabid=19397.

National Consortium for Justice Information and Statistics. (2009). *SEARCH Survey on State Compliance with the Sex Offender Registration and Notification Act (SORNA)*. www .search.org/files/pdf/SORNA-StateComplianceSurvey2009.pdf.

O'Sullivan, J., Hoggett, J., Kemshall, H., & McCartan, K. (2016). Understandings, Implications and Alternative Approaches to the Use of the Sex Offenders Register in the UK. *Irish Probation Journal, 13*, 84–101.

Petrunik, M. & Deutschmann, L. (2008). The Exclusion–Inclusion Spectrum in State and Community Response to Sex Offenders in Anglo-American and European Jurisdictions. *International Journal of Offender Therapy and Comparative Criminology, 52*(5), 499–519. DOI: 10.1177/0306624X07308108.

Police Service of Northern Ireland (2017). Child Protection Disclosure Arrangements. www .psni.police.uk/advice_information/child-protection/child-protection-disclosure-arrange ments/.

Sex Offender Registration and Notification Act (SORNA): Barriers to Timely Compliance by States: Hearing Before the Subcommittee on Crime, Terrorism, and Homeland Security of the Committee on the Judiciary House of Representatives. 111th Cong. 1 (2009).

Sex Offenders Act 1997 (c.51).

Sexual Offenses Act 2003 (c.42). www.legislation.gov.uk/ukpga/2003/42/contents.

Shin, J. & Lee, Y.-B. (2005). Korean Version of the Notification Policy on Sexual Offenders: Did it Enhance Public Awareness of Sexual Crimes Against Minors? *International Journal of Offender Therapy and Comparative Criminology, 49*(4), 376–391. DOI: 10.1177/0306624X04271255.

SMART Newsroom (2020). Available at https://smart.ojp.gov/press-releases-speeches (last visited February 28, 2020).

U.S. Department of Justice. (2008). The National Guidelines for Sex Offender Registration and Notification. *Federal Register, 73*(128), 38030–38070.

U.S. Department of Justice. (2011). Supplemental Guidelines for Sex Offender Registration and Notification. *Federal Register, 76*(7), 1630–1640.

U.S. Department of Justice. (2015). Prosecution, Transfer, and Registration of Serious Juvenile Sex Offenders. www.smart.gov/pdfs/smartjuvenilessum.pdf.

U.S. Department of Justice. (2016a). Supplemental Guidelines for Juvenile Registration Under the Sex Offender Registration and Notification Act. *Federal Register, 81* (147), 50552–50558.

U.S. Department of Justice. (2016b). Global Survey of Sex Offender Registration and Notification Systems. https://smart.gov/pdfs/global-survey-2016-final.pdf.

U.S. Department of Justice SMART Office. (2016). Substantial Implementation of SORNA. https://smart.gov/substantial_implementation.htm.

Vess, J., Langskaill, B., Day, A., Powell, M., & Graffam, J. (2011). A Comparative Analysis of Australian Sex Offender Legislation for Sex Offender Registries. *Australian & New Zealand Journal of Criminology, 44*(3), 404–424. DOI: 10.1177/0004865811419065.

Victorian Law Reform Commission (April 2017). Sex Offenders Registration. www .lawreform.vic.gov.au/sites/default/files/SOR_Final%20Report_Full%20text.pdf.

Whitting, L., Day, A., & Powell, M. (2017). An Evaluation of the Impact of Australia's First Community Notification Scheme. *Psychiatry, Psychology and Law, 24*(3), 339–355. DOI: 10.1080/13218719.2016.1247606.

Zgoba, K. M. (2017). Memorialization Laws in the United Kingdom: A Response to Fear or an Increased Occurrence? *American Journal of Criminal Justice, 42*(3), 628–643. DOI: 10.1007/ s12103-016-9376-0.

Zgoba, K. M., Miner, M., Levenson, J., Knight, R., Letourneau, E., & Thornton, D. (2016). The Adam Walsh Act: An Examination of Sex Offender Risk Classification Systems. *Sexual Abuse: A Journal of Research and Treatment, 28*(8), 722–740. DOI: 10.1177/1079063215569543.

3

Registries and Registrants:

Research on the Composition of Registries

Alissa R. Ackerman

Chapter 3 analyzes the demographic makeup and composition of state sex offender registries. The data reject the popular narratives of incomplete registries filled with dangerous individuals. The chapter begins by investigating the widely reported counts of registered individuals from the National Center for Missing and Exploited Children (NCMEC). While NCMEC reports that there are nearly one million registrants nationwide, no true national registry exists to confirm this claim. Further, independent studies indicate that many registrants simply do not live in their listed community – they may be incarcerated, committed, deported, or deceased. Additionally, the data refute common arguments that registries are systematically incomplete with regard to "missing" registrants. The chapter next examines how registries reflect broader racial dynamics. The typical registrant is middle-aged and white. However, registries are disproportionately black, and black registrants are overclassified with respect to recidivism risk. Finally, the chapter dissects the technical and data challenges affecting registries. While intra-registry duplicates plague few jurisdictions, many registries contain individuals present on other states' registries. This chapter contends that policymakers should account for these deficiencies when considering sex offender policy.

As noted in Chapter 1, while sex offender registration originated in California in the late 1940s, it did not come to fuller fruition for several decades, in the 1990s, when it was combined with community notification. In the early years, individuals who wanted information on specific registrants could request information from a local police department or could access information via a CD-ROM, provided directly from law enforcement. However, by 2003 all states had public internet sex offender registries.

This chapter focuses on the population makeup of state sex offender registries. The chapter begins by dissecting the aggregate counts compiled by the National Center for Missing and Exploited Children (NCMEC), which have typically served as the standard reference point in public discussion and policy discourse regarding sex offender registration and notification (SORN). The chapter then describes the research methodology and findings of the first attempt to disaggregate and better understand the mass of individuals targeted by SORN laws. Discussion then turns to the several studies later undertaken to expand our understanding of the composition of state sex offender registries. The chapter concludes by highlighting the significant data collection and analysis challenges that stand in the way of securing comprehensive and accurate information on the composition of registries and the major importance of having such information when devising SORN laws and policies.

3.1 THE NATIONAL CENTER FOR MISSING AND EXPLOITED CHILDREN

In 2005, NCMEC, an independent nonprofit entity, first generated its map concerning state sex offender registries, which included estimated raw counts and rates per 100,000 people. To produce the map, NCMEC conducted a telephone survey of all US states and territories twice a year. The map, which was recently discontinued for reasons that remain unknown, underwent periodic changes in its almost fifteen-year existence. For example, in some iterations, NCMEC highlighted states that included incarcerated individuals in their totals, but over time this was discontinued. As a result, it has been difficult to discern, from NCMEC estimates alone, how many individuals are actually living in the community, as opposed to being involuntarily civilly committed, incarcerated, deported, deceased, or living out of state.

In 2005, NCMEC estimated that there were roughly 549,038 registered sex offenders (RSOs) in the United States. In mid-year 2019, NCMEC reported 917,771 RSOs on state and US territory registries, 279 RSOs per 100,000 residents.

NCMEC has significant ties to the federal government. In 2015 alone, the organization received over thirty million dollars in federal contracts and grants (NCMEC, 2015). It has been in existence for nearly thirty years and continues to have a considerable voice in the expansion of federal responsibility for sex offender management policies (Harris, Levenson, & Ackerman, 2014). Until a few years ago, the NCMEC count was the only national level estimate available. As discussed next, however, this is no longer the case, and research has cast doubt on NCMEC's registry population data.

3.2 ADDITIONAL RESEARCH REGARDING REGISTRY POPULATIONS

3.2.1 *Counts of "Publicly" Registered Sex Offenders*

Research on the composition of registries has been undertaken for well over a decade. Until 2011, every study conducted focused on specific states or individual jurisdictions within states. This was in part because there was no national sex offender registry. Even today, the closest thing available is the amalgamation of state, tribal and US territory registries contained in the Dru Sjodin National Sex Offender Registry, maintained and operated by the US Department of Justice.[1]

---

[1] The Dru Sjodin National Sex Offender Registry site can be accessed at www.nsopw.gov/?AspxAutoDetectCookieSupport=1.

A second, more pragmatic reason is that no national data set existed. In this vacuum, the NCMEC population counts played a determinative role.

In 2011, Ackerman and her colleagues published the first study of the national RSO population, based on a data set that integrated information from every state registry (Ackerman, Harris, Levenson, & Zgoba, 2011). To create this database, the researchers worked with a computer programmer to develop software that would "scrape" all available information on every publicly registered individual. The database included information on 449,127 RSOs who were listed on a public registry in 2010. Registry information on forty-nine states (Michigan was excluded due to missing data), Washington, DC, Puerto Rico, and Guam were included in the data set. The database originally included 498,536 entries. After the exclusion of Michigan's data, duplicate listings (N=13,515), and nonsexual offenders (n=3,120),[2] the final data set represented 66 percent of the 2010 NCMEC total (Ackerman, et al., 2011).

The difference between the larger NCMEC estimates and the final Ackerman et al. (2011) data download is in significant part explained by the fact that NCMEC tallied all registrants. Many individuals, however, are not publicly registered (i.e., not subject to notification) and information about them remains accessible only to law enforcement agencies. For example, in 2010, NCMEC estimated that Minnesota had roughly 16,000 RSOs. However, the state only lists its highest risk offenders on its public registry. So while there may be 16,000 RSOs in the state, data about them would not have been publicly available for download (fewer than 200 individuals were actually publicly registered).

Finally, when considering data on "public" registries, it is important to keep in mind that registrants listed do not necessarily live in local communities. Ackerman et al. (2011) concluded that almost 11 percent of registrants on public registries nationwide are incarcerated or civilly committed, while another 1 percent remains on public registries despite being deported or deceased. Certain state registries reach more broadly than others. For example, Florida included the largest number of deported (n=1,991) and deceased (n=388) registrants.[3] Florida also listed individuals living in other states (n=16,925). When individuals not living in a Florida community (i.e., were confined, deported, deceased, or living in another jurisdiction) are subtracted, registrant counts are reduced by over half compared to the NCMEC Florida estimate (Ackerman, Levenson, & Harris, 2012). The same study by Ackerman et al. (2012) found that based on data from five states examined – Florida, Georgia, Illinois, New York, and Texas – that about 43 percent of registrants

---

[2] Kansas, for instance, publicly notifies communities about drug and violent offender registrants.

[3] According to the state's registry website (https://offender.fdle.state.fl.us/offender/sops/faq.jsf), registrants "reported deceased remain on the website for one year after the date of death as provided on the death certificate. This allows victims, the community, and local law enforcement time to be notified" (Florida Department of Law Enforcement (FDLE), n.d.).

reflected in NCMEC data for those states did not live in the community, with corresponding lower registrant rates per 100,000 residents.[4]

3.2.2 *"Missing" Registered Sex Offenders*

Another data misunderstanding concerns the common assertion by advocates that a large proportion of RSOs are "missing," that is, that accurate locational information on them is lacking, creating corresponding public safety risk. A 2003 survey from *Parents for Megan's Law* first articulated the contention that there are "100,000 missing sex offenders," which has figured centrally in public policy discussion regarding the need for more rigorous SORN laws and increased interstate conformity, culminating in adoption of the federal Adam Walsh Act (AWA) in 2006. (Lord, 2011; Parents for Megan's Law, 2010)

Research, however, has failed to substantiate the contention. Ackerman et al. (2011), in their study of national RSO counts, found the following: transient/homeless (n=6,942), absconding (n=5,349), in violation (n=4,152), and whereabouts/address unknown (n=1,254). When these numbers are combined, they do not even approach 20,000 RSOs, much less the 100,000 classified as "missing." In a follow-up study, Levenson and Harris (2012) came to a similar conclusion, finding little evidence to support the "100,000 missing" claim, even using the most inclusive and broad definition of "missing."

3.2.3 *Registered Sex Offenders: Demographics*

The publicly registered RSO population, based on 2010 data, is overwhelmingly white (66 percent) and male (98 percent) (Ackerman et al., 2011). This statistic, it is worth noting, should be interpreted in light of the fact that information distinguishing Hispanic/Latino individuals is often not provided, with registrants categorized as "white" or "black."[5] Nevertheless, the biracial data are noteworthy. Despite comprising 13 percent of the US population, more than 22 percent of registrants are Black (Ackerman et al., 2011).[6] This percentage is jurisdiction-dependent. For example, almost 50 percent of registrants in Louisiana are Black (Ackerman et al., 2011). Eight states have a percentage of Black registrants in excess of 30 percent. The Delaware, New Jersey, and Georgia registries range between 42 percent and 43 percent Black registrants, and between 36 percent and 37 percent of individuals on the registries in Minnesota, Alabama, and North Carolina are Black (Ackerman et al., 2011). In twelve jurisdictions,

---

[4] According to a recent government report, 60 percent of Florida registrants in 2018 did not reside in Florida communities (Office of Program Policy Analysis and Government Accountability [OPPAGA], 2018).

[5] Only thirteen jurisdictions utilize Hispanic or Latino as a demographic descriptor (Ackerman & Sacks, 2018).

[6] The study, it is important to note, did not contain data from the District of Columbia, Guam, Maine, Maryland, or Puerto Rico due to lack of sufficient available information on ethnicity and race.

less than 5 percent of the RSO population are Black. Three of the twelve state registries (those in North Dakota, New Hampshire, and Vermont) are 3 percent Black, and three state registries (Wyoming, Montana, and Idaho) are 2 percent—or less—Black (Ackerman et al., 2011).

Much like prison populations, in all jurisdictions the percentage of African-American RSOs exceeded their percentage in a jurisdiction's general population (Ackerman & Sacks, 2018). A more recent nationwide study focusing on the racial composition of publicly available registries produced some interesting findings. Ackerman & Sacks (2018) created a data set consisting of RSOs from fifty-four US jurisdictions,[7] during 2012–2014, N=488,260. Like the earlier study by Ackerman et al. (2011), the more recent study showed that Whites comprise the majority of registrants nationwide (72 percent) (Ackerman & Sacks, 2018). The percentage of African-American registrants was 26.5 percent, with the remaining percentages Asian, Native American/Pacific Islander, and Hispanic (Ackerman & Sacks, 2018).

Geographically, in every state, the percentage of African-American RSOs exceeded their corresponding state population percentage, although some states had dramatically higher percentages than others. As Ackerman & Sacks (2018) noted:

> African Americans comprise almost 50% of the Mississippi, Maryland, and Louisiana registries. Delaware, New Jersey and Georgia range between 43 and 45% African American and between 36 and 39% of individuals on the registries in South Carolina, Minnesota, Virginia, Alabama, North Carolina and Illinois are Black (Ackerman & Sacks, 2018, p. 8).

With respect to per capita rates, in every state except Michigan, African-American registrants had a higher rate of inclusion on registries. Whereas the per capita (per 10,000 residents) of whites nationally was 16.88, the African American per capita rate was 31.78 nationally, ranging from 3.90 in Minnesota to 98.29 in South Dakota (Ackerman & Sacks, 2018). Southern states, while often having a higher percentage of African Americans on their publicly available registries compared to other states, per capita manifested the least disparate impact:

> [I]n Florida, Mississippi, Alabama, Georgia, Arkansas, and South Carolina, the comparative rates of inclusion are 1.36, 1.50, 1.54, 1.56, 1.65 and 1.65, respectively. That is, African Americans are 1.36 times more likely to be included on public registries than Whites in Florida. Conversely, in Massachusetts, Rhode Island, New Jersey, Washington, Connecticut, Oregon, and Minnesota, African Americans are far more likely to be placed on public sex offender registries. African Americans are 3.61,

---

[7] Puerto Rico, American Samoa, and St. Croix were included, but Washington, DC, Maine, the US Virgin Islands, and the Nothern Mariana Islands were excluded because these registries could not be scraped using an automated process.

3.72, 4.00, 4.26, 4.32, 7.20, and 10.99 times more likely to be listed on public sex offender registries in Massachusetts, Rhode Island, New Jersey, Washington, Connecticut, Oregon, and Minnesota, respectively (Ackerman & Sacks, 2018, p. 10).

The study also examined the racial composition of the several states that subject only a subpopulation of registrants to community notification, targeting individuals thought to pose the highest risk of recidivism. Within these states, the racial effect was more noticeable compared to states that subject all registrants to notification, regardless of risk. In Washington State, for instance, among registrants subject to notification, African Americans were over four times more likely to be publicly listed than white RSOs (Ackerman & Sacks, 2018). In Oregon and Minnesota, African Americans were over seven and ten times as likely to be listed, respectively (Ackerman & Sacks, 2018).

Another recent study also detected disparate racial impact (Ticknor & Warner, 2020). In the study, researchers examined Ohio's SORN scheme, which is modeled on the federal AWA's I–III offense-based tiering system (Level I being least "dangerous" and III being most, with corresponding increased registration requirements and duration) (Ticknor & Warner, 2020). The study evaluated actual recidivism of registrants and concluded, inter alia, that in the five-year period studied, 26.46 percent of African Americans and 10.54 percent of the whites were "overclassified," that is, did not recidivate (Ticknor & Warner, 2020). African Americans were thus two-and-one-half times more likely to be overclassified, which the authors contended "raise[d] specific concerns about the utility of the tier designation but also suggest that there may be underlying racial bias in the tier system" (Ticknor & Warner, 2020, p. 14).

With respect to the age of RSOs, composite national RSO data indicate that registrants are predominantly middle-aged, with an average age of 44.9; almost 75 percent of registrants fall between the ages of 26 and 55 (Ackerman et al., 2011). As discussed later, securing accurate data on juvenile registrants is difficult, but based on the data analyzed comparatively, few registrants are under the age of 18 years. However, three jurisdictions – Delaware, Washington, DC, and Guam – have at least 2 percent of their registrants under the age of majority (Ackerman et al., 2011). On the other end of the age spectrum, 38 percent of California registrants are above the age of 55 years, a statistic that is perhaps explainable by the fact that California law at the time required lifetime registration and reached back retroactively several decades (Ackerman et al., 2011).[8] Notably, in all jurisdictions, 25 percent or more of all registrants were above the age of 46 (Ackerman et al., 2011). With lifetime registration requirements in many jurisdictions, and only modest opportunity available to exit registries, the mean age will likely continue to rise.

---

[8] In 2017, California amended its law, providing significantly greater opportunity for individuals to exit the state registry (Guitierrez, 2017).

3.3 REGISTERED SEX OFFENDERS: OFFENSE BACKGROUND AND RISK LEVELS

Reliable data on more registrant-specific matters has proven more difficult to secure. A study undertaken by Ackerman et al. (2011), for instance, concluded that only 24 states provided information on registrant risk level or sexual predator designation. Data analysis revealed that states either utilized multi-tiered systems, a sexual predator designation for certain offenders, or a one-tiered system that made little distinction between individuals. A small number of states (13) have a specific designation for sexually violent predators or sexually dangerous registrants, comprising 4.9 percent of the total nationwide RSO population (Ackerman et al., 2011). These findings, it is important to note, are complicated by variations in state definitions of the designations.

The same study by Ackerman et al. (2011) highlighted the difficulty in obtaining accurate victim age and gender data. The researchers found that in cases where victim status as a minor was specified (n=170,679), 86 percent of victims were 17 years of age or younger, with about 33 percent of victimized individuals 10 years of age or younger (Ackerman et al., 2011). Victim gender was available for just over 80,000 cases (n=80,742); 87 percent of these cases involved female victims (Ackerman et al., 2011). Viewed as a whole, in short, the vast majority of cases where victim age and gender were available involved female adolescents and children (Ackerman, et al., 2011).

The final phase of analysis focused on the offenses for which individuals were placed on public registries. When the data for this study were originally collected, two files were created: an offender file and an offense file. The offense file was linked to the offender file using a unique identifier. Approximately 460,000 offense records were tied to 350,000 offenders.[9] An offense-level analysis would have provided a more well-rounded and nuanced picture, but given the variation in how states provided offense data, the analysis was performed at the offender level. A series of text queries was created that combined like terminology. For instance, to ascertain the number of offenders with a minor age victim, a combination of phrases, including "minor," "child," and "juvenile" were utilized. While an individual may have had three offenses that included a particular child victim, he would only be counted once. Any individual flagged for a specific offense query was captured only one time, regardless of how many counts or offenses were listed.

Ten main items were included in this analysis (offense against a child, rape, sodomy, computer/internet, aggravated, pornography, kidnapping/abduction, solicitation/enticement, force/forcible, exhibitionism/voyeurism). When considering the data, it is important to keep in mind that other offenses were not captured and that the individual items are not mutually exclusive. This means that an individual flagged for an offense against a minor might also have been flagged for other

---

[9] Some states utilize one offense field per offender, even if that offender had multiple offenses. Other states utilized a row for each specific offense.

TABLE 3.1 *National snapshot of public registrants (2011)*

Mean Age	44.3
% white	66
% male	98
% with minor victims	90
% designated high risk	13 (25 states reporting)
# absconded	5,236
# homeless	6,943 (43 states reporting)
# in community (not deceased, deported, in another state)	392,867

combinations of queried terms. For example, an individual might have been flagged for both offense against a child and kidnapping, or rape and force.

With these caveats in mind, data analysis revealed that more than half of RSOs (55 percent, n=193,000) for whom an offense was provided had an offense against a child. Thirteen percent (n=45,974) and 11 percent (n=39,851) of offenders had a rape or aggravated offense, respectively. Five percent of RSOs used force or had a forcible offense (n=16,406). For each other query percentages ranged from less than 1 percent (computer/internet) to 4 percent (sodomy). Table 3.1 provides a national snapshot of the Ackerman, et al. (2011) study.

3.4 METHODOLOGICAL CHALLENGES

Data collection and analysis efforts regarding SORN face a number of significant methodological challenges. To a considerable extent, such challenges stem from the variability of state SORN laws and policies, which reflect the policy preferences of multiple state legislatures and agencies. Ambiguous and varied definitions of seemingly straightforward terms make comparing across jurisdictions problematic. In such an environment, researchers must remain mindful of the limits of cross-jurisdictional data collection and analysis. Despite the efforts of federal policy makers to standardize state registries, as a result of pressure imposed by the AWA in 2006, fewer than twenty states have substantially implemented its requirements,[10] and even within such jurisdictions significant variations remain.[11] Further, the specific information included on registries differs by jurisdiction, and significant gaps exist in the nature and extent of data available to researchers. Even within given jurisdictions, moreover, vague statutory definitions and data input and collection irregularities pose challenges.

---

[10] See the website for the Office of Sex Offender Sentencing, Monitoring, Apprehending, Registering, and Tracking. (www.smart.gov/newsroom_jurisdictions_sorna.htm) (last visited February 26, 2020). for the current status of SORNA implementation.

[11] For further discussion of state compliance with federal SORN policies see Chapter 2.

TABLE 3.2 *Five state disaggregation from Ackerman, Levenson, &*
Harris (2012)

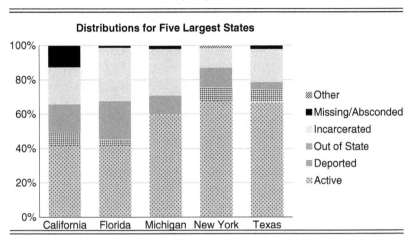

One important illustration of the difficulty concerns the methods used to report data on the racial background and juvenile status of registrants. With respect to race, as noted earlier, most states do not include data on race/ethnicity for categories other than white, black, and Asian/Pacific Islander, which presents difficulty in the many states with large Hispanic/Latino populations. Texas is one such state. Presumably, these individuals are classified as white or black. With respect to juveniles, in their 2011 study, Ackerman et al. found that less than 1 percent of the total registry nationwide consisted of juveniles (with age determined at the time of data collection). However, to determine how many individuals are on registries for offenses committed when they were juveniles, one must undertake a rather complex mathematical calculation. Varied state definitions of juvenile status also complicate data analysis.

Another potential pitfall of data analysis stems from the possibility that any given registrant might be counted more than once in registry population totals. To get a better understanding of actual state registry counts, amid the possibility of double counting, Ackerman and colleagues collected and analyzed data from five US states with substantial registry populations (Ackerman, Levenson, & Harris, 2012). The researchers provided refined counts and prevalence rates for RSOs actually living in the jurisdiction, after accounting for those who were incarcerated, living in another jurisdiction, deported, or deceased. Notably, 43 percent of individuals listed on the registries in these five states (Florida, Georgia, Illinois, New York, and Texas) were not living in the jurisdiction (Ackerman, Levenson, & Harris, 2012). The proportion ranged from 25 percent in Texas to 60 percent in Florida (Ackerman, Levenson, & Harris, 2012). Table 3.2 provides a visual representation of these findings.

In another study, Harris, Levenson, & Ackerman (2014) employed a similar rubric to that used by the NCMEC. The researchers developed a list of agencies responsible for administering and updating state sex offender registries and provided them with a link to a survey that focused on multiple registry information domains (Harris, et al., 2014). Ultimately, forty-two states and two US territories participated. One of the study's findings was that almost 9 percent of registrants were living in another jurisdiction (Harris, et al., 2014). Other categories included registrants who had been deported or were deceased. The latter two categories represented only 3 percent of cases, but appeared to be concentrated in specific jurisdictions (Harris, et al., 2014). The foregoing highlighted concern regarding the risk that registry populations reflect double counting of individuals.

To address this concern, Ackerman developed a new data set. It took almost a year to do so because each state utilizes its own internet code to populate its website and many states had changed their protocols in the ensuing years. The new data set included 502,740 registrants, which represented 67 percent of the NCMEC total at mid-year 2013. The first paper to be published using the new data looked specifically at whether and how double counting was a problem (Ackerman, 2015). In total, 3.4 percent of the rows (n=17,131) were duplicated, representing 8,436 registrants (Ackerman, 2015). Interestingly, fifteen jurisdictions did not have a single double counted individual while five jurisdictions (Tennessee, Illinois, North Carolina, New York, and Florida) included more than 1,000 duplicated rows (Ackerman, 2015).

In addition to determining which jurisdictions had the highest number of double-counted registrants, Ackerman (2015) created a matrix to determine whether registrants were double counted within or across jurisdictions. Most states did not have duplicate records within the state, with the exception of Colorado, where there were over 200 registrants (n=226) with 452 duplicate records (Ackerman, 2015). Most surprisingly, Ackerman found that duplicated RSO records appeared to involve particular combinations of jurisdictions. Tennessee, for instance, shares 354 duplicate records with Illinois, yet shares only 17 with Connecticut. Table 3.3 replicates the matrix provided in Ackerman (2015).

3.5 DATA LIMITATIONS

As noted, varied legal definitions and approaches to RSO classification among states present major obstacles to research seeking to document the nation's RSO populations. These limitations are compounded by missing data and human error introduced during the entry of information into registries.

Using an automated data-gathering process, such as the "scraping" programs noted earlier, highlights these limits. While scraping might be needed in order to collect state public registry data when it is otherwise lacking, it comes with some risk. In their first study, Ackerman et al. (2011) learned that in some instances missing data was not a result of the registries themselves but rather stemmed from the collection of the registry data.

TABLE 3.3 *Matrix of states with duplicate records*

Jurisdiction	TN	IL	NC	NY	FL	AL	CO	CA	TX	OH	IA	KY	MS	LA	MD	CT
TN	26															
IL	354	2														
NC	292	86	4													
NY	114	44	272	6												
FL	228	153	207	293	0											
AL	228	88	65	59	179	46										
CO	48	56	23	27	8	10	452									
CA	78	67	51	38	10	30	31	292								
TX	46	8	32	22	28	11	25	46	12							
OH	123	72	59	55	15	35	1	9	18	24						
IA	26	293	13	6	3	2	3	8	6	1	10					
KY	223	117	45	13	6	28	5	1	8	38	5	0				
MS	171	83	27	19	4	85	2	3	17	2	2	1	0			
LA	55	48	27	16	26	44	9	18	80	6	2	8	38	24		
MD	28	15	67	41	7	4	0	5	6	5	0	0	0	2	26	
CT	17	6	34	109	34	14	2	6	4	3	1	2	2	2	6	0

This was apparent after the researchers cross-checked data with other sources, which indicated that the data collection process failed to properly capture certain registrants and specific information about them. Altering the data "scraping" program and applying it again often remedied the problem, but the need for caution persists. Given the large number of registrants, it is difficult to ascertain exactly how much missing data exists. This is not to say that some state registries are not sufficiently comprehensive for robust research to be undertaken. Rather, it is a caution to future researchers to utilize data taken directly from states, not scraped data, whenever possible.

When obtaining data directly from the states is not possible, automatized scraping programs can be of use. However, it is crucial for anyone using such data to be cognizant of the possibility of missing data and understand why it is missing. There may be substantial differences between data missing from state registry sites and data that were not scraped by the automated process.[12] Further, researchers should be cognizant of variations in state definitions, particularly those related to offenses and offense-level data and those related to risk classifications.

3.6 CONCLUSION

The research findings discussed here permit several conclusions. First and foremost, it is clear that the NCMEC estimates of public registries, which have served as

---

[12] There are no specific standards with which states must comply regarding how to compile and disseminate state registry information. Most states utilize similar platforms, which allow for a seamless data scraping process, others use platforms that do not allow for automation.

a primary basis for public knowledge and discussion, are consistently inflated. Furthermore, research has also failed to substantiate the frequently made claim that 100,000 registrants are "missing." And, despite the common perception that registries are composed of high-risk individuals who have committed serious sex offenses, the RSO population actually comprised individuals who are mostly low or moderate risk: fewer than 20% fall in the high risk category.

Several other data points are worth mentioning. Based on research conducted to date, it appears that just above 80 percent of registrants actually live in the community. In terms of demographics, on average, they are middle-aged (mean=44.3 years of age) and overwhelmingly male (98 percent). For registrants where offense data are provided, over half have committed an offense against an individual under age 17 years and above 80 percent of the time that child is female. We also know that reliable information regarding individuals on public registries for crimes they committed as juveniles is not readily available. Finally, in terms of race/ethnicity, the registry population is predominantly white (66 percent) yet African Americans are overrepresented across several dimensions, as in the corrections system more generally.

This chapter has also sought to emphasize that methodological challenges and data deficits impede research concerning the composition of state registries. Moving forward, it is imperative that policy makers and researchers be aware of these deficits. Based on experience to date, state SORN laws and policies will continue to vary, making cross-jurisdictional comparisons difficult. However, governments should strive to ensure that their registries contain information that is as accurate as possible. And researchers should continue their efforts to surmount methodological obstacles and provide research findings of the highest quality possible. Evidence-based SORN law and policy demand no less.

REFERENCES

Ackerman, Alissa R. (2015). National estimates of registered sex offenders in the United States: Is double counting a problem?. *American Journal of Criminal Justice, 40,* 75–88.

Ackerman, Alissa R., Harris, Andrew, Levenson, Jill, & Zgoba, Kristen. (2011). Who are the people in your neighborhood? A descriptive analysis of individuals on public sex offender registries. *International Journal of Law and Psychiatry, 34,* 149–159.

Ackerman, Alissa R., Levenson, Jill S., & Harris, Andrew J. (2012). How many sex offenders really live among us? Adjusted counts and population rates in five U.S. states. *Journal of Crime and Justice, 35,* 464–474.

Ackerman, A.R. & Sacks, M. (2018). Disproportionate minority presence on U.S. sex offender registries. *Justice Policy Journal, 15,* 1–20.

Adam Walsh Sex Offender Registration and Notification Act, Pub. L. No. 109–248, § 111, Stat. 2466 (2006).

Florida Department of Law Enforcement (FDLE) (n.d.). Florida sexual offenders and predators, frequently asked questions. FDLE. https://offender.fdle.state.fl.us/offender/sops/faq.jsf.

Guitierrez, Melody. (2017, October 6). New California law allows sex offenders to be removed from the registry. SFGATE. www.sfgate.com/politics/article/California-law-sex-offenders-Jerry-Brown-12259564.php.

Harris, Andrew J., Levenson, Jill S., & Ackerman, Alissa R. (2014). Registered sex offenders in the U.S.: Behind the numbers. *Crime and Delinquency*, 60, 3–33.

Harris, A. J. & Lobanov-Rostovsky, C. (2009). Implementing the Adam Walsh Act's sex offender registration and notification provisions: A survey of the states. *Criminal Justice Policy Review*, 21, 202–222.

Jacob Wetterling Crimes Against Children and Sexually Violent Offender Registration Act, Pub. L. No. 103–322, § 170101, 108 Stat. 2038. (1994).

Levenson, J. S. & Harris, A. J. (2012). 100,000 sex offenders missing ... or are they? Deconstruction of an urban legend. *Criminal Justice Policy Review*, 23, 375–386.

Lord P. (2011). Palumbo says there are 500,000 registered sex offenders in the U.S. and 100,000 are unaccounted for. www.politifact.com/rhode-island/statements/2011/mar/03/peter-palumbo/palumbo-says-there-are-500000-registered-sex-offen/GoogleScholar.

National Center for Missing and Exploited Children (2015). *Annual Report*. www.missingkids.com/en_US/publications/NCMEC_2015.pdf.

Office of Program Policy Analysis and Government Accountability (OPPAGA), State of Florida. *Sex offender registration and monitoring triennial review 2018* (Report No. 18–08) www.oppaga.state.fl.us/MonitorDocs/Reports/pdf/1808rpt.pdf.

Parents for Megan's Law (2010). www.parentsformeganslaw.org/public/meganFederal.html.

Ticknor, B. & Warner, J.J. (2020). Evaluating the accuracy of SORNA: Testing for classification errors and racial bias. *Criminal Justice Policy Review*, 23, 3–21. doi.org/10.1177/0887403418786548.

4

Law Enforcement and SORN

Kristen M. Zgoba and Richard Tewksbury

Chapter 4 discusses the relationship between SORN laws and law enforcement. Since the inception of SORN laws, proponents of registration and notification have viewed them as tools for effective law enforcement. The significant financial costs to maintain and enforce these laws, however, may outweigh any usefulness they offer to law enforcement in terms of reducing sex offense victimization. The chapter first describes how states implement SORN laws. State and local law enforcement agencies are charged with the initial registration of covered individuals. Thereafter, these agencies monitor registrants and facilitate community notification. They conduct unannounced visits, maintain online registries, and inform community groups. These tasks impose substantial costs on the police, diverting resources from other criminal justice priorities. Many agencies form specialized units for SORN enforcement; others outsource aspects to private, for-profit companies. The chapter next analyzes how law enforcement personnel perceive SORN laws – in particular, their effectiveness. Studies show that individuals in law enforcement often doubt the efficacy of registration and notification, despite consistently supporting them. Law enforcement agents also recognize the costs SORN laws carry for their agencies and priorities. Ultimately, this chapter questions whether SORN laws are worth the costly burdens they impose on law enforcement.

Law enforcement has primary responsibility for maintaining and enforcing sex offender registration and notification (SORN) laws. As registries have grown in size and scope, the resources necessary for law enforcement to satisfy their responsibilities have grown and become a significant budgetary and personnel issue for agencies.

This chapter focuses on the range of duties and responsibilities that fall to law enforcement agencies in enforcing SORN laws and the costs (financial, organizational, and other) incurred by law enforcement in doing so. While other governmental entities can have significant and important responsibilities regarding SORN, the focus here will be on law enforcement.

As explored elsewhere in this volume, substantial literatures now exist regarding the effect of SORN on registrants (and their families), as well as community members, two of the three populations principally affected by SORN laws. The third population – law enforcement agencies and their officers (primarily local police, state police, and county sheriffs) – has been the subject of comparatively little study, which is both surprising and unfortunate, given the central role played by law enforcement in the operation of SORN laws.

4.1 EARLY REGISTRIES AND LAW ENFORCEMENT

The origins of sex offender registries date back to at least the nineteenth century (Logan, 2009). Predecessor methods included "rogues' galleries" of photographed criminals known to the police, as well as registries containing personal identifying information such as physical characteristics (Logan, 2009). In the early 1930s, local governments created registries of convicted criminal offenders more generally, with efforts starting in southern California but soon gaining popularity nationwide (Logan, 2009).

It was not until 1947 that a state – California – adopted a registry that singled out convicted sex offenders in particular. Whether focused exclusively on convicted sex offenders or more generally on ex-convict populations, the job of collecting and maintaining registry information fell to local law enforcement, which saw the utility of registration. According to a newspaper account from 1955, police in St. Paul, Minnesota would not engage in

> spectacular roundups of unregistered criminals ... But when a St. Paul detective recognizes a known felon on the street or gets a tip that he is in town (perhaps to case a job), the detective either knows where the man can be reached – if he has registered – or has grounds on which to pick him up and hold him – if he hasn't (Albuquerque Journal, 1955).

Birmingham, Alabama police embraced registration not only because it provided "an accurate check upon the criminal element," but also because it could "result in an exodus of a great many known criminals" (N.Y. Times, 1935). In Philadelphia, registration provided police a tool to "make it tough on a fellow" known to be "wrong," providing a basis to detain individuals until details of additional criminal activity they might be involved in could be obtained (University of Pennsylvania Law Review, 1954).

Law enforcement also played a key role in the genesis of community notification. As noted in Chapter 1, the idea of making registrants' identifying data publicly available originated in Washington State, in the wake of a brutal sexual assault of a boy in May 1989 by a recently released convicted sex offender, whose whereabouts in the community were known to police. In the wake of the crime, a task force was convened to assess ways in which public safety could be enhanced, and community notification was included in the final report issued based on the recommendation of Mountlake Terrace Police Chief John Turner. Turner, alarmed that an individual believed to pose a high risk of molesting children was to reside in his community, provided a physical description of the individual to the public and school authorities (Judd & Lobos, 1989).

4.2 LAW ENFORCEMENT RESPONSIBILITIES

Since its origin, a chief justification of registration has been that it can facilitate police investigation and apprehension of offenders if a registrant recidivates. As noted by the Center for Sex Offender Management (2008):

> Sex offender registration creates a mechanism for "keeping track" of convicted sex offenders and provides authorities with a natural starting point when investigating sex crimes. This is accomplished by collecting identifying information about convicted sex offenders (e.g., name, address, photograph, fingerprints, DNA sample) and entering this information into databases that are accessible to law enforcement agencies nationwide. The extensive information that is maintained in these databases can help investigators quickly rule in or rule out specific sex offenders as suspects.

The goal of notification differs: It seeks to allow community members to be proactive in their own security and safety by providing them with the knowledge needed to protect themselves – and their loved ones – from potential recidivist-registrants, whether by altering their own behavior or informing the police about suspicious behavior by registrants (Logan, 2009; Ragusa-Salerno & Zgoba, 2012). The principle underlying notification is "the more eyes, the better," allowing the public to be proactive in their own safety. As the New Jersey Legislature stated in its "legislative findings" in enacting the nation's first "Megan's Law," community notification is justified on the premise that "public safety will be enhanced by making information about certain sex offenders ... available to the public" (New Jersey Legislature, 2001).

Today, sex offender registries exist in all fifty states, the District of Columbia, US territories, and dozens of tribal jurisdictions (Harris, Lobanov-Rostovsky & Levenson, 2016). As a result, law enforcement agencies in every US jurisdiction are tasked with the responsibilities associated with collecting information from registrants, maintaining the SORN infrastructure (e.g., websites), and verifying registrants' information. Although the precise number of registrants nationwide remains unclear, as discussed in Chapter 3, the combined registry population in the United States now certainly numbers in the hundreds of thousands (Harris, Levenson & Ackerman, 2014).

State and local law enforcement are in the engine room, so to speak, in effectuating SORN. They collect registration information from registrants, manage registry databases, update information regarding registrants as it becomes available, monitor registrants in the community, conduct address and other registry information verifications, apprehend registrants in violation of registry requirements (e.g., failure to verify data at a required interval), and work with community members/groups in conducting community notification. Agencies employ differing methods to accomplish these tasks, in accord with state and local SORN laws and regulations.

Once released from prison, or upon entering to live in or visit a jurisdiction, individuals required to register must report in person to their local law enforcement agency (generally within 72 hours) and furnish the background information specified by law. Most large police departments have created internal SORN units to handle the ever-increasing number of registrants. At the outset of the registration process, individuals are photographed and fingerprinted, and DNA information is often collected and stored. Information typically includes an individual's name, any aliases, home address, height, weight, eye color, scars/tattoos, convictions, a description of the offense, car make and model, license plate number, place of employment or school, and email address, although some jurisdictions also collect additional information (Mustaine & Tewksbury, 2013). The information must be collected, recorded, and entered into the database, which is a time-consuming process.

After initial registration, individuals must thereafter verify (usually in person) the continued accuracy of their registry information, on at least an annual basis, and apprise authorities in the interim of any changes (e.g., a change of residence). Law enforcement agencies are also the most common places that registered sex offenders visiting a jurisdiction must personally go to and complete temporary registration, in the event they are visiting another jurisdiction (Rolfe, 2019). As noted, officers also perform unannounced visits at the homes of registrants, to ensure compliance. In the event the jurisdiction prevents registrants from living near places such as schools, police must also verify that the distance requirement is satisfied (Center for Sex Offender Management, 2008; Ragsua-Salerno & Zgoba, 2012).

To get a sense of the many obligations of law enforcement occasioned by SORN, consider a hypothetical case of Cityville, a city of approximately 500,000 residents. Such a city would be expected to have approximately 1,038 registered sex offenders in residence.[1] If law enforcement officials devote an hour to registration/updates regarding each registrant, conduct three home visits annually (at two hours each, including transportation, planning, etc.), and a combined five hours of other tasks per registrant monitoring, investigating reports/tips, and so on, then the Cityville police will require 12,456 person-hours to complete these tasks. If employees work a forty-hour week, there is a need for 311 additional workweeks, which would require more than six new full-time positions to handle the tasks for one year. Depending on how much Cityville pays its officers, the additional burdens will carry a significant financial cost.

In addition to their registration-related duties, law enforcement personnel figure centrally in effectuating community notification. In some jurisdictions, personnel hold community meetings to share information about local registrants with citizens. They often must also share registrant information with local schools, day care centers, local youth organizations, and other community entities (Bandy, 2011).

In response to the significant resource demands, and concern that registry information contains outdated or incorrect information regarding registrants, governments have turned to the private sector for help. In suburban New York City, for instance, in April 2013, the Suffolk County Legislature contracted with the private nonprofit organization Parents for Megan's Law to conduct address verifications,

---

[1] Estimate based on Tucson, Arizona's population of 530,000 in 2016 and total registrants in early 2017.

monitor registrants' use of social media, develop a system for reporting SORN violations, and provide community education regarding SORN (Jones v. County of Suffolk, 2019). The contract, which required use of retired law enforcement officers to carry out the tasks, paid the organization $2.7 million for its services over a three-year period (Newsday, 2016).

Agencies have also farmed out responsibility for maintaining registries to for-profit companies, with "OffenderWatch" attracting most business. The company's website relates that it "Specializes in Providing Sex Offender Services to Law Enforcement Agencies and to their Communities" and that "[m]ore than 3,000 local, state, and federal agencies trust their sex offender registries to OffenderWatch, the nation's most widely used sex offender registry management and community notification solution." The company stores and maintains registrant information received from law enforcement on the software it provides, which also sends email alerts to community members, uses pinpoints on maps to indicate registrants' addresses, and enables community members to conduct database searches regarding registrants (OffenderWatch, 2019).

4.3 FINANCIAL AND RESOURCE IMPACT ON LAW ENFORCEMENT

A few studies have evaluated the financial consequences associated with the operation of SORN laws. The first analysis found that in New Jersey the price tag and resource consequences were quite significant (Zgoba, Witt, & Dalessandro, 2008). The research team mailed a cost assessment questionnaire to the twenty-one SORN units housed within county prosecutor offices. In 2008, total expenses attributable to the ongoing implementation of the state Megan's Law were estimated to be $3,973,932 per annum (according to the participating counties). Of total per annum outlays, staffing costs accounted for $3,605,972, internet registry maintenance for $146,300, equipment/supplies for $130,483, and other/miscellaneous expenses for $91,177 (Zgoba et al., 2008).

According to completed surveys, the number of employees dedicated to SORN unit operations totaled 78, and an estimated 5,873 cases were processed during that time. Moreover, counties reported that law enforcement officers performed a total of 31 door-to-door notification events throughout that year (with 1 event equaling 300 households) for tier three sex offenders (those thought to pose greatest risk). The cost for Megan's Law implementation during the 2006 calendar year was estimated to be $1,557,978, whereas costs during calendar year 2007 totaled $3,973,932. This change represented a 155 percent increase in expenses (Zgoba et al., 2008). Given subsequent growth in the registry, it can reasonably be expected that these expenses have since grown significantly.

A recent report from Oregon sheds additional light on the major fiscal impact this can have on local departments. Budget cuts and insufficient staff for data entry and verification there caused a two-year backlog, resulting in the registry being disregarded by law enforcement (Bernstein, 2013).

4.4 LAW ENFORCEMENT PERCEPTIONS OF SORN

While a number of studies suggest significant community support of SORN (Levenson & Tewksbury, 2009; Tewksbury & Lees, 2006; Levenson, Brannon, Fortney & Baker, 2007; Armstrong, Miller, & Griffin, 2014), far fewer explore the sentiments of SORN's front-line actors–law enforcement. In an early study, Finn (1997) interviewed thirteen criminal justice officials and the consensus was that SORN was useful in managing sex offenders.

Farkas & Zevitz (2000) undertook one of the first large-scale studies of law enforcement views regarding SORN. The statewide survey of 312 Wisconsin police chiefs and sheriffs indicated use of interagency "notification teams." These teams entailed collaboration among police officers, corrections officers, district attorneys, and victim-witness representatives. Despite the shared responsibility, results indicated that SORN nonetheless required considerable law enforcement personnel time and budgetary resources. Respondents related that their main goal was to educate the public about sexual offending while not creating a panic (Farkas & Zevitz, 2000).

The Farkas and Zevitz study paved the way for a later study of twenty-one police agencies in the Midwestern and Western regions of the United States (Gaines, 2006). Among other findings, the study reported that police regarded staffing and funding for SORN as problematic, because it diverted money and man power from other important, but underemphasized responsibilities (Gaines, 2006).

In another study, Tewksbury and Mustaine (2013) surveyed law enforcement utilizing a Community Attitudes Toward Sex Offender (CATSO) scale, with a sample of 209 officers. They found that law enforcement held negative views of sex offenders, but a large majority (approximately 76 percent) disagreed that registrants are deterred by SORN, and only 38 percent believed that SORN was effective in preventing sexual offending. Moreover, 60 percent of respondents somewhat or strongly disagreed with the premise that being placed on a publicly available registry will deter a nonregistrant from committing a sexual offense. Paradoxically, respondents also conveyed that, even though they did not believe that a public registry would increase public safety, they still believed it was necessary: 63 percent believed that all convicted sex offenders should be placed on the registry, with 90 percent indicating support for the use of online registries. The study also noted that respondents with longer tenure in their positions were less likely to believe that SORN would successfully meet its goal of reducing sexual offending. For each additional year on the job, respondents were 4 percent less likely to believe that SORN was effective in preventing sexual offending.

A study of law enforcement perspectives initiated in 2014 produced a cluster of publications (Harris et al., 2016; Walfield et al., 2017; Harris, Levenson, Lobanov-Rostovsky & Walfield, 2018; Cubellis, Walfield & Harris, 2018). The mixed-methods study used data from 101 interviews of law enforcement personnel drawn from a nationwide survey sample.

One of the studies focused in particular on four areas of inquiry: (1) SORN as an information tool for the public; (2) SORN as an information tool for law enforcement; (3) matters concerning sex offender monitoring, supervision, and compliance enforcement; and (4) the challenges posed by homeless and/or transient registrants (Harris, Levenson, Lobanov-Rostovsky, & Walfield, 2018). As for the first inquiry, the study found generally strong support for "the public dimensions of registries and that [respondents] strongly support citizens' right to know about sex offenders living in their communities." Respondents, however, expressed reservations about the ability of citizens to understand and contextualize registry information. Moreover, a solid majority (62 percent) expressed concern that public registries created a false sense of security and almost half (46 percent) expressed concern that registries generated unfounded or misplaced fear, with many respondents (especially agency heads) indicating that the public would benefit from more detailed information regarding the public safety risk of particular registrants. The second inquiry, concerning the perceived benefit of SORN for law enforcement, garnered greater support, mainly as a means of monitoring registrants and somewhat less so in support of investigations. Despite this support, 60 percent of respondents expressed concern over the utility of registry data, especially uncertainty regarding lack of specificity of the offense histories of registrants. Regarding the third inquiry, monitoring of registrants, the study found that uniformed line staff were most concerned about issues relating to their monitoring caseloads, whereas respondents in agency leadership roles were more concerned about registry accuracy and efficiency. The last inquiry, concerning the challenges posed by registrants' transience and homelessness, elicited the greatest level of concern as a challenge, with almost three-quarters of respondents ranking it as either a major or moderate concern. The study authors concluded that the significant concerns elicited "are reflective of both pragmatic considerations as well as humanitarian or liberty-based ones" (Harris, Levenson, Lobanov-Rostovsky & Walfield, 2018).

Research has also compared the perceptions of front-line law enforcement with other criminal justice system officials. In 2015, Mustaine et al. published a comparative study of views regarding SORN among law enforcement; elected prosecutors from Ohio, Michigan, Kentucky, and Tennessee; prison wardens; parole board members; and community corrections officials. Results showed that law enforcement held the most negative views of sex offenders of all criminal justice officials (except prosecutors). Law enforcement was also less likely to believe that SORN was effective. With respect to the perceived fairness of SORN policies, law enforcement officials and prosecutors reported the greatest positive response (Mustaine, et al., 2015).

The result aligns with what is known as the "contact hypothesis," whereby the amount and intensity of contact one has with a particular type of individual is likely to positively influence the view of such an individual. Reflecting on the findings, Mustaine, et al. (2015) concluded that "criminal justice officials who do not commonly experience deep and intensive interactions with sex offenders may only see these offenders as 'cases' rather than individuals, which may explain [law enforcement's] more negative, cynical, and punitive viewpoints." When compared with experiences of community corrections officials, prison wardens and parole board members, police and prosecutors are likely to know offenders more superficially and in ways that reduce the individual to merely a "type" rather than an individual (Mustaine et al., 2015).[2]

Generally speaking, the existing literature shows that law enforcement sees value in SORN. Even though they acknowledge the limits of SORN as a public safety measure, officers still seem to approve of the continued use of SORN. Notably, the generally positive perspective among law enforcement contrasts with the low levels of support of SORN often found among mental health professionals (Connor & Tewksbury, 2017). Support among law enforcement has been consistent for over two decades, in large and small studies and with urban and rural departments.

4.5 CONCLUSION

Since its inception, registration has been viewed as an aid to law enforcement, providing a ready pool of potential suspects in the wake of commission of a sex offense. However, the actual utility of the registry as a tool for police to apprehend recidivists remains unclear, and as other chapters in this volume highlight, research continues to question whether SORN delivers promised public safety benefits for communities. At the same time, it is clear that SORN has significant financial impact on jurisdictions and imposes major burdens on law enforcement.

Considering the challenges and burdens imposed on law enforcement agencies by SORN, it is not surprising that there is at least some skepticism among law enforcement regarding the utility and wisdom of SORN. This is an interesting parallel to the results reported upon in Chapter 8 highlighting that the general public holds strongly favorable views of SORN, while often being skeptical of its efficacy and utility. Although the public strongly supports SORN, the level of support is significantly lower among those involved in the daily administration of SORN laws – law enforcement.

The costs of SORN are significant and varied, including financial outlays associated with paying law enforcement personnel to collect, maintain, and verify registrants' information, as well as implement community notification. Indeed, to

---

[2]   In a recent study, Call (2018) surveyed community corrections professionals (*n*=209) and disputed the contact hypothesis, finding instead that attitudes were most influenced by other factors such as parental status, political orientation, race, tenure, gender, and age.

satisfy these demands, governments increasingly are farming out SORN-related tasks to private entities, which while relieving law enforcement, only adds to the financial impact of SORN systems as a whole. Whether the substantial costs are warranted, in light of the benefits delivered by SORN, is a critically important question for citizens and policy makers to address. This is so because ultimately every SORN-related task required of law enforcement and every dollar spent on the operation of SORN distracts from other, perhaps more worthwhile public safety strategies.

REFERENCES

Albuquerque Journal (May 31, 1955), Two Laws Provide Invisible Weapons Against Crime in Minnesota City.

Armstrong, M., Miller, M., & Griffin, T. (2014). An examination of sex offender registration and notification laws: Can community sentiment lead to ineffective laws? In M. K. Miller, J. A. Blumenthal, & J. Chamberlain (eds.), *Handbook of Community Sentiment* (pp. 239–251). New York: Springer.

Bandy, R. (2011). Measuring the impact of sex offender notification on community adoption of protective measures. *Criminology & Public Policy*, 10(2), 237–264.

Belzer, R. (September 2015). The costs and benefits of subjecting juveniles to sex offender registration and notification. R Street, Study number 41.

Bernstein, Maxine. *Sex Offenders in Oregon: State Fails to Track Hundreds*, Oregonian (October 2, 2013), www.oregonlive.com/sexoffenders/special-presentation/.

Bonnar-Kidd, K. (2010). Sexual offender laws and prevention of sexual violence or recidivism. *American Journal of Public Health*, 100(3), 412–419.

Call, Corey (2018). The community corrections perspective toward sex offender management policies and collateral consequences: Does contact with sex offenders matter?. *Criminal Justice Studies*, 31(1), 1–7.

Carter, M., Bumby, K., & Talbot, T. (2004). Promoting offender accountability and community safety through the comprehensive approach to sex offender management. *Seton Hall Law Review*, 34, 1273–1297.

Center for Sex Offender Management (2008). *Key Roles of Law Enforcement in Sex Offender Management*. Washington, DC: Office of Justice Programs, U.S. Department of Justice.

Connor, D. P., & Tewksbury, R. (2017). Public and professional views of sex offender registration and notification. *Criminology, Criminal Justice, Law & Society*, 18(1), 1–27.

Cubellis, M., Walfield, S., & Harris, A. (2018). Collateral consequences and effectiveness of sex offender registration and notification: Law enforcement perspectives. *Intl. Journal of Offender Therapy and Comparative Criminology*, 62(4), 1080–1106.

Farkas, M., & Zevitz, R. (2000). The law enforcement role in sex offender community notification: A research note. *Journal of Crime and Justice*, 23(1), 125–139.

Finn, P. (1997). *Sex Offender Community Notification* (Volume 2, Number 2). Washington, DC: National Institute of Justice, U. S. Department of Justice.

Gaines, J. (2006). Law enforcement reactions to sex offender registration and community notification. *Police, Practice and Research*, 7(3), 249–267.

Government Accountability Office (2013). *Sex Offender Registration and Notification Act: Jurisdictions face challenges to implementing the Act, and stakeholders report positive and negative effects.* GAO-13–211: Published February 7, 2013.

Harris, A., Lobanov-Rostovsky, C., & Levenson, J. (2016). *Law Enforcement Perspectives on Sex Offender Registration & Notification.* Document Number 250181. Washington, DC: National Institute of Justice, U. S. Department of Justice.

Harris, A., Levenson, J., Lobanov-Rostovsky, C., & Walfield, S. (2018). Law enforcement perspectives on sex offender registration & notification: Effectiveness, challenges and policy priorities. *Criminal Justice Policy Review*, 29(4), 391–420.

Harris, A., Levenson, J., & Ackerman, A. (2014). Registered sex offenders in the United States: Behind the numbers. *Crime & Delinquency*, 60, 3–33.

Judd, R., & Lobos, I., "We're Just Waiting for Someone to Ruin Lives": School Officials Told of Release of Man with "Predatory" Nature, Seattle Times, July 21, 1989.

Justice Policy Institute. What will it cost states to comply with the Sex Offender Registration Notification Act www.justicepolicy.org/images/upload/08–08_fac_sornacosts_jj.pdf

Kabat, A. R. (1998). Scarlet letter sex offender databases and community notification: Sacrificing personal privacy for a symbol's sake. *American Common Law Review* (35).

Lawson, L., & Savell, S. (2003). Law enforcement perspective on sex offender registration and community notification. *APSAC Advisor*, 15(1), 9–12.

Levenson, J., & Tewksbury, R. (2009). Collateral damage: Family members of registered sex offenders. *American Journal of Criminal Justice*, 34, 54–68.

Levenson, J. S., Brannon, Y. N., Fortney, T., & Baker, J. (2007). Public perceptions about sex offenders and community protection policies. *Analyses of Social Issues and Public Policy*, 7, 137–161.

Logan, Wayne. (2009). *Knowledge as Power: Criminal Registration and Community Notification Laws in America.* Stanford, California: Stanford University Press.

Matson, S. (1999). Sex *Offender Registration: Policy Overview and Comprehensive Practices.* Washington, DC: Center for Sex Offender Management, Office of Justice Programs, U.S. Department of Justice.

Mustaine, E.E., & Tewksbury, R. (2013). What can be learned from a sex offender registry? An 8 year follow up. *Journal of Community Corrections*, 23(1), 5–10.

Mustaine, E. E., Tewksbury, R., Connor, D.P., & Payne, B. K. (2015). Criminal justice officials' views of sex offenders, registration and community notification. *Justice System Journal*, 36(1), 63–85.

New Jersey Legislature (2001). Legislative Findings and Declarations, sec. 2C:7–12.

Newsday, May 6, 2016, www.newsday.com/opinion/letters/letter-why-a-new-deal-for-megan -s-law-group-1.11769142

N.Y. Times (July 4, 1935), Birmingham Police to Register All Ex-Felons in the City.

OffenderWatch, https://offenderwatch.com/.

Ragusa-Salerno, L. M., & Zgoba, K. M. (2012). Taking stock of 20 years of sex offender laws and research: An examination of whether sex offender legislation has helped or hindered our efforts. *Journal of Crime and Justice*, 35(3), 335–355.

Rolfe, S. (2019). When a sex offender comes to visit: A national assessment of travel restrictions. *Criminal Justice Policy Review*, 30(6), 885–905.

Tewksbury, R., & Lees, M. (2006). Perceptions of sex offender registration: Collateral consequences and community experiences. *Sociological Spectrum*, 26(3), 309–334.

Tewksbury, R., & Mustaine, E. (2013). Law enforcement officials' views of sex offender registration and community notification. *International Journal of Police Science & Management*, 15(2), 95–113.

University of Pennsylvania Law Review (1954), Criminal Registration Ordinances: Police Control Over Potential Recidivists, v. –, p. 103.

Walfield, S., Levenson, J., Cubellis, M., Harris, A., & Lobanov-Rostovsky, C. (2017). Law enforcement views on sex offender compliance with registration mandates. *American Journal of Criminal Justice*. DOI: 10.1007/s12103-017-9386-6.

Whitting, L., Day, A. 7 Powell, M. (2016). Police officer perspectives on the implementation of a sex offender community notification scheme. *International Journal of Police Science and Management*, 18, 261–272.

Zgoba, K., Witt, P., & Dalessandro, M. (2008). *Megan's Law: Assessing the Practical and Monetary Efficacy*. Document Number 225370. Washington, DC: National Institute of Justice, U. S. Department of Justice.

Zgoba, K., Miner, M., Letourneau, E., Levenson, J., Knight, R., & Thornton, D. (2015). A Multi-state Recidivism Study Using Static-99 and Static-2002 Risk Scores and Tier Guidelines from the Adam Walsh Act. *Sexual Abuse: A Journal of Research and Treatment*. DOI: 10.1177/1079063215569543.

Zgoba, K., Veysey, B., Dalessandro, M. (2010). Do the best intentions predict best practices: An analysis of the effectiveness of Megan's law. *Justice Quarterly*, 27(5), 667–691.

CASELAW

Jones v. County of Suffolk, 936 F.3d 108 (2d Cir. 2019).

5

The Public and SORN Laws

Lisa L. Sample

Chapter 5 examines the role the public plays in passing and implementing SORN laws. It argues that understanding how the public views SORN laws and how it uses registry information is critical to reform efforts. The chapter begins with SORN laws' roots in public opinion toward individuals convicted of sexual offenses. High-profile crimes drive the public's strong and consistent support for SORN laws. However, altruistic fear rather than fear of personal victimization accounts for this support. The chapter also examines how people use publicly available registries. Studies indicate that only a minority of people access sex offender registries. Moreover, those who do access registry information do so primarily out of curiosity. Further, it is at best unclear whether registries induce users to take protective actions likely to reduce their risk of victimization – and whether registries even make people feel safer. The chapter concludes by arguing that the public's opinion about SORN laws turns ultimately on what the public intends them to accomplish. If public safety plays any role, public support may wane over time. Given the public's modest use of registries, it may be time to rethink public registries and prioritize providing actually useful information to the public.

Public sentiment, opinion, and behavior are important ingredients in the passage, continuation, and operation of sex offender registration and notification (SORN) laws. This is at least in part by design. Unlike many criminal justice policies, SORN laws are built on the idea that an alliance between law enforcement officials and the public can accomplish the primary goal of SORN – the reduction of sexual victimization. But SORN laws are more than just potential means to reduce sex offender recidivism. Collectively, they reflect values and ideals (symbolic policy), express notions of right and wrong (morality policy), and seek to protect the public from harm (protective regulatory policy) (Schwartz & Tatalovich, 2019; Wilson, 2013).

Sex offender registration and notification laws aim to inspire changes both in potential and repeat offenders' behaviors and in the beliefs and actions of community members. Although registration laws alone work to provide law enforcement with more information with which to monitor registrants, notification laws allocate protective regulatory functions away from the government and toward the public. Notification is intended to empower community members to assume responsibility for their personal safety by encouraging them to learn about registrants' backgrounds and whereabouts, help police monitor registrants, and take steps to protect themselves and their loved ones from sexual victimization (Logan, 2009; Sample, 2011).

This chapter will discuss public opinion regarding SORN laws. It will detail the origin and evolution of the public's views on SORN and the theories that may account for the development of these views (as well as related evidence). The chapter will also examine the public's use of registry information, and, importantly, it will explore whether individuals change their behavior based on the information they obtain from registries. The chapter will conclude with a discussion of the implications of public opinion for future potential SORN legal reforms.

5.1 PUBLIC OPINION AS A DRIVER OF SORN POLICY

In a democracy, political representatives are elected to hear, understand, and enact policies that address the concerns of their constituents. Although the causal ordering of the relationship between public opinion and policy reform is not always clear (Sample & Kadleck, 2008; Wood, 2009), opinions of the public are an integral part of the policy-making process. The commanding role of the public's opinion has proven especially visible and powerful in the creation and expansion of laws concerning sexual offenses and sexual offending (Anderson et al., 2015).

Surveys of public sentiment have long found that the public favors a punitive over a rehabilitative approach with individuals convicted of sex offenses (Manchak & Fisher, 2019; Reynolds et al., 2009; Roberts & Stalans, 2004). The public consistently supports repressive laws such as lifetime exposure to SORN, residency restrictions, and involuntary civil commitment (Berryessa & Lively, 2019; Pickett et al., 2013). Also, the "climate of public opinion" surrounding sexual offending aligns with a just deserts approach, or one that asserts that sex offenders deserve to be punished severely – even over their entire lifetime – for their crimes, just as victims will be forced to live for the rest of their lives with their victimizations (Pickett et al., 2013).

Sex offender-related laws named for specific victimized individuals (e.g., "Megan's Law") are especially emblematic of public disdain. Although an instrumental purpose of SORN laws is to help increase public safety by reducing either first-time sex offending or re-offending or both, there is significant evidence that SORN laws also serve an expressive purpose of satisfying the public's deep and abiding desire to demonstrate disdain for convicted sex offenders (Soothill & Francis, 2010).

To a significant extent, public opinion has been driven by high-profile media accounts of sexually related child homicides, which the public views as especially heinous (Cohen & Jeglic, 2007; Jenkins, 1998; Levenson et al., 2007; Sample, 2006; Sample & Bray, 2003, 2006; Sample & Kadleck, 2008; Tewksbury, 2002, 2005; Zevitz, 2003; Zevitz & Farkas, 2000). Research also suggests that legislators tend to rely on their own perceptions of how to address sexual offending (and in particular sex offender recidivism) to create a political climate favorable to draconian legislation targeting individuals who have been convicted of sex offenses (Sample & Kadleck,

2008). Public opinion surveys show consistently high levels of support for SORN laws for adults and for juveniles convicted of sex offenses (Call, 2020; Campregher & Jeglic, 2016; Harris & Socia, 2016; Salerno et al., 2014; Stevenson, Smith, Sekely, & Farnum, 2013). A 2005 survey of Florida residents, for instance, concluded that 95 percent of respondents supported SORN (Levenson et al., 2007). A national poll conducted in 2014 found that 53 percent of respondents strongly agreed that registry information should be made available to the public and another 23 percent somewhat agreed with this sentiment (Harris & Socia, 2016). Importantly, it appears that public support persists regardless of whether respondents believe SORN is an effective strategy to reduce sexual offending (Call, 2020; Koon-Magnin, 2015; Tewksbury & Jennings, 2010). This is even true for policy makers (Jung et al., 2020).

5.2 PERCEIVED RISK OF SEXUAL VICTIMIZATION AND PUBLIC OPINION

For someone new to the study of laws targeting sex offense recidivism, it is logical to assume that public opinion about the genesis and expansion of SORN laws would be tied to concern over rates of sexual offending – and, particularly, sex offense recidivism. Empirical reality, however, does not support this assumption. With respect to child and adult sexual victimizations alike, actual rates during the last quarter century have fallen, not risen (Anderson and Sample, 2008; Levenson et al., 2007; Mancini et al., 2010; Martin & Marinucci, 2006; Phillips, 1998; Pickett et al., 2013). And there is no evidence that recidivism rates have increased over time. Despite this, it is known that the public harbors inaccurate beliefs about the frequency of sexual offenses and their trends and that, because of these misperceptions, the public strongly supports the application of punitive laws to potential sex offenders and re-offenders (Levenson et al., 2007). The same dynamic is evidenced among legislators who craft and amend SORN laws (Meloy et al., 2013; Sample & Kaldeck, 2008).

Public misunderstandings about the incidence of sexual offending, it is important to note, do not neatly track individuals' concerns regarding their own potential victimization. Data suggest that most people do not personally fear being the victim of sexual assault (Gallup, 2020). Studies, however, do not always take into account an important motivation behind SORN: altruistic and vicarious fear of crime (Chadee et al., 2017). Altruistic fear of crime has long been defined as the fear of the perceived risk of victimization for others, not the self (Vozmediano et al., 2017; Warr, 1992; Warr & Ellison, 2000). Snedker (2006) draws further distinctions within altruistic fear of crime by suggesting that the notion of altruistic fear implies unselfish care generalized to all, regardless of relationship. She finds that altruistic fear can be mediated by kinship and introduces the term "vicarious" fear of crime, which is the specific concern about the victimization of loved ones in whom we are deeply invested and have strong and close attachments. It could be altruistic and/or vicarious fear of crime that accounts for public support for SORN, both of which can be influenced by "pragmatic" fear or "urban unease" (Chadee et al., 2017; Garofalo & Laub, 1978). Generally, urban unease reflects people's concerns and anxieties about broader structural conditions that pose a threat such as changes in the economy. Although personal fear of sexual victimization may not be driving public support for SORN, altruistic, vicarious, and pragmatic fear of crime may be central explanatory factors (Warr, 1992, 2000).

5.3 PUBLIC SUPPORT FOR SORN LAWS

What explains the consistently broad public support for SORN laws? In at least some cases, the simple existence of registries makes individuals feel safer, regardless of whether they actually have accessed registry information (Anderson & Sample, 2008). It also matters that, by supporting SORN, individuals implicitly make a statement about what matters, the seriousness of addressing sexual offending, and the relative importance of victims as compared to individuals convicted of crimes. Others support SORN because they believe that it reduces (or at least has the potential to reduce) sexual re-offending (Levenson et al., 2007).

DeVault, Miller, and Griffin (2016) refer to SORN laws as crime control theater, or laws with public support that offer simple solutions to complex criminal behaviors, the efficacy of which has yet to be validated or cannot be validated. They suggest support for laws in this framework relies on the use of cognitive schemes and heuristics accompanied by cognitive-experiential self-theory. In simpler terms, humans have two informational processing systems, one based on rationality, and one based on experience (Epstein, 1991). The experiential system operates automatically, effortlessly, and rapidly based on memories of experiences, or representations of many generalizations, such as those found in media accounts.

In this way, support for SORN laws is more symbolic than instrumental and is consistent with the crime control theater surrounding their enactment based on assumptions of offenders' high re-offending rates, existing mental health disorders, and the failure of treatment to "fix" perceived disorders (Kernsmith, Craun, & Foster, 2009a; Williams, Comartin, & Lytle, 2020). Support can also be based predominantly on psychological information processing, rather than on empirical evidence. Empirical evidence of the efficacy (or, rather, inefficacy) of SORN laws seemingly has little effect on citizens' positive view of SORN laws, which is consistent with the public's reaction to social science evidence more generally (Prescott, 2016).

Importantly, however, an individual's support for SORN laws does not always (or even most of the time) equate to that individual feeling an increased sense of safety once such laws are in place. Some research shows that as the public receives more information on where convicted sex offenders live, their fear of victimization (personal or altruistic) actually increases (Beck & Travis, 2004; Phillips, 1998; Zevitz & Farkas, 2000). Warr (2000) criticizes existing literature on the ability of SORN to make citizens feel safer, focusing on concerns with measurement issues that surround the use of the term "victimization." Warr contends that many studies fail to take into account "altruistic" fear, or fear for others' well-being, when evaluating someone's emotional response upon learning of the existence and location of sex offenders' residences in their community.

Additional explanations for the persistent support for SORN can found in the choices and actions of the media. A large body of scholarship highlights the critical influence of media coverage in shaping and driving public opinion regarding criminal justice policy and the public's fear of crime. Cucolo and Perlin (2013) suggest that inaccurate and misleading statistics in the media unduly influence public support for SORN. Indeed, inaccurate statistics promulgated by ultimately irresponsible sources on the nature of sexual offending and recidivism rates of convicted sex offenders have played a prominent role in important US Supreme Court decisions upholding SORN laws against constitutional challenges (Ellman & Ellman, 2015).

Finally, research shows interesting variation when it comes to support for SORN. Pickett et al. (2013), using a web-based survey of a national sample of 537 citizens, found support for punitive sex crime laws that is significantly related to gender (female), parenthood, education levels below college, conservative political views, and residence in areas with higher percentages of children younger than 18 years. Call (2020), in a web-based survey of 1,023 citizens, similarly found gender (female) and parenthood were associated with stronger support for SORN. Support is less robust among mental health practitioners (Malesky & Keim, 2001), compared to individuals not working in the mental health fields. Parents (Mancini et al., 2010) and judges (Bumby & Maddox, 1999) view SORN in a more positive light than others. More support for SORN is also found among those living in cities as compared to those living in rural areas (Calvert, 1999) and those living in the Midwest versus those living in the South (Pickett et al., 2013). Importantly, there is evidence that those providing support to registrants in treatment by and large do not support or believe in the effectiveness of SORN (Connor, 2020).

5.4 PUBLIC AWARENESS AND USE OF REGISTRY INFORMATION

More than a quarter century after SORN laws were first enacted, there is still no reliable evidence to support two of the basic operative assumptions of SORN: first, that the public is aware of registry information and, second, if they are aware of registry information, that they use the information to take precautionary or protective measures in order to reduce victimization risk. This gap is particularly instructive, as it may help us understand empirical work that indicates that SORN laws are generally ineffective and may even contribute to greater recidivism rates in some cases (Prescott & Rockoff, 2011; Prescott, 2011, 2012).

In one of the first studies undertaken to examine these questions, Anderson and Sample (2008) found that the majority of Nebraskans surveyed (89.8 percent) were aware of the existence of their state's publicly accessible website registry, but only 34.8 percent had actually ever accessed it. A study of Michigan respondents also found a high rate of general knowledge that a public registry existed (88.9 percent), but a similarly low rate of individuals who had actually engaged the registry by accessing its information (37 percent) (Kernsmith et al., 2009b). In a later sample of Nebraska residents, Sample et al. (2011) found an increase in the percentage of people who knew of the registry's existence on the web but perhaps surprisingly a slight decline in those who accessed it (31 percent), suggesting that low-use rates were not just a matter of people needing time to learn of and access a new resource.

As to why Nebraska respondents did not access the registry, Sample, Evans, & Anderson (2011) found that a majority related that they had no interest in sex offender information on the website (59.4 percent). An additional 20 percent of respondents received the website information on sex offenders from another source, and about 10 percent indicated that they lacked access to the internet as reasons for not accessing sex offender notification information. Of the minority of respondents who did access the registry website in Nebraska, over half (56.5 percent) claimed to have accessed information for safety purposes. To put it in other terms, they claimed to have accessed the registry information to devise and take preventative measures against the risk of sexual victimization, such as installing locks and more closely monitoring children. Other reasons given by respondents for accessing registry information included curiosity or personal interest (28.7 percent) and job obligations (10.4 percent). In a study of New Jersey residents, only 51 percent indicated awareness of the state's public website registry (Boyle et al., 2013). The study also found very low rates of access even considering this general lack of awareness, with only 17 percent of respondents (or less than one-third of those who were aware of the registry) indicating that they had accessed the registry at least once.

More recently, Harris & Cudmore (2016) surveyed a nationally representative random sample of US adults concerning their use of registry information. Although the study found a higher rate of access to sex offender information (45 percent) compared to previous studies, the majority of respondents (60 percent) had done so only once or twice, typically out of general curiosity rather than with a specific purpose, presumably one related to safety. Indeed, of those who did access registry information, many could be classified as "casual" users or users seeking entertainment, rather than as potential victims who access information more frequently and for the purpose of learning about nearby threats and how they might be mitigated.

Studies have also examined the key question of the effect of registry information on those who do access it, including whether the information actually results in behavioral changes. In their Nebraska study, Anderson & Sample (2008) discover that fewer than one third of respondents reported that they had taken protective actions as a result of accessing registry information. In New Jersey, Boyle et al. (2013) found that two-thirds of respondents who accessed information indicated that they had taken some form of protective measure. The differences in the results between the Nebraska and New Jersey studies, it should be noted, might reflect the different queries used by the researchers, with New Jersey (with its higher reported rates of action) respondents being asked a series of specific questions regarding a variety of possible protective measures (e.g., educating children about sexual-offending risks). Also using specific prompts (e.g., sharing information with family members), the national sample surveyed by Harris and Cudmore (2016) likewise reported a relatively modest rate of behavioral impact (60 percent of those accessing the registry).

Beck and Travis (2004), in a survey of an Ohio community, compared a sample of residents receiving notification about a designated high-risk registrant in the neighborhood and those who did not receive information. They found that notified residents were significantly more likely to engage in protective behaviors regarding themselves and others. A study by Bandy (2011) in Minneapolis, Minnesota, however, compared the reactions of a group of residents receiving notification via community meetings with police regarding a resident registrant with the behavior of those nearby who did not receive notice. She found no difference in self-protective behavior taken by subjects. However, like Beck and Travis (2004), Bandy found a small but statistically significant relationship between receiving notification and protective behaviors undertaken to protect children specifically (i.e., altruistic behavior).

Finally, research has examined the emotional and psychological effect of SORN laws and implementation on community members. In both Nebraska (Anderson & Sample, 2008) and New Jersey (Boyle et al., 2013), significant majorities of those who accessed registry information felt safer as a result (87 percent and 88 percent, respectively). However, it is important to recognize that this emotional reaction (feelings of safety) to registry access in the two jurisdictions does not appear to translate in any reliable way into individuals taking protective measures. Harris and Cudmore (2016) in their national sample of adults found that almost 60 percent of respondents who used the registry once or twice indicated that doing so had no impact on their sense of safety. Notably, the study also found that respondents with the highest level of registry use were more than three times as likely to feel less safe as a result of accessing information, compared to respondents with the lowest levels of usage (28.4 percent v. 9.4 percent). In an earlier study, Beck and Travis (2004), who compared sample populations in Ohio receiving active notification and those who did not, found that SORN is significantly related to higher levels of personal fear of general criminal victimization. By contrast, SORN was positively correlated with altruistic fear only with respect to the fear of sexual victimization.

5.5 FACTORS ASSOCIATED WITH ACCESSING AND USE OF REGISTRY INFORMATION

When trying to understand the factors that make some people more likely than others to access online sex offender registry websites, we must remember that access to computers and to the internet is not evenly distributed across the population

(Estacio et al., 2019). Age, education, income, and social isolation are sociodemographic factors associated with accessing information on the internet. Scholars have found many of these same factors—such as sex, age, race, political ideology, and religiosity (Harris & Cudmore, 2016) – also affect people's access to web-based registry information. Anderson et al. (2009) found that females, older citizens (above 65 years), those with less than a college education, parents, those living in urban areas, and those with internet access at home or work, are significantly more likely to access sex offender registries than men, younger individuals, and those with a high school education or less, those living in rural areas, those with no children, or those who do not have free internet access at home or work. Kernsmith et al. (2009b) reiterate these factors as influencing registry use but also identify a significant connection between being a victim of a sexual offense and registry access. Based on these findings, it seems that those who perceive themselves as the most vulnerable to sexual victimization (the elderly, women, those living in metropolitan areas, and those who have children) are the ones accessing information, but then again, variability across people in terms of access to computers, smart phones, internet connections, and technological skill, which might be correlated with the predictors identified in the research, could explain the variation in people accessing registry information.

Sometimes the factors that are not predictive of registry access and use are just as interesting as those that are. For instance, one would likely expect single women, or those living alone, to be more inclined to want registry information than married women. But there is no evidence of such a relationship (Anderson & Sample, 2008). Similarly, one might predict that the longer a person has lived in an area the greater the awareness of registry information they are likely to have, but this is not the case either (Kernsmith et al., 2009b).

Research regarding motivation for access also provides interesting and important results that are useful to understanding the full picture of SORN's effects and its role in our society. In a fairly recent study, among those who access the registry, "curiosity about sex offenders living in the area" was by far the most common motivation (74.4 percent), followed by general concern over family safety (38.2 percent), concern for personal safety (18.2 percent), concern about a particular individual in the community (14.2 percent), examining a neighborhood for potential relocation (11.8 percent), and conducting background checks on potential employees (2.0 percent) (Harris & Cudmore, 2016). If the goal of SORN laws is to inform citizens of nearby convicted sex offenders, regardless of the outcomes that result, it appears that nowhere near all citizens desire having the information or are even curious about it (although perhaps they value knowing it is available).

Thus, a paradox exists: the public strongly favors SORN policy but many fewer than one might expect actually access sex offender registries and, when they do, they do so once or rarely, most often out of curiosity, raising questions about the usefulness of the information to those individuals, given that registrants are a fairly transient population. Furthermore, even for residents who do obtain registry information, research suggests that the information does not foster much in the way of protective behavioral change. Indeed, according to perhaps the most comprehensive study conducted to date (Harris & Cudmore, 2016), almost three-quarters of the public feel they have no use for registry information (71.1 percent) and almost a quarter (24.7 percent) do not believe the registry will keep themselves and their families safe.

It is important to note that the use of registries and notification procedures by the public, to some degree, rests on citizens' trust that the information they learn through notification is accurate. Research, however, has questioned the quality of registry information (Harris & Pattavina, 2009; Lees & Tewksbury, 2006; Levenson et al., 2014; Tewksbury, 2002). Both journalistic investigations and empirical research suggest data entry errors, data entry lag times, incomplete address information, unauthorized travel, and homelessness plague the information found on registries (Harris & Pattavina, 2009). Of course, registrants can also provide false addresses, leave the state, or otherwise abscond after registering (Levenson et al., 2014). However, it seems that the percentage of registrants who fail to maintain registry information is relatively small (11.5 percent), with only 1.2 percent of all registrants listed as absconders (Levenson et al., 2010).

Finally, several factors can influence the reliability of empirical evidence and conclusions derived from surveys regarding the use of registration information, including sample bias, concerns about the honesty of subjects, and pressure to offer socially desirable responses.[1] In particular, some of these concerns may suggest inaccurately high access and use rates. It is possible that survey respondents report they have checked the registry when they have not, believing this is the response surveyors expect and what society would like them to have done. For instance, Craun (2010) found that survey respondents claim to know sex offenders who live in their communities who in fact do not live there.

5.6 PRACTICAL CONCERNS REGARDING NOTIFICATION

Today, community members generally obtain registry information from online websites, which can be seen as a form of passive notification, compared to more active forms such as community meetings conducted by police or the distribution of leaflets. Research shows that active notification methods result in greater awareness of registrant information as compared to passive methods, such as merely making registry information available on a website (Beck & Travis, 2006; Harris & Cudmore, 2016). This should not be surprising. The mode of delivery, context, and the specific information provided by notification is likely to influence whether

---

[1] Because all survey research is based on voluntary participation, it is possible that those who choose not to participate in survey research have very different opinions than those who do. It is also common in survey research for participants to want to answer questions in ways the researcher wants to hear. The honesty of subjects answering survey questions is similarly a concern for survey research, but all research based on survey responses shares these limitations.

residents access registries (e.g., ease of use concerns) and whether they are able to use the information to take protective measures (e.g., specificity about a registrant's previous crimes).

A consistent criticism levied against the information the public receives online is that it is devoid of meaningful content and context (Anderson & Sample, 2008). Of course, sometimes information about a registrant's conviction history or the risk posed by a particular registrant is absent. But, even when that is not the case, when examining registrants in a zip code, registries often provide community members vague information or statutory legalese regarding registrants' criminal history. For instance, if one is listed on the registry as having been convicted of a second-degree sexual assault of a "minor," the community does not likely know what this means in practical terms, nor do they know the victim's age at the time of the crime or the victim-offender relationship. The crime could involve the molestation of a seven-year-old stranger to the offender, a "consensual" sexual encounter between an 18-year-old male and 15-year-old girlfriend whose parents filed charges, or the fondling of the 14-year-old son of the registrant. Each of the aforementioned scenarios would understandably trigger different cognitive and perhaps behavioral responses for the individual consuming the registry information.

Today, a significant majority of states use a conviction-based approach to SORN, not one that relies on individual assessments of recidivism risk, which exacerbates the information deficit. The fact that registries combine in the same place those convicted of very serious offenses (e.g., aggravated rape) and less serious offenses (e.g., public indecency) perhaps explains Harris and Cudmore's (2016) conclusion that the more frequently people view registry information, the more fearful they become of sexual victimization. At the same time, if all registrants present equal risk of sexual predation, requiring maximum vigilance, we ought to be concerned that fatigue will arise (Logan, 2009). Aggravating matters, registry websites provide raw information but generally offer no advice about what to do with that information or what it means in practical terms in terms of risk (Anderson & Sample, 2008). Perhaps, even in the absence of individualized risk determination for registrants, if governments explained that not all registrants have the same risk for re-offending and that the risk diminishes over time as offenders age and desist from committing crimes (Hanson et al., 2014), the public would be less fearful after viewing registry information.

5.7 IMPLICATIONS FOR THE FUTURE OF SORN

While we have learned a great deal in recent decades about how the public views SORN laws and individuals convicted of sex offenses, and we have made important progress in assessing whether and how community members access and use sex offender registries, there is still much we do not know. In particular, research on these topics has identified gaps in our understanding of how and why the public supports SORN. Notably, for instance, while scholarship confirms that the public strongly supports the idea of and philosophy behind SORN, in practice only a minority of community members actually access registry information. Why might this be?

The answer in large measure likely lies in what the public expects from SORN laws. If the mere passage of *any* law ostensibly directed toward the goal of reducing sex re-offending is sufficient to address the public's concerns, citizens would be supportive of SORN laws the minute they were passed, regardless of their content, use, or public safety impact. In contrast, if the public believes that SORN laws are meant to address re-offending and expects that they will reduce recidivism and help reduce the incidence of sex crime by providing law enforcement with ready-made lists of suspects, then the evidence is, at the very best, mixed (Bierie, 2015; Harris & Cudmore, 2016; Maurelli & Ronan, 2013; Prescott & Rockoff, 2011; Zgoba et al., 2016). We can thus expect that over time the public may become less supportive in light of this evidence (Williams, Comartin, & Lytle, 2020). If instead SORN is intended simply to stigmatize, express moral outrage and satisfy a need for public vengeance regarding individuals convicted of sex offenses, then SORN may be considered to have achieved its goal, because SORN does socially isolate and ostracize registrants and make their lives more difficult (e.g., finding housing and employment). In short, until we have a better sense of what the public expects of SORN and the laws that make it a reality, it will be difficult to determine how to generate more public buy-in for its use and better fulfillment of its now only theoretical promise of community self-protection.

Given that only a minority of the public reviews registry information, and that those who do access registries do so rarely, and often only out of curiosity, perhaps it is time to rethink public dissemination of registrant information. The government can instead provide the public with information only on those individuals assessed as most at risk for re-offending, increasing the salience of the information. Although community members voice support for SORN, their actions clearly show a disconnect between the goals and the impact of these laws—only a minority of citizens access registry information. Rather than continuing to throw "good" money after "bad," resources should be dedicated to strategies that tangibly help reduce sexual victimization. We should be selective about what information we provide the public and be precise about the goal society aims to achieve by sharing this information with a broader group of people.

Providing background and locational information on registrants was and is intuitively thought to empower citizens (Anderson & Sample, 2008), but it offers a false sense of security at best because most sex offenders do not sexually re-offend (Hanson et al., 2018; Levenson et al., 2007; Maguire & Singer, 2011) and most sex crimes are committed by individuals who are not registered (Socia & Stamatel, 2010). Approximately 15–18 percent of sex offenders re-offend (Bench & Allen, 2013; Hanson et al., 2018; Kim et al., 2016), so notification laws are providing citizens with a great deal of information on a large number of individuals (the majority) who will likely never re-offend. Furthermore, the lengthy registration periods used in jurisdictions, often extending to an offender's lifetime, are inapt given research showing significant decline in recidivism likelihood over time (Hanson et al., 2018).

In light of modest actual public use of registry information and the low re-offending rates of registrants as a group, rather than websites depicting where convicted sex offenders live, it may be more effective to increase public safety by providing citizens with essential empirical information about sex offending generally, such as: that the vast majority of sex crimes are committed by non-strangers (RAINN, 2020a); sexual offenses are more likely to occur in private residences than in school zones or public spaces (RAINN, 2020b); sexual predation is not associated with residential proximity (Agan & Prescott, 2014; Socia & Stamatel, 2010); and by far most sex offenses are committed by first-time offenders (who by definition are not on registries) (Socia & Stamatel, 2010). Also, the public should be informed about the behaviors of adults used to "prime" children for sexual victimization (called grooming behaviors) (Wolf & Pruitt, 2019). Such information would likely far better serve public safety than lists of where prior offenders live. Of course, this suggestion is premised on the notion that SORN laws are intended to improve public safety. If SORN laws serve primarily a retributive function, suggestions designed to increase public safety will fall on deaf ears. Although born of significant public fervor, often referred to as a "moral panic," the actual limited public use of registries is perhaps surprising, unless, again, SORN laws serve expressive rather than instrumental purposes.

Perhaps, to foster the use of SORN laws, instead of asking community members how often they access registry information and why, we should start asking what purposes they believe registries serve, what they know about sexual offending (both in terms of recidivism and etiology), and how they believe they can prevent sexual victimization. Similarly, it would be useful to learn community members' views on SORN so it can be improved to better serve public safety.

Despite punitive public attitudes toward sex offenders, the twenty-first century has witnessed innovations in evidence-based sex offender treatment (Levenson & Prescott, 2014; Planty et al., 2013). Research suggests that offender treatment can help individuals manage their behaviors in the community (Kim et al., 2016) and reduce the likelihood of re-offending (Schmucker & Lösel, 2015). Although pinpointing a particular reason for a crime decline is always difficult, treatment might help explain falling rates of sexual victimization from 2014, compared to victimization rates for robbery and nonsexual assault (Morgan & Oudekerk, 2019).

Sex offender registration and notification is a resource-intensive strategy. Perhaps the public would rather see, or should be made to see, that allocating resources to treatment of convicted sex offenders, and enhancing prospects for their successful reentry, are preferable. If punitiveness is the animating concern of SORN, we should query the public as to how much money it wishes to expend to express its disdain. More importantly, we should determine if the public has considered the lost opportunities for funding matters such as health care and quality public education. The time has come to ask citizens, and their elected representatives, whether the realities of SORN, compared to its avowed original goals, are worth its significant cost, both in terms of money expended and perhaps more efficacious public safety initiatives not undertaken. That should be the question going forward.

5.8 CONCLUSION

Public opinion about social problems and the strategies policy makers deploy to address them is important to any representative form of government. Surveys and polls provide insight into problems that the public wants addressed and the potential boundaries of legislative solutions the public is willing to tolerate. Public opinion data has demonstrated the public's acceptance of and support for SORN laws, resulting in the continued legislative expansion of SORN. What lawmakers do not seem to recognize is that the public supports registries but seldom accesses them, and that individuals who do access registries often do so out of curiosity.

In the 1990s, there arose the idea that SORN would help prevent sexual offending by providing communities with knowledge of where previously convicted sex offenders lived, their names, and what they looked like. The public believed it when they were told that convicted sex offenders have the highest rates of re-offending rate among criminals, that once someone is a sex offender, they will always be a sex offender, and that there is no "cure" for sexual offending (Mancini & Budd, 2016; Sample & Bray, 2003). We now know that these premises are scientifically unfounded.

Although punitively minded citizens may want lifelong incarceration for convicted sex offenders, they would not likely relish paying for it. Lifelong registration, complemented by notification, might seem an attractive alternative, but is public safety served as a result? At least to date, the evidence suggests a negative answer. The achievement of other potential public goals, however, such as shaming and other forms of additional punishment for individuals convicted of sex offenses seem to follow directly and naturally from the enforcement of SORN laws.

Future researchers should ask citizens if they prioritize their support for registries over public services that could be better funded, such as health care and education. Relatedly, we know little about the public's more general views regarding sex offender management in the community. Do people value and support probation for noncontact sex offenders over incarceration; would they rather spend their tax dollars on treatment, community reentry programs, and housing for convicted sex offenders over building new prisons? These are important questions to ask going forward as states allocate scarce budgetary resources.

When polling for public opinion, it will be important to remain cognizant of how issues are framed. For instance, the label "sex offender" decidedly elicits different responses than the term "registrants" or individuals convicted of sex crimes (Harris &

Socia, 2016). Rather than forcing responses into pre-determined categories, perhaps we should embrace more open-ended responses from citizens regarding what they want to see in sex offender policy, what frightens them the most about sexual offending, and what they believe might be most beneficial in combatting it. Also, those conducting surveys should be mindful of the particularities of state SORN laws in effect, which vary considerably, and can therefore possibly affect public sentiment.

The study of public opinion of sex offense laws is still in its infancy as few scholars have had the time or resources to conduct large-scale public surveys. Despite methodological limitations of survey research generally, and internet surveys specifically, we should embrace new technologies (Burchfield et al., 2014) to uncover what the public thinks, knows, and hopes to accomplish by continuing current sex offender policies. After all, in democratic societies with representative forms of government, public opinion can and should matter.

REFERENCES

Agan, A. Y. & Prescott, J.J. (2014). Sex offender law and the geography of victimization. *Journal of Empirical Legal Studies*, 11, 786–828.

Anderson, A. L., Evans M. K., & Sample, L. L. (2009). Who accesses the sex offender registries? A look at legislative intent and citizen action in Nebraska. *Criminal Justice Studies: A Critical Journal of Crime, Law, and Society*, 22(3), 1–23.

Anderson, A. L. & Sample, L. L. (2008). Public awareness and action resulting from sex offender community notification laws. *Criminal Justice Policy Review*, 19(4), 371–396.

Anderson, A. L., Sample, L. L., & Cain, C. (2015). Residency restrictions for sex offenders: Public opinion on appropriate distances. *Criminal Justice Policy Review*, 26 (3), 262–277.

Armstrong, M. M., Miller, M. K., & Griffin, T. (2015). An examination of sex offender registration and notification laws: Can community sentiment lead to ineffective laws? In M. K. Miller, J. A. Blumenthal, & J. Chamberlain (eds.), *Handbook of Community Sentiment* (pp. 239–251). New York: Springer.

Avrahamian, K. A. (1998). A critical perspective: Do "Megan's Laws" really shield children from sex predators? *Journal of Juvenile Law*, 19, 301–317.

Bandy, R. (2011). Measuring the impact of sex offender notification on community adoption of protective behaviors. *Criminology & Pub. Pol'y*, 10, 237.

Beck, V. S. & Travis, L. F. (2004). Sex offender notification and fear of victimization. *Journal of Criminal Justice*, 32(5), 455–463.

Beck, V. S. & Travis, L. F., (2006). Sex offender notification: An exploratory assessment of state variation in notification processes, *Journal of Criminal Justice*, 34(1), 51–55.

Bench, L. L. & Allen, T. D. (2013). Assessing sex offender recidivism using multiple measures: A longitudinal analysis. *The Prison Journal*, 93(4), 411–428.

Berryessa, C. & Lively, C. (2019). When a sex offender wins the lottery: Social and legal punitiveness toward sex offenders in an instance of perceived injustice. *Psychology, Public Policy, and Law*, 25(3), 181–195.

Bierie, D. M. (2015). Enhancing the National Incident–Based Reporting System: A Policy Proposal. *International Journal of Offender Therapy and Comparative Criminology*, 59(10), 1125–1143.

Boyle, D. J., Ragusa-Salerno, L. M., Marcus, A. F., Passannante, M. R., & Furrer, S. (2013). Public knowledge and use of sex offender internet registries: Results from a random digit dialing telephone survey. *Journal of Interpersonal Violence, 29*, 1914–1932.

Bumby, K. M. & Maddox, M. C. (1999). Judges' knowledge about sexual offenders, difficulties presiding over sexual offense cases, and opinions on sentencing, treatment, and legislation. *Sexual Abuse, 11*(4), 305–315.

Burchfield, K., Sample, L. L., & Lytle, R. (2014). Public interest in sex offenders: A perpetual panic. *Criminology, Crim. Just. L & Soc'y, 15*, 96.

Calvert, J. F. (1999). Public opinion and knowledge about childhood sexual abuse in a rural community. *Child Abuse & Neglect, 3*(7), 671–682.

Call, C. (2020). The influence of victim type on the public's perception of sex offender registration and notification. *Justice Policy Journal, 17*(1), 1–22.

Campregher, J., & Jeglic, E. L. (2016). Attitudes toward juvenile sex offender legislation: The influence of case-specific information. *Journal of Child Sexual Abuse, 25*(4), 466–482.

Caputo, A. A. & Brodsky, S. L. (2003). Citizens coping with community notification of released sex offenders. *Behavioral Sciences & the Law, 22*(2), 239–252.

Chadee, D., Ali, S., Burke, A., & Young, J. (2017). Fear of crime and community concerns: Mediating effect of risk and pragmatic fear. *Journal of Community & Applied Social Psychology, 27*(6), 450–462.

Cohen, M. & Jeglic, E. L. (2007). Sex offender legislation in the United States: What do we know? *International Journal of Offender Therapy and Comparative Criminology, 51*(4), 369–383.

Comartin, E. B., Kernsmith, P. D., & Kernsmith, R. M. (2009). Sanctions for sex offenders: Fear and public policy. *Journal of Offender Rehabilitation, 48*(7), 605–619.

Connor, D. (2020). Impressions of ineffectiveness: Exploring support partners' attitudes toward sex offender registration and notification. *Psychology, Crime & Law, 26*(2), 128–147.

Cooley, B. N., Moore, S. E., & Sample, L. L. (2017). The role of formal social control mechanisms in deterring sex offending as part of the desistance process. *Criminal Justice Studies, 30*(2), 136–157.

Craun, S. W. (2010). Evaluating awareness of registered sex offenders in the neighborhood. *Crime & Delinquency, 56*(3), 414–435.

Cucolo, H. E. & Perlin, M. L. (2013). They're planting stories in the press: The impact of media distortions on sex offender law and policy. *University of Denver Criminal Law Review 3*, 185–246.

DeVault, A., Miller, M. K., & Griffin, T. (2016). Crime control theater: Past, present, and future. *Psychology, Public Policy, and Law 22*(4), 341–348.

Ellman, I. M. & Ellman T. (2015). "Frightening and high": The supreme court's crucial mistake about sex crime statistics, *Constitutional Commentary, 30*, 495–508.

Epstein, S. (1991). Cognitive-experiential self-theory: An integrative theory of personality. In R. C. Curtis (ed.), *The Relational Self: Theoretical Convergences in Psychoanalysis and Social Psychology* (pp. 111–137). New York, NY: Guildford Press.

Estacio, E. V., Whittle, R., & Protheroe, J. (2019). The digital divide: Examining socio-demographic factors associated with health literacy, access and use of internet to seek health information. *Journal of Health Psychology 24*(12), 1668–1675.

Gallup. (2020). *Crime.* Gallup.com. https://news.gallup.com/poll/1603/crime.aspx.

Garofalo, J. & Laub, J. (1978). The fear of crime: Broadening our perspective. *Victimology, 3* (3–4), 242–253.

Green, L. (1996). The concept of law revisited. *Michigan Law Review, 96*(6), 1687–1717.

Hanson, R. K., Harris, A. J. R., Helmus, L., Thornton, D. (2014). High-risk sex offenders may not be high risk forever, *Journal of Interpersonal Violence*, 29(15), 2792–2813.

Hanson, R. K., Harris, A. J. R., Letourneau, E., Helmus, L. M., & Thornton, D. (2018). Reductions in risk: Once a sexual offender not always a sexual offender, *Psychology, Public Policy, and Law*, 24(1), 48–63.

Harris, A. J. & Pattavina, A. (2009, November). Missing sex offenders and the utility of sex offender registration systems. Paper presented at the America Society of Criminology, Philadelphia, PA.

Harris, A. J. & Cudmore, R. (2016). Community experience with public sex offender registries in the United States: A national survey. *Criminal Justice Policy Review*, 29(3), 258–279.

Harris, A. J. & Socia, K. M. (2016). What's in a name? Evaluating the effects of the "sex offender" label on public opinions and beliefs. *Sexual Abuse*, 28(7), 660–678.

Higgins, E. M. & Rolfe, S. M. (2016). "The sleeping army": Necropolitics and the collateral consequences of being a sex offender. *Deviant Behavior*, 38(9), 1–16.

Jenkins, P. (1998). *Moral Panic, Changing Concepts of the Child Molester in Modern America*. London: Yale University Press.

Jung, S., Allison, M., Toop, C., & Martin, E. (2020). Sex offender registries: Exploring the attitudes and knowledge of political decision makers. *Psychiatry, Psychology and Law*, 1–15.

Kernsmith, P. D., Craun, S. W., & Foster, J. (2009a). Public attitudes toward sexual offenders and sex offender registration. *Journal of Child Sexual Abuse*, 18(3), 290–301.

Kernsmith, P. D., Comartin, E., Craun, S. W., & Kernsmith, R. M. (2009b). The relationship between sex offender registry utilization and awareness. *Sexual Abuse*, 21(2), 181–193.

Key, V. O. (1961). *Public Opinion and American Democracy*. New York, NY: Alfred A. Knopf.

Kim, B., Benekos, P. J., & Merlo, A. V. (2016). Sex offender recidivism revisited: Review of recent meta-analyses on the effects of sex offender treatment. *Trauma, Violence, & Abuse*, 17 (1), 105–117.

Koon-Magnin, S. (2015). Perceptions of and support for sex offender policies: Testing Levenson, Brannon, Fortney, and Baker's findings. *Journal of Criminal Justice*, 43(1), 80–88.

Lees, M. & Tewksbury, R. (2006). Understanding policy and programmatic issues regarding sex offender registries. *Corrections Today*, 68(1), 54–56.

Letourneau, E. J., Levenson, J. S., Bandyopadhyay, D., Sinha, D., & Armstrong, K. S. (2010). Effects of South Carolina's sex offender registration and notification policy on adult recidivism. *Criminal Justice Policy Review*, 21(4), 435–458.

Levenson, J. S. (2008). Collateral consequences of sex offender residence restrictions. *Criminal Justice Studies*, 21(2), 153–166.

Levenson, J. S. (2007). The new scarlet letter: Sex offender policies in the 21st century. In D. Prescott (ed.), *Applying knowledge to practice: Challenges in the treatment and super-visions of sexual abusers* (pp. 21–41). Oklahoma City, OK: Wood 'N' Barnes Publishing & Distribution.

Levenson, J. S., Ackerman, A. R., & Harris, A. J. (2014). Catch me if you can: An analysis of fugitive sex offenders. *Sexual Abuse* 26(2), 129–148.

Levenson, J. & Prescott, D. S. (2014). Déjà vu: from Furby to Långström and the evaluation of sex offender treatment effectiveness. *Journal of Sexual Aggression*, 20(3), 257–266.

Levenson, J. & Tewksbury, R. (2009). Collateral damage: Family members of registered sex offenders. *American Journal of Criminal Justice*, 34(1–2), 54–68.

Levenson, J. S., Brannon, Y. N., Fortney, T., & Baker, J. (2007). Public perceptions about sex offenders and community protection policies. *Analyses of Social Issues and Public Policy*, 7 (1), 137–161.

Levenson, J., Letourneau, E., Armstrong, K., & Zgoba, K. M. (2010). Failure to register as a sex offender: Is it associated with recidivism?. *Justice Quarterly*, 27(3), 305–331.

Logan, W. A. (2009). *Knowledge as Power: Criminal Registration and Community Notification Laws in America*. Stanford University Press.

Lovell, E. (2007). *Megan's Law: Does it Protect Children?* London: Policy and Public Affairs, NSPCC.

Maguire, M. & Singer, J. K. (2011). A false sense of security: Moral panic driven sex offender legislation. *Critical Criminology*, 19(4), 301–312.

Malesky, A. & Keim, J. (2001). Mental health professionals' perspectives on sex offender registry web sites. *Sexual Abuse: A Journal of Research and Treatment*, 13(1), 53–63.

Manchak, S. M. & Fisher, L. R. (2019). An examination of multiple factors influencing support for sex offender policy. *Criminal Justice Policy Review*, 30(6), 925–947.

Mancini, C., Shields, R. T., Mears, D. P., & Beaver, K. M. (2010). Sex offender residence restriction laws: Parental perceptions and public policy. *Journal of Criminal Justice*, 38(5), 1022–1030.

Mancini, C. & Budd, K. M. (2016). Is the public convinced that "nothing works?" Predictors of treatment support for sex offenders among Americans. *Crime & Delinquency*, 62(6), 777–799.

Martin, M. & Marinucci, C. (2006). Support behind tough sex offender initiative. *San Francisco Chronicle*, 3B.

Maurelli, K. & Ronan, G. (2013). A time-series analysis of the effectiveness of sex offender notification laws in the USA. *The Journal of Forensic Psychiatry & Psychology*, 24(1), 128–143.

Meloy, M., Curtis, K., & Boatwright, J. (2013). The sponsors of sex offender bills speak up: Policy makers' perceptions of sex offenders, sex crimes, and sex offender legislation. *Criminal Justice and Behavior*, 40(4), 438–452.

Morgan, R. E. & Oudekerk, B. A. (2018). Criminal Victimization. U.S. Department of Justice: Bureau of Justice Statistics.

Morgan, R. E. & Oudekerk, B. A. (2019). Criminal victimization, 2018 (NCJ 253043). Bureau of Justice Statistics Special Report. (US Department of Justice, Washington, DC.).

Phillips, D. M. (1998). *Community Notification as Viewed by Washington's Citizens*. Washington: Washington State Institute for Public Policy.

Planty, M., Langton, L., Krebs, C., Berzofsky, M., & Smiley-McDonald, H. (2013). *Female Victims of Sexual Violence, 1994–2010* (pp. 3–4). Washington, DC: US Department of Justice, Office of Justice Programs, Bureau of Justice Statistics.

Petrosino, A. J. & Petrosino, C. (1999). The public safety potential of Megan's Law in Massachusetts: An assessment from a sample of criminal sexual psychopaths. *Crime and Delinquency*, 45(1), 140–158.

Pickett, J. T., Mancini, C., & Mears, D. P. (2013). Vulnerable victims, monstrous offenders, and unmanageable risk: Explaining public opinion on the social control of sex crime. *Criminology*, 51(3), 729–759.

Prescott, J.J. (2016). Portmanteau ascendant: Post-release regulations and sex offender recidivism. *Connecticut Law Review*, 47, 1035–1078.

Prescott, J.J. (2012). Do sex offender registries make us less safe? *Regulation*, 35(2), 48–55.

Prescott, J.J. (2011). Child pornography and community notification: How an attempt to reduce crime can achieve the opposite. *Federal Sentencing Reporter*, 24, 93–101.

Prescott, J.J. & Rockoff, J. E. (2011). Do sex offender registration and notification laws affect criminal behavior? *Journal of Law and Economics*, 53, 161–206.

RAINN. (2020a). *Perpetrators of Sexual Violence: Statistics*. RAINN.org. www.rainn.org/statis tics/perpetrators-sexual-violence.

RAINN. (2020b). *Scope of the Problem: Statistics*. RAINN.org. www.rainn.org/statistics/scope-problem.

Redlich, A. D. (2001). Community notification: Perceptions of its effectiveness in preventing child sexual abuse. *Journal of Child Sexual Abuse*, 10(3), 91–116.

Reynolds, N., Craig, L. A., & Boer, D. P. (2009). Public attitudes towards offending, offenders and reintegration. In Wood, J. L., Gannon, T. A. (eds.), *Public opinion and criminal justice* (pp. 166–186). Portland, OR: Willan.

Roberts, J. V. (1992). Public opinion, crime, and criminal justice. *Crime and Justice*, 16, 99–180.

Roberts, J. V. & Stalans, L. J. (2004). Restorative sentencing: Exploring the views of the public. *Social Justice Research*, 17(3), 315–334.

Saad, L. (2005, June 9). *Sex offender registries are underutilized by the public*. Gallup. https://news.gallup.com/poll/16705/sex-offender-registries-underutilized-public.aspx.

Salerno, J. M., Murphy, M. C., & Bottoms, B. L. (2014). Give the kid a break—but only if he's straight: Retributive motives drive biases against gay youth in ambiguous punishment contexts. *Psychology, Public Policy, & Law*, 20(4), 398.

Sample, L. L. (2001). The social construction of the sex offender. [Unpublished dissertation]. University of Missouri–St. Louis.

Sample, L. L. (2004). The relationship between burglary and sex offending. *Sex Offender Law Report*, 5(3), 23–26.

Sample, L. L. (2006). An examination of the degree to which sex offenders kill. *Criminal Justice Review*, 31(3), 230–250.

Sample, L. L. (2011). The need to debate the future of community notification laws. *Criminology and Public Policy*, 10(2), 265–274.

Sample, L. L. & Bray, T. M. (2003). Are sex offenders dangerous? *Criminology & Public Policy*, 3(1), 59–82.

Sample, L. L. & Bray, T. M. (2006). Are sex offenders different? An examination of re-arrest patterns. *Criminal Justice Policy Review*, 17(1), 83–102.

Sample, L. L., Evans, M. K., & Anderson, A. L. (2011). Sex offender community notification laws: Are their effects symbolic or instrumental in nature? *Criminal Justice Policy Review*, 22 (1), 27–49.

Sample, L. L. & Kadleck, C. (2008). Sex offender laws: Legislators' accounts of the need for policy. *Criminal Justice Policy Review*, 19(1), 40–62.

Schmucker, M. & Lösel, F. (2015). The effects of sexual offender treatment on recidivism: An international meta-analysis of sound quality evaluations. *Journal of Experimental Criminology*, 11(4), 597–630.

Schram, D. D. & Milloy, C. D. (1995). *Community Notification: A Study of Offender Characteristics and Recidivism*. Olympia: Washington State Institute for Public Policy.

Schwartz, M. A. & Tatalovich, R. (2019). Public opinion and morality politics: lessons from Canada and the United States. *Comparative Sociology*, 18(1), 1–32.

Snedker, K. A. (2006). Altruistic and vicarious fear of crime: Fear for others and gendered social roles. *Sociological Forum*. 21(2),163–195.

Sobel, R. (2001). *The Impact of Public Opinion on US Foreign Policy since Vietnam: Constraining the Colossus*. Oxford University Press on Demand.

Socia Jr., K. M. & Stamatel, J. P. (2010). Assumptions and evidence behind sex offender laws: Registration, community notification, and residence restrictions. *Sociology Compass*, 4 (1) 1–20.

Soothill, K. & Francis, B. (2010). Public/Human rights: The debate rumbles on. *New Law Journal*, 160, 94.

Stevenson, M. C., Smith, A. C., Sekely, A., & Farnum, K. S. (2013). Predictors of support for juvenile sex offender registration: Educated individuals recognize the flaws of juvenile registration. *Journal of Child Sexual Abuse*, 22(2), 231–254.

Tewksbury, R. (2002). Validity and utility of the Kentucky sex offender registry. *Federal Probation*, 66(1), 21–26.

Tewksbury, R. (2005). Collateral consequences of sex offender registration. *Journal of Contemporary Criminal Justice*, 21(1), 67–81.

Tewksbury, R. & Jennings, W. G. (2010). Assessing the impact of sex offender registration and community notification on sex-offending trajectories. *Criminal Justice and Behavior*, 37(5), 570–582.

Tewksbury, R. & Lees, M. (2006). Perceptions of sex offender registration: Collateral consequences and community experiences. *Sociological Spectrum*, 26(3), 309–334.

Vozmediano, L., San-Juan, C., Vergara, A. I., & Alonso-Alberca, N. (2017). "Watch out, sweetie": The impact of gender and offence type on parents' altruistic fear of crime. *Sex Roles*, 77(9–10), 676–686.

Warr, M. (1992). Altruistic fear of victimization in households. *Social Science Quarterly*, 73(4), 723–736.

Warr, M. (2000). Fear of crime in the United States: Avenues for research and policy. *Criminal Justice*, 4(4), 451–489.

Warr, M. & Ellison, C. G. (2000). Rethinking social reactions to crime: Personal and altruistic fear in family households. *American Journal of Sociology*, 106(3), 551–578.

Williams, M., Comartin, E., & Lytle, R. (2020). The politics of symbolic laws: State resistance to the allure of sex offender residence restriction. *Law & Policy*, 42(3), 209–235.

Wilson, A. R. (2013). *Situating Intersectionality: Politics, Policy, and Power*. New York, St. Martin Press.

Wolf, M. R. & Pruitt, D. K. (2019). Grooming hurts too: The effects of types of perpetrator grooming on Trauma symptoms of child sexual abuse in adult survivors. *Journal of Child Sexual Abuse*, 28(3), 345–359.

Wood, J. (2009). Why public opinion of the criminal justice system is important. In J. Wood & T. Gannon (eds.), *Public Opinion and Criminal Justice*, Portland, OR: Willan Publishing.

Yankelovich, D. (1991). *Coming to Public Judgement. Making Democracy Work in a Complex World*. Syracuse, NY: Syracuse University Press.

Zevitz, R. G. (2003). Sex offender community notification and its impact on neighborhood life. *Crime Prevention and Community Safety: An International Journal*, 20(1), 41–61.

Zevitz, R. G. & Farkas, M. A. (2000). Sex offender community notification: Examining the importance of neighborhood meetings. *Behavioral Sciences and the Law*, 18(2/3), 393–408.

Zevitz, R. G. (2006). Sex offender community notification: Its role in recidivism and offender reintegration. *Criminal Justice Studies*, 19(2), 193–208.

Zgoba, K. M., Miner, M., Levenson, J., Knight, R., Letourneau, E., & Thornton, D. (2016). The Adam Walsh Act: An examination of sex offender risk classification systems. *Sexual Abuse*, 28(8), 722–740.

6

The Ancillary Consequences of SORN

Kelly Socia

Chapter 6 explores the broad range of ancillary consequences that stem from registration and notification laws. These consequences disrupt nearly every facet of daily life for registrants, their families, and their communities. The chapter begins with the most acutely felt consequences – the difficulty registrants experience finding jobs and housing. Since locating employment and housing is critical to successful reentry, the negative effects of SORN laws on both inhibit registrants' ability to reintegrate. These difficulties have also led to the spatial clustering ("ghettoization") of registrants. Other consequences include increased vigilantism by the public and decreased property values near registrant residences. All these consequences may lead to negative secondary effects on nonsexual criminal behavior and mental health outcomes, and in turn may affect the wellbeing of the family members of registrants and the overall community. Importantly, these wide-ranging consequences may also have hydraulic effects on charging and reporting decisions. Ultimately, this chapter concludes that SORN laws' wide-reaching deleterious effects, and their high implementation costs, outweigh their supposed benefits. As a result, it maintains that SORN laws must be tailored to higher-risk offenders and that community notification must be curtailed.

6.1 INTRODUCTION

Sex offender registration and notification (SORN) laws were enacted to reduce instances of sexual recidivism by individuals previously convicted of sex offenses. Over time, however, it has become apparent that the laws themselves, and several social control strategies that emanate from them, have an array of ancillary negative consequences. These consequences are in addition to those stemming from a felony conviction more generally. This chapter will examine these consequences, including SORN's effects on registrants' employment, housing options, personal safety, and family life, as well as its impact on real estate values, governmental spending, and justice system outcomes. The chapter will also discuss the effects of policies associated with SORN, such as residence restrictions.

6.2 EMPLOYMENT EFFECTS

A predominant unintended consequence of SORN, and the public registry especially, concerns the reduced employment potential of registrants. Employment is
a key factor for successful reentry (Anderson-Facile, 2009; Travis, 2005). As a general
matter, the stigmatization of a criminal conviction generally can result in reduced
employment chances (e.g., Apel & Sweeten, 2010; Holzer et al., 2003; Pettit &
Lyons, 2007; Solomon et al., 2004). For example, research in Ohio regarding
39,000 general population prisoners entering prison after 1993 and released between
1999 and 2004 found that more than half of them had not found a job six months
after release; after one year, 42.5 percent were still unemployed (Sabol, 2007).

On top of this, the effects of a sex-related conviction can be uniquely damaging.
Indeed, as noted by the Center for Sex Offender Management (CSOM, 2007, p. 10),
the "inability of offenders to secure ... employment is among the most significant
barriers to effective reentry, and this challenge becomes even more pronounced
when sex offenders are involved." Surveys of registrants have found that a high
percentage say their conviction and SORN laws have negatively affected employment options (Mercado et al., 2008; Tewksbury & Lees, 2006; Tewksbury & Zgoba,
2010). Studies find these effects are some of the most commonly reported negative
consequences experienced by registrants. They can range from the loss of previously
held jobs to difficulty in obtaining new employment (Griffin & Evans, 2019; Mercado
et al., 2008; Robbers, 2009). Registrants that do find jobs frequently do so below their
qualifications (Robbers, 2009). This is not surprising given that residence restrictions,
which are tied to registration, limit housing options near viable employment options
(see Socia, 2011a).[1] Follow-up interviews with 105 respondents found that a major
concern among registrants is finding *both* employment and suitable housing (Cubellis
et al., 2018). Families of registrants echo the view of the paramount importance of
adverse employment effects (Levenson & Tewksbury, 2009).

A common barrier in securing employment for registrants is the reaction of
employers and coworkers to their status. Many employers may fear being publicly
associated with registrants, being legally prohibited from hiring them, or merely be
averse to employing those with felony convictions more generally (Burchfield &
Mingus, 2008; Tewksbury & Lees, 2006). These concerns do not necessarily depend
on a public registry or public notification, as a conviction can be discovered through
a background check, but public registries are uniquely suited to allowing customers,
coworkers, or the public generally to become aware of a registrant's status. This
dynamic is *compounded* when registrants are required to list their place of employment on a public registry, disclosing their employer to members of the public who

---

[1] A nationwide online survey of 115 nonregistrant participants found that a majority did not believe
residence restrictions hindered registrants' employment options (Schiavone & Jeglic, 2009). Even so,
the difficulty of finding housing when publicly known as a sex offender may independently make
securing gainful employment difficult, especially when any housing found is unstable.

are particularly motivated to research registrants, sometimes in the wake of a sex offense making the local news (Robbers, 2009). Perhaps consequently, survey research by Robbers (2009) found that many registrants lie about their employment status. In other instances, employers may knowingly hire registrants but do so with an implicit condition that if their status is revealed, as when coworkers uncover the information on a public registry, the registrant will be terminated to mitigate potential problems for the employer (Robbers, 2009).

A variety of other negative employment-related consequences flow from SORN. For instance, registrants have reported being mistakenly arrested, which can threaten job status if the arrest occurs at work, becomes public, or otherwise restricts the individual's ability to attend work (Robbers, 2009). Further, if listing a place of employment is a condition of successful registration, registrants may be arrested for failure to report such employment, even if it is done solely with the intent to keep their jobs. Wary landlords and residence restrictions can relegate registrants to areas possibly far away from employment opportunities and public transportation (Levenson, 2008; Mercado et al., 2008). In particular, if securing housing is more difficult for registrants, registrants will likely have longer commutes on average and will be less flexible to the needs of their employer. The areas where registrants are able to live are frequently econom-ically depressed, further restricting employment prospects (Mustaine & Tewksbury, 2011). Ancillary requirements and limits, like electronic monitoring, parole limitations, mandatory therapy sessions, and/or simple exclusions from certain professions, exacerbate employment-related difficulties (Burchfield & Mingus, 2008; Robbers, 2009). Certain laws also direct law enforcement to track registrants with GPS devices, impose curfews, and even limit access to cell phones, further chilling their freedom of movement and increasing barriers to their full integration and rehabilitation (Daskal, 2013; Mogulescu & Goodmark, 2020).

Clearly, finding and keeping employment can be a challenge for registrants. However, stable employment is a key (and well-established) factor in successful reentry. Prescott (2016) suggests that the extent to which recidivism decreases in response to laws addressing sexual re-offending may turn largely on whether the law succeeds in creating an environment in which registrants have something to lose from engaging in future violations. When SORN laws ostracize, isolate, and geographically cluster registrants, they may inadvertently facilitate recidivism by limiting healthy social and economic lives that promote successful reentry and rehabilitation (Prescott & Rockoff, 2011).

6.3 HOUSING EFFECTS

Not surprisingly, under SORN laws, registrants have considerable difficulty finding high-quality and stable housing. Recently, Kunstler & Tsai (2020) documented that a sizable share of landlords simply will not rent to sex offenders. Indeed, the authors report that 44 percent will not rent to individuals with a history of sexual offending under any circumstances. An additional 36 percent report being willing to rent to individuals convicted of a sex offense but only under conditions not necessarily required of other applicants (e.g., stable housing history). SORN laws, by design, make it easier for landlords to obtain sex offense-related criminal history of their applicants; SORN also makes it easier for nearby residents or community members to pressure landlords to exclude registrants from housing – or to refuse to renew their leases. In light of research that makes plain that stable housing is an important factor in reducing recidivism (e.g., Jacobs & Gottlieb, 2020), the ancillary effects of SORN laws on housing opportunities for registrants are extremely policy-relevant.

An important but less obvious consequence of SORN laws (indirectly, through reduced housing and employment options for registrants) and residence restriction laws is the increased likelihood that registrants will cluster in particular geographic areas. This effect is seen among registrants whose offenses involved child and adult victims alike (Tewksbury & Mustaine, 2007). Research has shown that the areas containing such clusters are often marked by concentrated socioeconomic disadvantage and residential instability (Navarro & Rabe-Hemp, 2018; Socia, 2016; Socia & Stamatel, 2012). Race may also play a role. Mustaine and Tewksbury (2008) found that white registrants were more likely to live among higher concentrations of registrants, and their African-American counterparts were more likely to find themselves living in areas exhibiting more indicators of social disorganization (e.g., more poverty and unemployment, lower education levels).

Residential density may also be a factor in whether registrants cluster in socially disorganized neighborhoods. Amin (2019) found a strong correlation between social disorganization and clustering in the Queens and Bronx boroughs of New York City. These areas were marked by severely limited access to support services and high concentrations of minority populations. Other studies have found similar results (e.g., Wang et al., 2020). Williams (2018), however, found limited evidence that social disorganization was correlated with the presence of registrants in Dallas and that registrants in her study were likely to move to areas of less rather than more social disorganization. She suggested that her divergent results may be explained by Dallas's lower density compared to larger cities. On the other hand, Navarro and Rabe-Hemp's (2018) study of rural McLean County, Illinois, found a correlation between registrant clustering and social disorganization.

While registrants may opt to live in socially disorganized areas to secure a measure of anonymity, and perhaps protection if they re-offend, research supports the idea that registrants by and large reside where they do out of necessity (Mustaine et al., 2006). Yet it is often the case that densely packed urban areas offer very little legally acceptable (i.e., unrestricted) housing as a result of SORN-based residence restriction policies (Socia, 2011b), and thus such areas may offer limited housing options to registrants whose residences are not "grandfathered" under such laws.[2] Consequently, even in

---

[2] "Grandfathered" residences are generally those (1) where a registrant lives at the time a residence restriction policy is first implemented in an area and (2) that happen to fall inside the policy's restricted "buffer zone." While a registrant is not considered to be in violation of the restriction while they

a scenario in which landlords are willing to rent to (and nearby tenants and neighbors are willing to tolerate) individuals listed on a public sex offender registry, many registrants find themselves trapped between the pressures of an already-limited selection of affordable and available housing in a given area and simultaneously having to maintain compliance with residence restrictions that may place many of these otherwise accessible housing options out of reach. Thus, SORN laws, especially but not only when they interact with residence restrictions, can affect where registrants live, relegating them to areas that offer unrestricted, affordable, available – but often low-quality – housing.

These housing pockets might, in practice, lead to registrants clustering into a handful of large apartment buildings or low-cost daily motels that are outside residence restriction buffer zones and that are willing to tolerate individuals who are publicly listed as potential recidivists, possibly on the outskirts of a city or town. Such housing options may have very low-quality living conditions (Dum, 2016) for the same reasons they are open to registrants, and this clustering may in turn raise the concerns of nearby residents or local policy makers (Dum et al., 2017) about its public safety consequences. However, clustering may also make it easier for law enforcement to monitor multiple registrants (Casady, 2009; Goldman, 2009), reducing the costs of enforcing SORN and related laws.

The criminogenic effect of clustering, if any, is unclear. While some argue that grouping registrants together may encourage further deviant behavior, others maintain that there is little evidence that is the case (see Bain & German, 2006). Some research on formal shared living arrangements (e.g., halfway housing) finds that such situations may be beneficial to reentry chances and law enforcement monitoring aims. As noted by a report by the Colorado Department of Public Safety (2004, p. 4), "Shared Living Arrangements appear to be a frequently successful mode of containment and treatment for higher risk sex offenders and should be considered a viable living situation for higher risk sex offenders living in the community." Further, some research on residential motels (Dum, 2016) suggests that living among other similarly stigmatized individuals can yield a supportive environment. While formal shared living arrangements and residential motels are not the same as registrants simply living nearby one another in a community, some evidence exists that, under certain circumstances, registrant clustering may have some benefits beyond simply reducing the number of necessary law enforcement visits (Savage & Winsor, 2018).

To the extent residence restrictions have any potential to reduce clustering by forcing registrants to reside in less dense areas, research finds that any such effects may be short lived. At the neighborhood level, a cross-sectional study of upstate New York found that residential areas subject to residence restrictions had less clustering compared to those without any registrant residential restrictions (Socia, 2013a). Yet this relatively diminished clustering was not present in block groups with

---

continue to live at this residence, any movement out of this residence may permanently remove the grandfathered status.

restrictions in place longer than about two years, suggesting that any anti-clustering effects of residence restrictions could be temporary in nature (Socia, 2013a). While longitudinal data would be required to confirm this hypothesis, these findings point to a particular pattern of behavior among registrants that could be studied in the future to demonstrate how registrants respond to residence restrictions and whether such constraints affect community safety. It is plausible that in the wake of newly enacted residence restrictions, registrants scramble among their limited options and settle on dispersed, rural areas (Socia, 2013b). However, as residence restrictions age, registrants may either cluster in more convenient, newly discovered, unrestricted housing options, or simply find restricted options where enforcement is lax (Socia, 2013b). Supporting the latter possibility, some research indicates that many registrants simply do not comply with residence restrictions (Socia, 2013b). It is then possible that a mixture of lax enforcement, broad noncompliance, and willing landlords in disorganized neighborhoods generates clustering (Socia, 2013b). Importantly, if registrants are less likely to report their *actual* addresses, due to fears of being forced to move or being found in violation of the law, then residence restrictions would work to undermine the information dissemination goals of SORN itself.

In response to real or perceived increases in clustering, some communities have imposed additional residence restrictions that limit the number of registrants either living at the same location or limit the ability of one registrant to live within a given distance of another. While no research has examined the efficacy of these anti-clustering policies, it is useful to compare similar laws restricting "adult" businesses from operating within certain distances of schools or residences. These adult zoning laws are predicated ostensibly on fears of increased crime, decreased housing values, and similar secondary negative effects (Paul et al., 2001), which are comparable to the fears associated with registrant clusters. While the containment of certain businesses might have public appeal, *too much* clustering might provoke concern and increase fears regarding crime and related social ills. Yet many of these fears are empirically unfounded, with more sound research finding there is little evidence supporting the presence of these secondary effects for adult businesses (Paul et al., 2001). As such, we are in need of more research specifically addressing SORN-related registrant clustering and its effects, if any.

Reflecting this need for research, Grubesic (2010) notes that there are few benchmarks for even identifying an actual cluster of registrants. Perhaps as a result, some researchers have attempted to use spatial statistics to more scientifically identify clusters (Grubesic, 2010), predict where registrants are most likely to cluster (Mack & Grubesic, 2010), and/or outline methods to optimize the distribution of registrants (Grubesic & Murray, 2008, 2010). Yet these studies typically focus on methodological concerns, not so much the effects of clusters.

In extreme cases, the difficulty in obtaining housing due to SORN and related restrictions may force registrants to leave jurisdictions entirely in search of available compliant housing. Mercado et al. (2008) found that some major municipalities are using zoning laws to all but preclude housing for registrants. For instance, Morgan (2008) found that in Bay County, Florida, registrants became less likely to live in municipalities that passed residence restrictions and more likely to live in those without such restrictions. Similarly, Nobles et al. (2012) found more restrictive housing restriction spurred a greater dispersal of registrants throughout the surrounding areas, dissipating the potential for clustering.

In response to severe housing constraints, some registrants have assembled their own communities – in Southern Florida, for instance, the City of Refuge (Kirk, 2015). While such a community would sidestep clustering concerns, compliance with severe residence restrictions, and/or backlash from neighbors, it is hard to describe such an outcome as anything other than banishment. However, for those registrants living in Refuge, such a community represents a place where they can live in relative safety. As noted by Kirk (2015):

> Here is exile that is also asylum from the larger, unforgiving world. Here is, weirdly enough, real community ... the kind of community that would protect you from vigilantes intent on dragging you out of bed in the middle of the night to take turns kicking your teeth down your throat (Paragraph 13).

Any tendency to construct a separate community in response to fear of persecution is a paradigmatic example of an ancillary effect of SORN laws, which presumably aid would-be vigilantes and others in learning the identities and whereabouts of registrants. Whether such a threat is real or imagined, it is hard to fault individuals with sex offense convictions for establishing their own communities as a form of self-preservation. Refuge not only allows former offenders to live without concerns about how close their home is to a school or day care, or even how close they are to other registrants, but also makes it easier to locate stable housing, a willing landlord, and neighbors who are unlikely to object to a registrant.

Similar to the importance of rewarding employment options, finding stable housing is key to successful reentry. Whether through landlords prescreening and denying applicants based on their public registry status (Kunstler & Tsai, 2020), or through legal restrictions on where registrants can reside, finding housing can be difficult for registrants. When living with family members is not an option, such as when laws impose residence restrictions or inhibit clustering, registrants may face increased risk of homelessness and/or transience. In South Carolina, Cann and Isom Scott (2019) found the implementation of residence restrictions correlated with rapidly increasing rates of homelessness. In New York City, this burden fell disproportionately on registrants with disabilities, many of whom found themselves effectively banished (Frankel, 2019). Compounding this issue, some homeless shelters have policies that prohibit convicted sex offenders from staying there (Rolfe et al., 2017). And homelessness makes tracking registrants more difficult.

6.4 IMPACT ON NONSEXUAL CRIMINAL AND ANTISOCIAL BEHAVIOR AND MENTAL HEALTH

While most of the concern regarding individuals with sex offense convictions living in the community clearly involves the possibility of sexual recidivism, SORN laws may have negative effects on other kinds of behavior. In particular, for those concerned about public safety more broadly, SORN laws may exacerbate criminogenic risk factors that can increase nonsexual criminal behavior as well as legal but antisocial and counter-productive behavior (see Grossi, 2017; Rydberg, 2018). As noted earlier, SORN laws can interfere with the employment potential of registrants and disrupt stable housing options. The financial and emotional strains of either of these may lead to criminal coping, such as burglarizing homes as a means of financial support or using alcohol or drugs to weather the emotional pressures of being unemployed and/or transient.

The direct and indirect effects of SORN may increase mental health problems and feelings of isolation among registrants (Bailey & Klein, 2018). Such consequences may follow directly from public registration status – including the more visual signs of a registrant's status, such as placing signs outside of their homes on Halloween, or requiring that they carry special licenses identifying themselves as a registered sex offender (Warford, 2015) – but may also result indirectly from the inability to obtain employment and the financial burdens and time requirements associated with SORN compliance. Such stigmatizing measures and economic barriers may cause distress and associated mental health problems for registrants.[3]

6.5 EFFECTS ON REGISTRANTS' FAMILIES

In addition to effects on registrants themselves, research has documented the variety of ways that SORN laws negatively affect registrants' family members and friends. For example, a survey of 584 family members of registrants revealed financial hardships to be the most consequential result they experienced due to their family member's registrant status (Levenson & Tewksbury, 2009). Other issues identified by family members included housing disruption and forced relocation, threats and other harassment, vandalism of property, stigmatization (particularly for registrants' children), and emotional and psychological problems (Bailey & Klein, 2018; Levenson & Tewksbury, 2009; Tewksbury & Levenson, 2009). These burdens can lead family members to condemn SORN laws as unfair, and cause them to discount the potential of their related registrant to re-offend, regardless of actual risk (Levenson & Tewksbury, 2009). In turn, this may reduce the willingness of a registrant's family and friends to monitor, report, or otherwise cooperate with law enforcement. For registrants with children, this blindness to risk may hinder

---

[3] Deleterious effects may be even more important for juveniles forced to register after adjudication for a sex crime. The negative effects of SORN on juvenile registrants more generally are discussed at length in Chapter 9.

registrants' rehabilitation and reintegration into society and increase the risk of re-offense (Levenson & Tewksbury, 2009). These consequences undermine the aims of SORN to rehabilitate registrants and promote public safety.

6.6 VIGILANTISM

Even though SORN laws, law enforcement, and registries themselves expressly prohibit the misuse of registry information, it is not uncommon for registrants to be the target of harassment and to experience harm to themselves, family members, or their property. While individuals with criminal records, especially those con-victed of committing violent crimes against vulnerable populations, have always been at risk of extrajudicial punishment and social shaming within their communi-ties, community notification makes such vigilante behavior easier by informing strangers of the current whereabouts of registrants and by allowing individuals to infer a shared societal preference for the further punishment of registrants.

Among the most notorious instances of such behavior to date concerned regis-trants Joseph Gray and William Elliott. In April 2006, Canadian Stephen Marshall used the Maine sex offender registry to identify the addresses of Gray and Elliott. Armed with two handguns and a rifle, Marshall shot Gray through his living room window at 3 a.m. on a Sunday morning, and then shot Elliott five hours later after knocking on the door at his separate residence (Harrison, 2016). Although not common, fatal acts of vigilantism have occurred elsewhere. In South Carolina, for instance, a registrant and his wife were murdered (Williams, 2018). In Alaska, an individual just released from prison himself attacked three registrants over a five-day span, using a hammer to cause debilitating injuries to one of the men (Boroff, 2018).

One of the more comprehensive studies regarding vigilantism examined media reports of vigilantism against individuals accused, arrested, convicted, or registered for a sex offense, finding 279 such incidents occurring between the years of 1983 and 2015 in the United States (Cubellis et al., 2019). Of these 279 incidents, most attacks targeted a single victim (95 percent) living in the community (80.3 percent); those targeted most often had a male victim (95 percent), and were charged with crimes involving child molestation (68.3 percent) (Cubellis et al., 2019). About half of the attacks involved lone offenders (51 percent), and of the 302 total victims, nine (3 percent) were collateral victims who were not registrants, and sixty victims (20 percent) were killed as a result of the attack (Cubellis et al., 2019).

Other research has been based on interviews with registrants and treatment providers. Malesky and Keim (2001), for example, found that more than 50 percent of the 133 mental health professionals surveyed believed that registrants were at risk for vigilantism victimization. Levenson and Tewksbury (2009) found that 44 percent of family members of registrants experienced threats or harassment, and 7 percent reported being physically assaulted or injured. Further, 47 percent of children of registrants had been harassed, and the vast majority of them reported feelings of depression, anxiety, or anger (Levenson & Tewksbury, 2009). In contrast, a survey of forty-five sheriffs and police chiefs in Washington State found that less than 4 percent of registrants reported acts of harassment between 1990 and 1996 (a total of thirty-three incidents) (Matson & Lieb, 1996), although SORN was somewhat new at the time. These conflicting findings suggest perhaps a diminished inclination to report instances of harassment by registrants and their family, arguably an additional consequence of their undermined faith in the system into which they are thrust.

Vigilantism and harassment are not limited to the United States, where community notification is most expansive and pervasive. Internationally, a qualitative study of twenty-one police officers involved in running a sex offender management squad in Australia found that anxiety over increased vigilantism from a new notification scheme was a major concern of both officers and registrants (Whitting et al., 2016). The officers also noted a potential chain reaction from vigilantism that would decrease the ability of registrants to find suitable housing options and would negatively affect family members (Whitting et al., 2016). In Canada, an Alberta judge withheld the identity of a convicted sex offender out of fear of vigilantism (Johnston, 2016). Thus, it is unsurprising that both English (Kemshall et al., 2010) and Scottish (Manson, 2015) evaluations of pilot community notification schemes suggest that limiting the amount of available information concerning registrants, and the number of community members with access to such information, may result in fewer acts of vigilantism and fewer difficulties for registrants, such as employment problems.

While any vigilantism is obviously concerning, among the most concerning cases are those involving vigilantism perpetrated against individuals wrongly targeted, either due to mistaken identity or errors in registry data, which are not uncommon (Salmon, 2010). A number of such cases have been reported. For example, a disabled man in the United Kingdom was murdered by an individual who thought the man had been convicted of a sex offense (Morris, 2013), and another individual's car was destroyed after vigilantes mistakenly thought it belonged to a convicted child molester (Gilbert, 2017). In Ireland, a man had to be escorted out of a town after being confronted by an angry mob who mistakenly believed he was a child sex offender (Gallagher, 2017), and another man was abducted and threatened after being (mistakenly) suspected of committing a sexual assault (Brennan & Gallagher, 2016). Similar cases of mistaken identity have also occurred in Canada (Soloducha, 2017).

Even when photos of registrants are made available on a registry, it is easy to see how cases of mistaken identity can occur. Horn (2019) reviewed how inaccurate and incomplete criminal data and complex statutory schemes contribute to the mistaken targeting of nonregistrants. Presumably similar errors, although not resulting in extrajudicial violence, interfere with the ostensible purpose of SORN laws to allow community members to engage in monitoring and self-protective behavior. What may be more worrying is that registries are unlikely to become more accurate over time. Indeed, Logan and Ferguson (2016) charted how SORN databases have been largely immunized in the law from consequences arising from errors, under-mining incentives to rectify errors and avoid misdirected harms.

6.7 COMPLIANCE COSTS

The consequences of SORN are not borne only by registrants, their families, and their communities. Governments (and hence taxpayers) bear them as well. SORN is not cost-free to implement, and compliance costs can vary widely, both at the state and local level. Indeed, while some members of the public might infer that SORN costs must be relatively modest (at least from the taxpayer's perspective), involving mainly the cost of running a public registry website, costs can actually be quite substantial. For instance, one study of New Jersey's Megan's Law estimated that in 2007, it would cost $555,565 in start-up expenses, and a further $3.9 million in annual expenses, for the fifteen counties responding to the survey (Zgoba et al., 2008).[4] The Justice Policy Institute compiled a list of estimates associated with state compliance with changes required by the Adam Walsh Act (AWA), which threatens to withhold a percentage of federal criminal justice funding if a state fails to comply with its heightened requirements. These estimates ranged from $848,000 for Wyoming up to $59 million for California (Petteruti & Walsh, 2008). A partial breakdown of California's estimate included $21 million for probation, $9 million for police personnel, and $27 million to renovate the state's existing registry system, not counting "tens of millions" to link California's registry to the public Megan's Law website. The Virginia Department of Planning and Budget estimated initial compliance would cost $12.5 million in start-up expenses, along with almost $9 million in annual expenses.

As Chapter 2 discusses, fewer than twenty states are now in compliance with AWA requirements. According to Justice Policy Institute estimates, the amount lost in federal funding is typically a small fraction of the costs associated with compliance (Petteruti & Walsh, 2008), suggesting that the sheer magnitude of SORN law expenses are at least partly to blame for this state of affairs. Indeed, the Texas Senate Criminal Justice Committee estimated SORN compliance would cost the state $38.7 million going forward, while loss in allocated federal money would only amount to $1.4 million (Wang, 2014).

Another fiscal consideration is the impact of SORN on other potential strat-egies that might be effective in reducing sexual offending. Every dollar spent retooling registry systems, purchasing hardware and software, or hiring personnel to maintain SORN systems, is a dollar that cannot be dedicated to substance abuse or mental health treatment, educational resources, parole and probation services, or similar measures. Further, in many jurisdictions, registrants must pay fees as part of their registry requirements. According to Makin et al. (2018),

---

[4] Start-up expenses included establishing the registry, equipment costs, and any other miscellaneous expenses. Ongoing costs included items such as salaries, maintenance, equipment/supplies, and other miscellaneous expenses accumulating on a yearly basis.

twenty-eight states require registrant payments, with varying costs. For instance, Massachusetts requires a $75 fee for new registrants (Commonwealth of Massachusetts, 2018), while Alabama mandates a $200 fee (Shim, 2014). These charges, while possibly helping to offset some small portion of the registry costs for the state, may be better used by the registrant to pay for housing, out-of-pocket behavioral health costs, care of dependents, or other matters that would help with successful reentry and rehabilitation.

6.8 REAL ESTATE VALUES

Unsurprisingly, people are not keen on living near where registrants live, and as a general matter, people learn where registrants live (and possibly that a registrant lives near them) through SORN-related public registries. While theoretically there might be a compensating benefit to SORN in terms of reduced risk of sexual victimization, housing markets suggest that awareness of a nearby registrant amounts to a local disamenity. As such, the financial impacts of SORN extend to real estate values as well, as research finds that registrants' residences can negatively affect the value of spatially proximate real estate. In some cases, these financial impacts can be surprisingly large.

For instance, using cross-sectional data from Montgomery County, Ohio, Larsen et al. (2003) found that houses within a third of a mile of a registrant sold for significantly less than houses further away and those within one-tenth of a mile sold for 17 percent less. Incorporating intertemporal and cross-sectional data, Linden and Rockoff (2008) found that registrant residences in Mecklenburg County, North Carolina, reduced the property values of nearby houses within a tenth of a mile. Specifically, compared to baseline property values, homes within one-tenth of a mile of a registrant sold for about 4 percent less, while houses next door to a registrant sold for about 12 percent less than they otherwise would have. These impacts were extremely localized, however, as houses more than a tenth of a mile away saw no decline in property values (Linden & Rockoff, 2008), but also suggest significant losses of property value for those unlucky enough to live proximate to North Carolina's many registrants.

Pope (2008) found similar results in Hillsborough County, Florida, when incorporating longitudinal data on registrant residential histories. Specifically, homes within one-tenth of a mile of a registrant sold for 2.3 percent less. Perhaps most importantly, Pope (2008) found that this decrease vanished once the registrant moved away from the area. This research suggests SORN laws enable homebuyers to trade-off their perceived risks with home values (Pope, 2008), and also that a registrant's arrival and departure are like lightning strikes mediated through public registries, likely disrupting plans and neighborhoods, and creating windfall gains (for those willing to buy near a registrant) and losses (for those who seek to leave a neighborhood) unrelated to housing fundamentals.

Caudill et al. (2015) conducted a recent study on this issue using a cross-sectional hedonic spatial error model on housing data from Memphis, Tennessee. They found that average property values decreased by about 2 percent for every *additional* registrant living within a one-mile radius, and that registrants caused a total housing value loss of about 7 percent within one-mile, and 14 percent within one tenth of a mile (Caudill et al., 2015). Navarro and Rabe-Hemp (2018) found that these property impacts also manifested in rural areas. Studying McLean County, Illinois, they examined the relationships between home sale values and the distance from and prevalence of registrants. They also looked at a subgroup of registrants who had re-offended and been classified as sexual predators (SPs). Their findings are in line with previous research. They found that each foot of added distance from the nearest registrant or SP is correlated with a $17.03 and $15.25 increase in home values, respectively. Further, the presence of more than one registrant or SP nearby correlated with decreases in home values of $12,750 and $17,797, respectively.

One study, it is worth noting, found no relationship between registrants and decreased property values. Navarro and Ruther (2018), focusing on Jefferson County, Kentucky, included neighborhood fixed effects in their model to control for fixed features of a neighborhood that do not change over time. The authors hoped that, by doing so, they would account for unexplained differences between neighborhoods, possibly eliminating any significant relationship between distance from and density of registrants and home prices. The authors suggested several potential explanations for their failure to detect any relationship, including diminished awareness in the county of the presence of registrants, high transience of registrants, and registrants' tendency to live in already socially disorganized neighborhoods.

Importantly, the impact on housing values documented by the majority of the research is not supported by actual changes in crime risk. Agan and Prescott (2014) found the risk of sex crime victimization was broadly lower in neighborhoods with additional registrants. Their research suggested that there may be a relationship between risk and the types of crimes for which the registrants were convicted (Agan & Prescott, 2014). When registrants were convicted for pornography or crimes against adults, their neighborhoods were found to be safer than neighborhoods without registrants, though slightly less so following the implementation of community notification (Agan & Prescott, 2014). Neighborhoods with registrants convicted for violent sex crimes or crimes against children were found to be as safe or less safe upon registration, but they became safer than comparison neighborhoods post-notification (Agan & Prescott, 2014).

In any event, the impact on housing value does comport with public perceptions of registrant behavior and risk (Levenson et al., 2007). A survey of 193 residents in Melbourne, Florida, found that the public perceives registrants as posing a uniform and significant risk to community safety, regardless of their particular criminal history (Levenson et al., 2007). These views were held despite respondents reporting very little exposure to notification activities (Levenson et al., 2007). Thus, the public seems to entertain systematic misperceptions regarding the risk of registrants (see Chapter 5), and these misperceptions may be behind the sometimes-dramatic effects on real estate values.

6.9 HYDRAULIC EFFECTS

An additional impact of SORN may be its distortion of how the criminal justice system handles SORN-eligible offenses. As noted decades ago by McCoy (1984), when discretion is removed from one part of the judicial system, the change may result in increased discretion in another part of the system that effectively undoes the original reform, an outcome known as a hydraulic effect. The many negative consequences of SORN on the criminal justice system exemplify this dynamic in several ways.

6.9.1 *Plea-Bargaining and Trials*

The specter of being subject to SORN laws is a major potential downside for defendants, with the potential of substantially influencing the plea bargaining process and its likely outcome. Logically, individuals charged with a registerable offense may be more likely to plead guilty to *other nonregisterable* crimes to avoid registrant status. Conversely, if prosecutors are unable to reduce charges for a plea bargain enough to avoid such penalties due to more minor crimes being included as registerable offenses, then it may entice defendants to try their luck in court, which requires much more in the way of government resources. Thus, SORN policies may result in hydraulic effects: an increased likelihood of a plea bargain for nonregisterable offenses or an increased likelihood of a trial for defendants initially charged with registrable offenses.

However, as noted by Socia and Rydberg (2016), there is conflicting evidence on the question whether SORN policies have increased the number or proportion of plea bargains as compared to trials. For instance, using twenty-one years of longitudinal arrest data, Freeman et al. (2009) concluded that New York State's SORN law did not increase plea-bargaining rates. Failing to find any evidence of a change hints that SORN policies may not be achieving much with respect to their goals of deterring sex crimes (Freeman et al., 2009). Conversely, in examining South Carolina data, Letourneau et al. (2013) found that plea bargains increased in *juvenile* sex crime cases after both an initial and a revised SORN policy were implemented. Specifically, their findings indicated that the juvenile SORN policy increased the likelihood of plea bargains, both changing the *type* of charges and lowering the severity of the charges (Letourneau et al., 2013).

6.9.2 *Reduced Charges*

Regarding adults, Letourneau et al. (2010) found that the South Carolina SORN changes led to more charge reductions (from a sexual to a nonsexual crime) both after the initial registration law and after the implementation of community notification provisions. Further, while the initial SORN law increased the probability of a guilty disposition (from 55 percent pre-SORN to 65 percent post-SORN), this decreased slightly (to 60 percent) after community notification was adopted (Letourneau et al., 2010).

In terms of juveniles, after South Carolina's 1995 registration law, Letourneau et al. (2009) found that prosecutors became 41 percent less likely to move forward with sexual assault charges.[5] After a 1999 revision to the law, the odds of a guilty disposition for juvenile sexual charges increased (Letourneau et al., 2009). These findings matched the authors' theory that the stiffer penalties had increased the likelihood of a plea bargain, and this was further supported by the increase in the proportion of less serious cases in the system at the time of disposition (Letourneau et al., 2009). Overall, Letourneau et al. (2009) concluded:

> that one effect of applying a lifetime, charge-based (vs. risk-based) registration policy to juvenile sexual offenders is that prosecutors became significantly less likely to move forward on cases, thus undermining the primary aims of registration policies (i.e., increase police and community surveillance of sexual offenders (P. 161).

6.9.3 *Sex Offense Reporting Rates*

Scholars have suggested that SORN laws may discourage reporting of intrafamilial sex crimes and/or self-reporting by offenders seeking treatment (Edwards & Hensley, 2001; Hlavka & Uggen, 2008). In effect, the concern is that SORN laws are sufficiently burdensome that at least some classes of victims would report being victimized less often so as not to subject their assailants to registration and notification, often for life. This is a similar argument to the one made by anti-rape activists in the 1970s, who maintained that strict penalties for sexual assault might discourage reporting and prosecution (Corrigan, 2006).

The potential for SORN laws to decrease reporting rates is important, particularly given that the vast majority of sex crimes, especially against children, are committed by acquaintances and family members who would be the ones subject to the SORN requirements after conviction (Greenfield, 1997). Given the direct negative effects of SORN requirements, plus the negative consequences in employment, housing, and increased harassment and mental health effects for registrants and their families, it is plausible many family members, including victims, would feel pressured to not report their offenders. Additionally, there may be real or perceived fears that *other* family members will blame the victim for the perpetrator-family member being subjected to SORN. Aggravating matters, requirements such as mandatory reporting laws covering treatment providers may hinder self-reporting and help-seeking behaviors.[6]

All of that said, there is relatively little generalizable statistical evidence to support or discount a relationship between SORN laws and victim reporting behaviors. Much of the research that does exist comes from surveys of convenience samples with limited generalizability. For example, in an online survey of sexual violence

---

[5]   They also found that prosecutors became less likely to proceed with assault charges, though not to the same extent as sexual assault charges (Letourneau et al., 2009).

[6]   However, Elbogen et al. (2003) found that about half of the forty sex offenders they surveyed would be *more likely* to seek treatment due to SORN policies.

survivors, very few suggested the sex offender registry affected their reporting deci-sion (Craun & Simmons, 2012). One exception to the convenience sampling in the literature is a study by Sandler et al. (2017). Using a National Incident-Based Reporting System (NIBRS) time series analysis of four states, they found no change in juvenile sex crime rates (which are based on reports of crimes to law enforcement) after policy enactments requiring juvenile registration/notification. While that does not confirm that reporting *likelihood* stayed consistent, it does suggest as much.

6.10 CONCLUSION

Clearly, there is an array of important consequences stemming either directly or indirectly from SORN laws, especially public registries. As outlined in this chapter, these consequences can affect the emotional, mental, financial, and physical well-being of not just registrants but also their family members and the communities in which they live. Further, SORN laws may influence the criminal justice system directly, resulting in hydraulic effects that may hinder the interests of justice for either the accused or their victims, higher costs needed to enforce and comply with SORN provisions, and ultimately increased budgetary outlays for governments.

In significant part, negative consequences flow from how the public instinctively reacts to the label of "sex offender." Illustrating this effect, Harris and Socia (2016) found that respondents in a nationally representative survey were more likely to support SORN, residence restrictions, and social networking bans when asked about "sex offenders" as compared to a control group asked about "individuals convicted of crimes of a sexual nature." The public sees "sex offenders" as uniformly high risk, and thus deserving of harsh policies and the associated consequences (Socia & Harris, 2016). Other experimental studies have found similar consequences relating to the use of stigmatizing labels (e.g., Lowe & Willis, 2019; Imhoff, 2015). Unfortunately, it is unlikely that members of the public will change their instinctive disdain for and fear over "sex offenders" as a group.

Thus, it may be more useful to identify specific language to use when describing this population or subsets of this population (such as "high risk sex offenders"), particularly when targeting individuals who must comply with a specific policy. As there is a very wide range of characteristics (and recidivism risk) under the umbrella of the "sex offender" label, policy makers and practitioners must be careful to design and support policies that are less hammer-like, applying to any and all individuals convicted of sex offenses, and more scalpel-like, identifying and applying to precisely those individuals likely to respond in a socially beneficial way.[7] As the next Chapter indicates (Chapter 7), there is little reason to think that SORN laws have achieved

---

[7] In a non-SORN context, for instance, the blanket application of residence restriction laws against publicly registered individuals is not supported by any existing research. Indeed, research indicates they likely would not have stopped any prior sex crimes from occurring had they been in place at an earlier time (see Minnesota Department of Corrections, 2007), leaving us no reason to think they are

their main goals of reducing recidivism, and so the ancillary effects of such policies should take center stage. If such effects are large and negative, we have good reason to question the use of SORN laws when any positive effects on recidivism are small at best.

Fortunately, there are ways to maintain some control over potentially dangerous individuals while at the same time minimizing ancillary negative consequences. For instance, registering an address with law enforcement theoretically allows those in charge of public safety to monitor convicted sex offenders in the community. Such a list can also be used to inform relevant businesses and organizations (e.g., schools and day cares) about potential issues with employees, volunteers, or nearby residents. However, the most serious consequences occur when this information is publicly disseminated. The ancillary consequences stem not from the registration itself, but rather when this list is used as a basis for discriminatory practices related to housing and employment, for stigmatizing or vigilante purposes by community members, or for related policies with no empirical support (e.g., residence restrictions).

Overall, the consequences that stem from SORN can be mitigated if three main practices are adopted. First, more care should be exercised when identifying which subset of the sex offender population is targeted by a given policy. Simply applying a policy to "sex offenders" is neither efficient nor effective. Second, the public registry should return to its original use only by law enforcement, with strict controls on what data are released to whom and under what conditions. While the latter may be challenging in the short run, given the ubiquity of privately hosted copies of electronic registry data, changing policies now would at least be helpful in mitigating many negative consequences in the future. Third, policies that build on SORN, such as residence restrictions, should be restricted to those that are empirically supported. Taking these steps will not be easy, but would ultimately result in policies that are more effective at protecting society from sex offender recidivism.

REFERENCES

Agan, A. Y. & Prescott, J.J. (2014). Sex offender law and the geography of victimization. *Journal of Empirical Legal Studies*, 11(4), 786–828.

Amin, A. (2019). *Mapping Sex Offenders and Treatment Centers in Relation to Social Disorganization* (119). [Master's Thesis, University of New Haven]. Criminology and Criminal Justice Commons.

disrupting crimes today. Scenarios in which such restrictions would stop a crime from occurring are rare, despite the fact that sex offenses garner intense media focus and policymaker interest. Realistically, if residence restrictions applied *only* in cases where an individual had solicited a stranger victim at or around a school or day care that was also located near their own residence, few if any individuals would be subjected to such restrictions in even the largest city. This would help mitigate some of the housing problems the registrant population experiences, and the negative economic and social consequences that accompany them, especially in municipalities whose policy makers are using these laws as ways to block all registrants from living there.

Anderson-Facile, D. (2009). Basic challenges to prisoner reentry. *Sociology Compass*, 3, 183–195. doi:10.1111/j.1751-9020.2009.00198.x.

Apel, R. & Sweeten, G. (2010). The impact of incarceration on employment during the transition to adulthood. *Social Problems*, 57(3), 448–479. DOI: 10.1525/sp.2010.57.3.448.

Bailey, D. J. S. & Klein, J. L. (2018). Ashamed and alone: Comparing offender and family member experiences with the sex offender registry. *Criminal Justice Review*, 43(4), 440–457. DOI: 10.1177/0734016818756486.

Bain, B. & German, E. (2006, September 26). *How a Cluster Grew so Large: Low Rents, Willing Landlords and Politics Play Roles*. Newsday. http://find.galegroup.com/gtx/info mark.do?&contentSet=IAC-Documents&type=retrieve&tabID=T004&prodId=SPN. SP04&docId=CJ151896742&source=gale&srcprod=SP04&userGroupName=albanyu& version=1.0.

Boroff, D. (2018, January 2). Vigilante pleads guilty to beating three sex offenders, implores others not to take law into own hands. N.Y. Daily News. www.nydailynews.com/news/ crime/man-beat-sex-offenders-admits-vigilante-justice-wrong-article-1.3733638.

Brennan, D. & Gallagher, C. (2016). Man threatened to cut off penis of man he wrongly thought was a sex offender. The Journal. www.thejournal.ie/innocent-man-kidnapped-3154544-Dec2016/.

Town of Brookhaven, New York. (2008, June 10). *Brookhaven Child Protection Act Passes with 7-0 Vote*. Brookhaven, NY. www.brookhaven.org/PressRoom/tabid/56/newsid970/363/ Brookhaven-Child-Protection-Act-Passes-with-7-0-Vote/Default.aspx.

Burchfield, K. B. & Mingus, W. (2008). Not in my neighborhood: Assessing registered sex offenders' experiences with local social capital and social control. *Criminal Justice and Behavior*, 35(3), 356–374. DOI: 10.1177/0093854807311375.

Cann, D. & Isom Scott, D. A. (2019). Sex offender residence restrictions and homelessness: A critical look at South Carolina. *Criminal Justice Policy Review*, Advance online publication. DOI: 10.1177/0887403419862334.

Casady, T. (2009). A police chief's viewpoint: Geographic aspects of sex offender residency restrictions. *Criminal Justice Policy Review*, 20(1), 16–20. DOI: 10.1177/0887403408327692.

Caudill, S. B., Affuso, E., & Yang, M. (2015). Registered sex offenders and house prices: A hedonic analysis. *Urban Studies*, 52(13), 2425–2440. DOI:10.1177/0042098014547368.

Claiborne, W. (1997, March 27). Registration Laws Unleashing Public Fury on Sex Offenders; Police in California City Acknowledge Underestimating Response. *Washington Post*, p. A03.

Colorado Department of Public Safety. (2004). *Report on Safety Issues Raised by Living Arrangements for and Location of Sex Offenders in the Community*. http://dcj.state.co.us/ odvsom/sex_offender/SO_Pdfs/FullSLAFinal.pdf.

Commonwealth of Massachusetts. (2018). *Register as a Sex Offender*. Mass.gov. www .mass.gov/how-to/register-as-a-sex-offender.

Corrigan, R. (2006). Making meaning of Megan's law. *Law & Social Inquiry*, 31(2), 267–312. DOI: 10.1111/j.1747-4469.2006.00012.x.

Craun, S. W. & Simmons, C. A. (2012). Taking a seat at the table: Sexual assault survivors' views of sex offender registries. *Victims & Offenders*, 7(3), 312–326. DOI: 10.1080/ 15564886.2012.685217.

CSOM. (2007). *Managing the Challenges of Sex Offender Reentry*. www.csom.org/pubs/ reentry_brief.pdf.

Cubellis, M. A., Evans, D. N., & Fera, A. G. (2019) Sex offender stigma: An exploration of vigilantism against sex offenders. *Deviant Behavior* 40(2), 225–239. DOI: 10.1080/ 01639625.2017.1420459.

Cubellis, M. A., Walfield, S. M., & Harris, A. J. (2018). Collateral consequences and effectiveness of sex offender registration and notification: Law enforcement perspectives. *International Journal of Offender Therapy and Comparative Criminology*, 62(4), 1080–1106. DOI: 10.1177/0306624X16667574.

Daskal, J. C. (2013). Pre-crime restraints: The explosion of targeted, noncustodial prevention. *Cornell Law Review*, 99(2), 327–386.

Denniston, S. E. (2016). *The Relationship between Juvenile Sex Offender Registration and Depression in Adulthood* (1883). [Doctoral Dissertation, Walden University]. Criminology and Criminology Justice Commons.

Dum, C. P. (2016). *Exiled in America: Life on the Margins in a Residential Motel*. New York: Columbia University Press.

Dum, C. P., Socia, K. M., & Rydberg, J. (2017). Public support for emergency shelter housing interventions concerning stigmatized populations: Results from a randomized experiment. *Criminology & Public Policy*, 16(3), 835–877. DOI: 10.1111/1745-9133.12311.

Edwards, W. & Hensley, C. (2001). Contextualizing sex offender management legislation and policy: Evaluating the problem of latent consequences in community notification laws. *International Journal of Offender Therapy and Comparative Criminology*, 45(1), 83–101. DOI: 10.1177/0306624X01451006.

Elbogen, E. B., Patry, M., & Scalora, M. J. (2003). The impact of community notification laws on sex offender treatment attitudes. *International Journal of Law and Psychiatry*, 26(2), 207–219. DOI: 10.1016/S0160-2527(03)00016-5.

Farkas, M. A. & Miller, G. (2007). Reentry and reintegration: Challenges faced by the families of convicted sex offenders. *Federal Sentencing Reporter*, 20(2), 88–92. DOI: 10.1525/fsr.2007.20.2.88.

Frankel, A. (2019). Pushed out and locked in: The catch-22 for New York's disabled, homeless sex offender registrants. *The Yale Law Journal Forum*, 279–324.

Freeman, N. J., Sandler, J. C., & Socia, K. M. (2009). A time-series analysis on the impact of sex offender registration and community notification on plea bargaining rates. *Criminal Justice Studies: A Critical Journal of Crime, Law, and Society*, 22(2), 153–165. DOI: 10.1080/14786010902975424.

Gallagher, C. (2017, May 30). Woman defends wrongly identifying man as sex offender. *The Irish Times*. www.irishtimes.com/news/crime-and-law/woman-defends-wrongly-identifying-man-as-sex-offender-1.3101998.

Gilbert, D. (2017, September 22). Two arrested after vigilantes targeting sex offender mistakenly destroy neighbour's car. *Eastern Daily Press*. www.edp24.co.uk/news/crime/two-arrested-after-vigilantes-targeting-sex-offender-mistakenly-destroy-neighbour-s-car-1-5206765.

Goldman, R. (2009). Dense Population of Sex Offenders in Fla. Case Is Alarmingly Typical. *ABC World News with Diane Sawyer* (Vol. 2012).

Greenfield, L. A. (1997). *Sex Offenses and Offenders: An Analysis of Data on Rape and Sexual Assault*. U.S. Department of Justice: Bureau of Justice Statistics. www.ncjrs.gov/App/Publications/abstract.aspx?ID=163392.

Griffin, V. W. & Evans, M. (2019). The duality of stigmatization: an examination of differences in collateral consequences for black and white sex offenders. *Justice Quarterly*, Advance online publication. DOI: 10.1080/07418825.2019.1666906.

Grossi, L. M. (2017). Sexual offenders, violent offenders, and community reentry: Challenges and treatment considerations. *Aggression and Violent Behavior*, 34, 59–67. DOI: 10.1016/j.avb.2017.04.005.

Grubesic, T. H. (2010). Sex offender clusters. *Applied Geography*, 30(1), 2–18. DOI: 10.1016/j.apgeog.2009.06.002.

Grubesic, T. H. & Murray, A. T. (2008). Sex offender residency and spatial equity. *Applied Spatial Analysis and Policy*, 1(3), 175–192. DOI: 10.1007/s12061-008-9013-5.

Grubesic, T. H. & Murray, A. T. (2010). Methods to support policy evaluation of sex offender laws. *Papers in Regional Science*, 89(3), 669–684. DOI: 10.1111/j.1435-5957.2009.00270.x.

Harris, A. J. & Socia, K. M. (2016). What's in a name? Evaluating the effects of the "Sex Offender" label on public opinions and beliefs. *Sexual Abuse: A Journal of Research and Treatment*, 28(7), 660–678. DOI: 10.1177/1079063214564391.

Harris, A. J., Walfield, S. M., Shields, R. T., & Letourneau, E. J. (2016). Collateral consequences of juvenile sex offender registration and notification: Results from a survey of treatment providers. *Sexual Abuse: A Journal of Research and Treatment*, 28(8), 770–790. DOI: 10.1177/1079063215574004.

Harrison, J. (2016, April 15). 10 Years after sex offender murders, questions linger about registry. *Bangon Daily News*. https://bangordailynews.com/2016/04/15/news/state/10-years-after-sex-offender-murders-questions-linger-about-mainesregistry/?ref=relatedBox.

Hlavka, H. R. & Uggen, C. (2008). Does stigmatizing sex offenders drive down reporting rates? Perverse effects and unintended consequences. *Northern Kentucky Law Review*, 35(4), 347–369.

Holzer, H., Raphael, S., & Stoll, M. A. (2003). *Employment Barriers Facing Ex-Offenders*. Washington, DC: www.urban.org/UploadedPDF/410855_holzer.pdf.

Horn, A. E. (2019). Wrongful collateral consequences. *George Washington Law Review*, 87(2), 315–372.

Imhoff, R. (2015). Punitive Attitudes Against Pedophiles or Persons With Sexual Interest in Children: Does the Label Matter? *Archives of Sexual Behavior*, 44(1): 35–44. DOI: 10.1007/s10508-014-0439-3.

Jacobs and Gottlieb (2020). https://journals.sagepub.com/doi/pdf/10.1177/0093854820942285

Justice Policy Institute. (2008). *Registering Harm: How Sex Offense Registries Fail Youth and Communities*. www.justicepolicy.org/uploads/justicepolicy/documents/walsh_act.pdf.

Johnston, J. (2016). Fearing vigilantes, judge protects privacy of Alberta sex offender. *CNC News*. www.cbc.ca/news/canada/edmonton/fearing-vigilantes-judge-protects-privacy-of-alberta-sex-offender-1.3847897.

Kemshall, H., Wood, J., Westwood, S., Stout, B., Wilkinson, B., Kelly, G., & Mackenzie, G. (2010). Child Sex Offender Review (CSOR) Public Disclosure Pilots: A Process Evaluation. Great Britain Home Office Research Development and Statistics Directorate. www.ncjrs.gov/App/Publications/abstract.aspx?ID=259713.

Kilgannon, C. (2007, February 17). Suffolk County to Keep Sex Offenders on the Move. *New York Times*, p. 3.

Kilgannon, C. (2008, January 24). Fears Anew in an Area Rife With Sex Offenders. *New York Times*, p. B3.

Kirk, J. (2015, April 27). *Welcome to Pariahville: The American City Where Sex Offenders Live*. GQ, Online Edition. www.gq.com/story/sex-offender-community.

Koeppel, B. (2018, May 4). Sex Crimes and Criminal Justice. *Washington Spectator*. https://washingtonspectator.org/koeppel-sex-crimes-and-criminal-justice/.

Kunstler, N. & Tsai, J. (2020). Understanding Landlord Perspectives on Applicants with Sex Offenses. *Housing, Care and Support*, 23(1), 27–34. DOI: 10.1108/HCS-10-2019-0022.

Larsen, J. E., Lowrey, K. J., & Coleman, J. W. (2003). The effect of proximity to a registered sex offender's residence on single-family house selling price. *Appraisal Journal*, 71(3), 253–265.

Letourneau, E. J., Armstrong, K. S., Bandyopadhyay, D., & Sinha, D. (2013). Sex offender registration and notification policy increases juvenile plea bargains. *Sexual Abuse: A Journal of Research and Treatment,* 25(2), 189–207. DOI: 10.1177/1079063212455667.

Letourneau, E. J., Bandyopadhyay, D., Sinha, D., & Armstrong, K. (2009). Effects of sex offender registration policies on juvenile justice decision making. *Sexual Abuse: A Journal of Research and Treatment,* 21(2), 149–165. DOI: 10.79063208328678.

Letourneau, E. J., Levenson, J. S., Bandyopadhyay, D., Armstrong, K. S., & Sinha, D. (2010). The effects of sex offender registration and notification on judicial decisions. *Criminal Justice Review,* 35(3), 295–317. DOI: 10.1177/0734016809360330.

Levenson, J. S. (2008). Collateral consequences of sex offender residence restrictions. *Criminal Justice Studies,* 21(2), 153–166. DOI: 10.1080/14786010802159822.

Levenson, J. S., Brannon, Y. N., Fortney, T., & Baker, J. (2007). Public perceptions about sex offenders and community protection policies. *Analysis of Social Issues and Public Policy,* 7 (1), 137–161. DOI: 10.1111/j.1530-2415.2007.00119.x.

Levenson, J. S. & Cotter, L. P. (2005). The effect of Megan's law on sex offender reintegration. *Journal of Contemporary Criminal Justice,* 21(1), 49–66. DOI: 10.1177/1043986204271676.

Levenson, J. S. & Tewksbury, R. (2009). Collateral damage: Family members of registered sex offenders. *American Journal of Criminal Justice,* 34(1–2), 54–68. DOI: 10.1007/s12103-008-9055-x.

Linden, L. L. & Rockoff, J. E. (2008). Estimates of the impact of crime risk on property values from Megan's law. *American Economic Review,* 98(3), 1103–1127. DOI: 10.1257/aer.98.3.1103.

Logan, W. A. (2015). Database Infamia: Exit from the sex offender registries. *Wisconsin Law Review,* 2015(2), 219–246.

Logan, W. A. & Ferguson, A. G. (2016). Policing criminal justice data. *Minnesota Law Review,* 101, 541–616.

Lowe, G. & Willis, G. (2019). "Sex Offender" Versus "Person": The Influence of Labels on Willingness to Volunteer With People Who Have Sexually Abused. *Sexual Abuse,* Advance online publication. DOI: 10.1177/1079063219841904.

Mack, E. & Grubesic, A. (2010). Sex offenders and residential location: A predictive-analytical framework. *Environment and Planning A,* 42(8), 1925–1942. https://doi.org/10.1068/a42370.

Makin, D. A., Walker, A. M., & Campbell, C. M. (2018). Paying to be punished: A statutory analysis of sex offender registration fees. *Criminal Justice Ethics,* 37(3), 215–237.

Malesky, A. & Keim, J. (2001). Mental health professionals' perspectives on sex offender registry web sites. *Sexual Abuse: A Journal of Research and Treatment,* 13(1), 53–63.

Manson, W. (2015). "Keeping children safe": The child sex offender disclosure scheme in Scotland. *Journal of Sexual Aggression,* 21(1), 43–55.

Matson, S. & Lieb, R. (1996). *Community Notification in Washington State: 1996 Survey of Law Enforcement.* Washington State Institute for Public Policy. www.wsipp.wa.gov/rptfiles/sle.pdf.

McCoy, C. (1984). Determinate sentencing, plea bargaining bans, and hydraulic discretion in California. *Justice System Journal,* 9(3), 256–275.

Mercado, C. C., Alvarez, S., & Levenson, J. S. (2008). The impact of specialized sex offender legislation on community reentry. *Sexual Abuse: A Journal of Research and Treatment,* 20 (2), 188–205. DOI: 10.1177/1079063208317540.

Minnesota Department of Corrections. (2007). *Residential Proximity & Sex Offender Recidivism in Minnesota.* www.doc.state.mn.us/documents/04-07SexOffenderReport-Proximity.pdf.

Mogulescu, K. & Goodmark, L. (2020). Surveillance and Entanglement: How Mandatory Sex Offender Registration Impacts Criminalised Survivors of Human Trafficking. *Anti-Trafficking Review*, 14, 125–130.

Morgan, J. K. (2008). *Spatial Implications of Municipal Sex Offender Residency Restrictions in Bay County, Florida, 2005–2007*. [Unpublished Master's Thesis]. Northwest Missouri State University, Maryville, MO. www.nwmissouri.edu/LIBRARY/theses/MorganJenniferK/jmorgan_thesis.pdf.

Morris, S. (2013, November 28). Vigilante jailed for killing man he mistakenly thought was paedophile. *The Guardian*. www.theguardian.com/uk-news/2013/nov/28/vigilante-lee-james-life-murdering-bijan-ebrahimi.

Mustaine, E. E. & Tewksbury, R. (2008). Registered sex offenders, residence, and the influence of race. *Journal of Ethnicity in Criminal Justice*, 6(1), 65–82. doi:10. 1300/J222v06n01_05.

Mustaine, E. E. & Tewksbury, R. (2011). Residential relegation of registered sex offenders. *American Journal of Criminal Justice*, 36(1), 44–57. DOI: 10.1007/s12103-010-9102-2.

Mustaine, E. E., Tewksbury, R., & Stengel, K. M. (2006). Social disorganization and residential locations of registered sex offenders: Is this a collateral consequence? *Deviant Behavior*, 27, 329–350. DOI: 10.1080/01639620600605606.

Navarro, J. C. & Rabe-Hemp, C. (2018). The financial impact of registered sex offenders on home sale prices: A case study of Mclean county, Illinois. *International Journal. of Rural Criminology*, 4(1), 87–109.

Navarro, J. C. & Ruther, M. (2018). A Geospatial Analysis Between the Sale Prices of Single-Family Properties and the Presence of Registered Sex Offenders in Jefferson County, Kentucky. *Urban Studies*, 1–15.

Nobles, M. R., Levenson, J. S., & Youstin, T. J. (2012). Effectiveness of residence restrictions in preventing sex offender recidivism. *Crime & Delinquency*, 58(4), 491–513.

Paul, B., Shafer, B. J., & Linz, D. (2001). Government regulation of "Adult" businesses through zoning and anti-nudity ordinances: Debunking the legal myth of negative secondary effects. *Communication Law & Policy*, 6(2), 355–391. DOI: 10.1207/S15326926CLP0602_4.

Petteruti, A. & Walsh, N. (2008). *Registering Harm: How Sex Offense Registries Fail Youth and Communities*. Washington, DC: Justice Policy Institute. www.justicepolicy.org/uploads/justicepolicy/documents/walsh_act.pdf.

Pettit, B. & Lyons, C. J. (2007). Status and the stigma of incarceration: The labor-market effects of incarceration, by race, class, and criminal involvement. In S. Bushway, M. A. Stoll, & D. F. Weiman (eds.), *Barriers to Reentry? The Labor Market for Released Prisoners in Post-industrial America* (pp. 203–226). New York: Russell Sage Foundation.

Pope, J. C. (2008). Fear of crime and housing prices: Household reactions to sex offender registries. *Journal of Urban Economics*, 64(3), 601–614. DOI: 10.1016/j.jue.2008.07.001.

Prescott, J.J. (2016). Portmanteau ascendant: Post-release regulations and sex offender recidivism. *Connecticut Law Review*, 48(4), 1035–1078.

Prescott, J.J. & Rockoff, J. E. (2011). Do sex offender registration and notification laws affect criminal behavior? *Journal of Law and Economics*, 54(1), 161–206.

Robbers, M. L. P. (2009). Lifers on the outside: Sex offenders and disintegrative shaming. *International Journal of Offender Therapy and Comparative Criminology*, 53(1), 5–28. DOI: 10.1177/0306624x07312953.

Rolfe, S. M., Tewksbury, R., & Schroeder, R. D. (2017). Homeless shelters' policies on sex offenders: Is this another collateral consequence? *International Journal of Offender Therapy and Comparative Criminology*, 61(16), 1833–1849. DOI: 10.1177/0306624x16638463.

Rydberg, J. (2018). Employment and Housing Challenges Experienced by Sex Offenders during Reentry on Parole. *Corrections*, 3(1): 15–37. DOI: 10.1080/23774657.2017.1369373.

Sabol, W. J. (2007). Local labor-market conditions and post-prison employment experiences of offenders released from Ohio state prisons. In S. Bushway, M. A. Stoll, & D. F. Weiman (eds.), *Barriers to Reentry? The Labor Market for Released Prisoners in Post-industrial America* (pp. 257–303). New York: Russell Sage Foundation.

Salmon, T. (2010). *Sex Offender Registry: Report of the Vermont State Auditor*. State of Vermont: Office of the State Auditor. https://auditor.vermont.gov/sites/auditor/files/files/reports/performance-audits/Final_SOR_report.pdf.

Sandler, J. C., Letourneau, E., Vandiver, D. M., Shields, R. T., & Chaffin, M. (2017). Juvenile Sexual crime reporting rates are not influenced by juvenile sex offender registration policies. *Psychology, Public Policy, & Law*, 23(2), 131–140.DOI: 10.1037/law0000118.

Savage, J. & Winsor, C. (2018). Sex offender residence restrictions and sex crimes against children: A comprehensive review. *Aggression and Violent Behavior*, 43, 13–25. DOI: 10.1016/j.avb.2018.08.002.

Schiavone, S. K. & Jeglic, E. L. (2009). Public perception of sex offender social policies and the impact on sex offenders. *International Journal of Offender Therapy and Comparative Criminology*, 53(6), 679–695. DOI: 10.1177/0306624x08323454.

Shim, J. (2014, August 13). *Listed for Life*. Slate. https://slate.com/news-and-politics/2014/08/sex-offender-registry-laws-by-state-mapped.html.

Socia, K. M. (2011a). The policy implications of residence restrictions on sex offender housing in Upstate NY. *Criminology & Public Policy*, 10(2), 351–389. DOI: 10.1111/j.1745-9133.2011.00713.x.

Socia, K. M. (2011b). *Residence Restriction Legislation, Sex Crime Rates, and the Spatial Distribution of Sex Offender Residences* (Publication No. 3454528). [Doctorate Dissertation]. University at Albany, SUNY, Albany, NY. Proquest Dissertations Publishing.

Socia, K. M. (2013a). Residence restrictions and the association with registered sex offender clustering. *Criminal Justice Policy Review*, 24(4), 441–472. DOI: 10.1177/0887403412445613.

Socia, K. M. (2013b). Too close for comfort: Registered sex offenders spatial clustering and recidivistic sex crime arrest rates. *Sexual Abuse: A Journal of Research and Treatment*, 25(6), 531–556. DOI: 10.1177/1079063212469061.

Socia, K. M. (2016). Examining the concentration of registered sex offenders in Upstate New York census tracts. *Crime & Delinquency*, 62(6), 748–776. DOI: 10.1177/0011128714526563.

Socia, K. M. & Harris, A. J. (2016). Evaluating public perceptions of the risk presented by registered sex offenders: Evidence of crime control theater? *Psychology, Public Policy, & Law*, 22(4), 375–385. DOI: http://dx.doi.org/10.1037/law0000081.

Socia, K. M. & Rydberg, J. (2016). Sex offender legislation and policy. In T. G. Blomberg, J. Mestre Brancale, K. M. Beaver, & W. D. Bales (eds.), *Advancing Criminology and Criminal Justice Policy* (pp. 187–202). New York, NY: Routledge.

Socia, K. M. & Stamatel, J. P. (2012). Neighborhood Characteristics and the Social Control of Registered Sex Offenders. *Crime & Delinquency*, 58(4), 565–587. DOI: 10.1177/0011128711142011.

Soloducha, A. (2017). *"Creep catcher" arrested after confronting wrong man in Lloydminister*. CBC News. www.cbc.ca/news/canada/saskatchewan/creep-catcher-arrested-after-confronting-wrong-man-in-lloydminster-1.4227752.

Solomon, A. L., Johnson, K. D., Travis, J., & McBride, E. C. (2004). *From Prison to Work: The Employment Dimensions of Prisoner Reentry*. Urban Institute. www.urban.org/url.cfm?ID=411097.

Tewksbury, R. & Lees, M. (2006). Perceptions of sex offender registration: Collateral consequences and community experiences. *Sociological Spectrum, 26*(3), 309–334. DOI: 10.1080/02732170500524246.

Tewksbury, R. & Levenson, J. S. (2009). Stress experiences of family members of registered sex offenders. *Behavioral Sciences & the Law, 27*(4), 611–626. DOI: 10.1002/bsl.878.

Tewksbury, R. & Mustaine, E. E. (2007). Collateral consequences and community re-entry for registered sex offenders with child victims: Are the challenges even greater? *Journal of Offender Rehabilitation, 46* (1–2), 113–131. DOI: 10.1080/10509670802071550.

Tewksbury, R. & Zgoba, K. M. (2010). Perceptions and coping with punishment: How registered sex offenders respond to stress, Internet restrictions, and the collateral consequences of registration. *International Journal of Offender Therapy and Comparative Criminology, 54*(4), 537–551. DOI: 10.1177/0306624x09339180.

The Associated Press. (2010, June 22). Sex offender confinement costing states too much. *CBS News.* www.cbsnews.com/news/sex-offender-confinement-costing-states-too-much/.

Travis, J. (2005). *But They All Come Back: Facing the Challenges of Prisoner Reentry.* Washington, DC: Urban Institute Press.

Wang, J. N. (2014). Paying the piper: The cost of compliance with the federal sex offender registration and notification act. *New York Law Review, 59,* 681–705.

Wang, X., Pei, F., Wu, S., & Dillard, R. (2020). Neighborhood Characteristics of Registered Sex Offender Residential Locations: Evidence from the State of Ohio, *Journal of the Society for Social Work & Research.* https://doi.org/10.1086/707310.

Warford, A. (2015). *Mistake on Driver's License Labeled Man as Sex Offender.* Action News JAX. www.actionnewsjax.com/news/local/mistake-drivers-license-labeled-man-sex-offender/29710847.

Whitting, L., Day, A., & Powell, M. (2016). Police officer perspectives on the implementation of a sex offender community notification scheme. *International Journal of Police Science & Management, 18*(4), 261–272. DOI: 10.1177/1461355716668539.

Williams, A.J. (2018). The Role of Social Disorganization Theory in Explaining Where Sex Offenders Reside: Do Some Neighborhoods Get More than Their Fair Share? (Doctoral Dissertation, University of Texas at Dallas). University of Texas at Dallas: Eugene McDermott Library.

Williams, M. (2018). *The Sex Offender Housing Dilemma: Community Activism, Safety, and Social Justice.* New York: New York University Press.

Younglove, J. A. & Vitello, C. J. (2003). Community notification provisions of "Megan's Law" from a therapeutic jurisprudence perspective: A case study. *American Journal of Forensic Psychology, 21*(1), 25–38.

Zgoba, K. M., Witt, P., Dalessandro, M., & Veysey, B. (2008). *Megan's Law: Assessing the Practical and Monetary Efficiency.* The Research & Evaluation Unit Office of Policy and Planning New Jersey Department of Corrections. www.ncjrs.gov/pdffiles1/nij/grants/225370.pdf.

7

Offenders and SORN Laws

*Amanda Agan and J.J. Prescott**

Chapter 7 describes what we know about the effects of SORN laws on criminal behavior. A coherent story emerges from this review: there is virtually no evidence that SORN laws reduce recidivism or otherwise increase public safety. The chapter first delineates the various ways registration and notification alter the legal environment not only for registrants but also for nonregistrants, the public, and law enforcement. There are many channels through which SORN laws might impact the frequency of sex offenses, including some that would produce an *increase* in overall offending. The chapter assesses these possibilities in light of a large body of relevant empirical research, focusing on potential changes in registrant recidivism, nonregistrant criminal behavior, the geography of victimization, and the distribution of types of sex offenses and victims. Scholars have plumbed many different data sources using a range of methodologies, yet nearly every study finds no evidence that SORN laws – in particular, community notification laws – reduce sexual recidivism. In fact, notification laws may increase recidivism risk. The final section discusses registrant beliefs about the effects of SORN laws. In sum, the chapter comprehensively engages with the pressing question of whether SORN laws protect the public and concludes that they do not.

7.1 INTRODUCTION

Perhaps the central empirical questions regarding sex offender registration and notification (SORN) laws involve their direct effects on sexual offending. The basic premise advanced in support of SORN laws is that they will reduce the frequency (or perhaps severity) of sex offenses. Specifically, proponents contend that registration and notification will diminish the total harm of sexual offending by reducing the likelihood that an individual previously convicted of a registerable sex offense will recidivate or by increasing the likelihood that law enforcement will more quickly apprehend any registrant who does recidivate.

But a full analysis reveals that this hypothesis is just one of many potential outcomes – and that SORN laws may actually *increase* the frequency of sexual offending (Prescott, 2016). At the same time, SORN may also change criminal

* We are grateful to Ira Ellman and Guy Hamilton-Smith for comments, and to Patrick Balke, Sophia Nocera, and Chris Pryby for excellent research and editorial assistance.

behavior in other important ways, including (1) by deterring sexual offenses by nonregistrants, who may wish to avoid the burdens of registration and notification that come with conviction, and (2) by altering the costs and benefits of re-offending in particular locations (and thus the geographic pattern of sexual offenses) or against particular victims. For policy makers who wish to understand the underlying determinants of sexual offending and to design and implement effective post-release regimes, it is crucial to consider this broad range of plausible behavioral consequences and relevant available evidence.

In this chapter, we discuss the various potential effects that SORN laws might have on sexual offending and related criminal behavior and summarize the available empirical evidence on the direction and magnitude of these effects. The story that emerges across dozens of papers, data sources, and empirical methods is coherent and convincing: there is scant evidence that SORN reduces recidivism or otherwise increases public safety, with the possible exception of some tentative evidence that registration alone (i.e., without notification, which no jurisdiction currently uses) might reduce sexual offense recidivism.[1] This conclusion is at odds with the basic premises upon which politicians and advocates have defended SORN laws from the outset, but it is not altogether surprising given what we now know about the very minor role recidivism plays in the overall incidence of sexual offending.

We also occasionally touch on evidence of the possible effects of SORN on non-sex offense crimes and on the role and usefulness of failure-to-register (FTR) offenses. Sex offender registration and notification "derivative" criminal behavior (such as FTR) is important to consider separately because, while technically criminal, such violations are not clearly connected to the goal of reducing the frequency of sex offenses. Finally, we address existing empirical research on registrant "beliefs" about the behavioral consequences of SORN laws. Although their value vis-à-vis the actual efficacy of SORN laws is uncertain, reported registrant beliefs may nevertheless be considered measures of the impact of SORN and can aid in our collective understanding of what drives the behavioral patterns we identify in the literature.

7.2 DELINEATING THE TYPES OF SORN EFFECTS ON SEXUAL OFFENDING

There are two basic ways SORN laws might affect the frequency and severity of sex offenses: (1) changing the behavior of potential sex offenders (e.g., deterrence); and (2) changing law enforcement or potential victim behavior. For example, if registration and notification only make it easier for the public to monitor and the police to apprehend registrants, we might observe the frequency of sex offenses decline for two reasons.[2] First,

---

[1] We define and distinguish registration (or "private" registration) and notification (or community notification or "public" registration) later.

[2] As other chapters demonstrate, there is considerable evidence that SORN has collateral consequences, and in theory, these changes can themselves have criminogenic effects.

individuals at risk of offending might alter their behavior in response to what they believe is a different information and enforcement environment.[3] Second, at least in theory, potential offenders might *not* respond at all to SORN laws (perhaps because they are impulsive in the extreme), yet we might still observe fewer sex offenses if SORN helps police or potential victims prevent sex offenses or if SORN makes apprehension and conviction easier and allows earlier incapacitation (and thus the commission of fewer total crimes).

We can obtain a fuller picture of the potential effects of SORN laws by assuming the possibility of behavioral changes both by potential offenders (in anticipation of changes in monitoring, enforcement, and victim precautionary behavior) *and* by the public and law enforcement (via access to sex offender registry information). There are other moving parts in this analysis, however. To begin with, sex offenses vary along many dimensions (i.e., type of offender, type of crime, type of victim, and offense location), and SORN may affect the various offense scenarios very differently. In particular, some potential offenders are already registered under SORN laws (i.e., "registrants," those previously convicted of registerable sex offenses), while others are not registered ("nonregistrants") because they either have not previously committed or have not been convicted of a registerable sex offense. In addition, because SORN is supposed to work by making information available to the police and the public, a potential offender's proximity to "informed" individuals may now matter – both to how a registrant (or even a nonregistrant) behaves and to how effective precaution-taking and monitoring by the public and law enforcement may be at disrupting any criminal behavior.

There are at least three other second-order dynamics at work in accounting for the impact of SORN on sexual offending. First, SORN laws may affect behavior by imposing affirmative administrative obligations on registrants and enforcing these requirements through separate criminal provisions (e.g., FTR penalties). Complying with SORN requirements can be burdensome and difficult, and inevitably, at least some individuals who are required to register will fail to register, keep their information current, or otherwise satisfy technical rules. Such failures produce an entirely new tally of (non-sex) offenses, and out-of-compliance status and convictions may, in turn, influence behavior. Second, and relatedly, potential offenders will have "beliefs" about SORN and its effects, and these beliefs may not align with reality. Because people operate based on their beliefs, even inaccurate beliefs about the requirements and enforcement of SORN laws may impact behavior. Third, the effects of SORN will depend at least in part on the accuracy of registry information, which is by no means perfect (e.g., Lasher and McGrath, 2012; Salmon, 2010).

A basic economic model of criminal behavior can help us understand what we need to measure empirically in order to fully account for the potential effects of

---

[3]   This is true even if the actual environment never changes – for example, if SORN laws were rarely enforced. Of course, if SORN does not produce real and lasting environmental changes, potential offenders might eventually realize this fact and revert to behavior suited to the pre-SORN world.

SORN laws.[4] Following the approach of Prescott and Rockoff (2011) and Agan and Prescott (2014), imagine that an individual is considering whether to commit a particular sex offense against a particular victim in a particular location, which may require costly travel and may involve more or less uncertainty about the likelihood of success or detection.[5] The potential offender faces a trade-off between either committing the crime against that victim in that place or choosing some other action instead (as a default, let's say "doing nothing").

In this setting, potential offender i's decision whether to commit a crime against victim j in location l is a function of the probability of punishment for committing the crime against victim j in location l (p_{ijl}), the victim-specific level of punishment if caught and convicted (f_{ij}), the cost of carrying out the crime against victim j in location l (c_{ijl}), and the assumed victim- and location-invariant utility (benefit) of engaging in lawful alternatives relative to committing the sex offense (u_i). The frequency of sex offenses is thus essentially the sum of all of these decisions across all individuals. Accordingly, if SORN laws, by whatever means, cause fewer of these individual decisions to end in crime, then the total number of sex offenses should decline.[6] To model how sexual offending behavior will react to SORN laws, we next isolate the ways that SORN might change the behavioral environment for potential registrants and nonregistrants alike.

We begin with sex offender registration alone – or what some refer to as "private" or "non-public" registration. At their core, registries assemble and store the identifying information of individuals previously convicted of sex offenses (e.g., name, physical description, age, home and work location, criminal history), and registration laws require that these individuals confirm and update their registry information on a regular basis. When unaccompanied by a community notification law that allows or requires public disclosure of registrant criminal history information, a registry (and the information it contains) can only be accessed by law enforcement entities and certain public agencies (as well as private employers who seek to access a specific individual's registry status for employment screening purposes).

In theory, easy access to registration information by law enforcement may allow officers to monitor registrants more effectively or easily and thereby increase the likelihood that registrants who re-offend will be detected and apprehended (i.e., registration may increase p_{ijl}). Officers might concentrate their monitoring efforts in predictable ways, too, potentially increasing detection probabilities even further for offenses against likely potential targets (e.g., former victims or victims similar to past victims) or for offenses committed in locations registrants are likely to visit (such as

---

[4] This discussion draws on the analysis in Agan and Prescott (2015).

[5] In this model, and in most of our discussion of existing evidence, we ignore the choice between different types of sex offenses, and we make some simplifying (but unnecessary) assumptions about how law enforcement works – for example, we assume in the text that the level of punishment may turn on the identity of the victim but that punishment severity is insensitive to a crime's location.

[6] As we will see, with SORN laws in effect, certain plausible conditions produce more crime and others produce less crime. This implies not only that the total frequency of sex offenses may change but also that the *composition* of sex offenses may change when SORN laws are enacted.

any location within a mile of a registrant's address).[7] Registration may also affect offending behavior through increasing the severity of punishment upon conviction for a sex offense: specifically, *nonregistrants* may change their offending behavior under a registration system if they perceive the prospect of complying with registration requirements in the future (and the associated law enforcement monitoring) as unpleasant (i.e., registration may increase f_{ij}). Finally, note that registration regimes impose burdens on *all* registrants, even those who would otherwise never recidivate. Requiring regular information updates – and thus imposing the significant costs that come with complying with these obligations, including anxiety over the serious consequences for even accidental oversights – can make staying on the straight and narrow more difficult (i.e., reducing u_i).

Community notification makes registration information available to the public. Today, registrants' identifying information is made publicly available primarily through free government websites often referred to as "internet registries." Governments have used other forms of community notification methods over the years as well (e.g., newspaper notification), some of which have been effectively superseded by internet registries (e.g., paper registries located in police departments). One form of notification that remains important is "active notification," in which officials proactively inform potential victims – usually neighbors – of the identity, history, and proximity of a registrant in person or by letter.

The motivation behind making registration information public is that it may encourage community members to monitor registrants and take protective precautionary measures. If the public uses the information to monitor potential recidivists, any sex offense (or potentially any offense) committed by a registrant will be more likely to be detected (further increasing p_{ijl}), especially in particular locations (e.g., near the registrant's home address) where relevant registry information may be better known and thus better able to help someone identify a registrant as the offender. Precautionary behavior by informed potential victims can increase the cost of committing an offense (e.g., by disrupting or diminishing registrants' offending opportunities), reducing the relative attractiveness of offending against those victims in those locations (increasing c_{ijl}). But, perversely, access to registry information might also distract potential victims or their caregivers from threats posed by nonregistrants (particularly those familiar to a victim, such as family members, neighbors, or coaches) and by registrants who live some distance away (reducing p_{ijl} for some potential offenders).

Although fear of being subject to community notification in the future is a nonissue for those already registered (unless the registration term is short or near its end), nonregistrants may find the total punishment associated with the commission of a sex crime much higher under a community notification regime (increasing

---

[7] This approach to reducing sex offense frequency comports in the abstract with criminology research, which generally shows that greater certainty of punishment (via an enhanced threat of apprehension) is more important to deterring crime than increasing punishment severity (Nagin, 2013). As we note immediately below, SORN laws potentially operate along both dimensions.

f_{ij}). The possibility of being publicly shamed as a sex offender upon conviction may be very salient and perhaps more important than an ambiguous and uncertain increase in detection probability alone. Moreover, if community notification reduces employment, housing, and social opportunities following release (e.g., Levenson and Cotter, 2005), and nonregistrants anticipate these collateral consequences, we might observe even greater deterrence effects for these potential first-time sex offenders. Registrants, of course, must suffer the same adverse effects of community notification for many years whether or not they recidivate. Because these consequences do not depend on post-release behavior, community notification effectively reduces the threat of criminal punishment for recidivism, at least in a relative sense (reducing u_i). In other words, because post-release life is relatively much worse for registrants subject to notification, the gravity of the threat of returning any recidivist among them to prison for committing another sex crime is significantly diminished. This effect might be particularly important if community members use registration information not only to shame or discriminate against registrants but also to harass and victimize them.

Despite the conventional wisdom that SORN laws will reduce recidivism and thus decrease the total number of sex offenses (see, e.g., Prescott, 2016), the analysis above shows that SORN laws can have multifaceted and ambiguous effects on offending behavior – with difficult-to-predict ramifications for recidivism, total sex offense frequency, and the specific kinds of sex crimes committed.[8] These effects may magnify or offset each other in the aggregate; effects may also be heterogeneous across groups of potential offenders, potential victims, and sex offenses. Thus, for example, SORN laws may work more or less as intended for some registrants, may increase recidivism risk among others, and may have offsetting effects for the rest. Changes in nonregistrant offending behavior may have an entirely different character (e.g., SORN may lead to higher recidivism levels but fewer first-time offenses).

It is therefore inappropriate to conceive of SORN laws, even in a single jurisdiction at a particular time, as having just one ex ante outcome of interest – for example, the recidivism rate. Even a simple behavioral model shows that SORN laws may produce (1) spillovers to other forms of criminal behavior (through changes in u_i), (2) re-ordering in the overall composition of sex offenses (e.g., variation in the types of offenses and victims making up any particular category of crime), (3) repercussions for the geographic distribution of sex offenses (e.g., relative to the location of registrants), and (4) a shift in the relative role of registrants and nonregistrants in driving the total frequency of sex offenses. In effect, SORN laws seem likely to have

---

[8] Questions about the effectiveness of SORN laws are distinct from – albeit not unconnected to – questions about sex offender recidivism risk generally. If, on average, SORN laws reduce or increase rates of recidivism or total sex offense frequency, policy makers should not care whether recidivism rates start at a relatively high or low level. For example, if research demonstrates that SORN makes recidivism *worse*, the fact that recidivism began at a high level would not make SORN any more attractive (unless the legislature's primary motivation was simply to soothe the public by "doing something" and it was willing to tolerate greater actual risk in doing so).

at least some "distributional" consequences, with certain potential victims "winning" but others – perhaps a larger group – "losing."[9]

7.3 EMPIRICAL EVIDENCE ON THE EFFECTS OF SORN LAWS

Over the last few decades, a considerable body of empirical work has studied how SORN laws affect the frequency of sex offenses and the likelihood of registrant recidivism. The methods and data these studies employ vary a great deal. Most studies look at data from one or two states and follow offenders over time, using criminal history trajectories (arrest, prosecution, conviction, incarceration, and FTR incidents) and the enactment timing or scope of SORN laws to identify their consequences for recidivism. Other studies use data from multiple states to unravel the potentially confounding role of state-level idiosyncrasies and control for countrywide trends by leveraging different laws' effective dates. Among these multistate studies, researchers often present evidence on the effects of SORN on total offense frequency – rather than just recidivism among registrants – but a few researchers have deployed strategies capable of isolating recidivism effects alone.

Examining the impact of SORN laws on *total* criminal incident frequency has advantages. In particular, this approach accounts for changes in nonregistrant sexual offending, avoids any bias resulting from prosecutorial charging and offender plea-bargaining behavior, and at least partly addresses any effects the laws may have on victim reporting and cooperation (e.g., victim refusal to cooperate with prosecutors, which makes charging and conviction less likely).[10] In the end, policy makers should care about *all* effects of SORN laws. But for our purposes, it is useful to distinguish evidence of effects on recidivism among registrants from evidence of effects on the deterrence of nonregistrants (e.g., potential first-time offenders). As we will see, these effects may offset each other in the case of notification, and this highly policy-relevant empirical possibility can be missed in studies that do not separately consider SORN effects on registered and nonregistered potential offenders.

---

[9] This complexity still reflects only a narrow slice of the potential costs (and benefits) SORN laws may create for society. A full accounting is beyond the scope of this chapter, but it would include much more than just the direct effect of the laws on sexual offending. For instance, administering and enforcing registration and notification laws are quite costly for governments. These costs amount to dollars not being spent on other crime reduction policies, many of which are presumably cost effective. Chapter 4 of this volume discusses the challenges SORN laws create for law enforcement. As a further example, SORN imposes costs not only on registrants but also on their families, neighbors, and communities. These consequences, reviewed in Chapter 8, ripple through society in many potentially noncriminogenic but important ways – for example, families lose bread winners, employers lose employees, and governments lose taxpayers. Such effects, beyond recidivism, are important in assessing whether SORN laws are worth their considerable costs.

[10] A few studies also use registrant surveys and interviews to draw tentative conclusions about the effects of SORN laws. In these analyses, registrants are expressly asked about the effects of SORN on their behavior and sexual offending generally. We discuss this line of research later in the chapter when we address registrant beliefs about the effects of SORN on sexual offending.

In what follows, we summarize existing empirical research concerning the various behavioral dimensions we identify above – in particular, the frequency, composition, and geographic effects of SORN laws on registrant recidivism and on the deterrence of nonregistrants. Rigorous published research on the effects of SORN has accreted for almost 25 years; we cannot exhaustively cite, much less discuss, all of the relevant research. Instead, we aim to present an overarching perspective and the consensus views of the experts in the field. We note, where it exists, any evidence running counter to these views, and we catalog the reasons to feel confident in the reliability of the scholarship standing behind the consensus.

The body of research on the consequences of SORN laws strongly suggests that typical SORN laws have essentially no effect on registrant sex offense recidivism. While empirical work necessarily produces results that retain some margin of error, there is enough peer-reviewed research behind this conclusion to feel reasonably certain that any reduction in recidivism has been, at best, very small. If anything, there is stronger evidence that SORN laws – particularly community notification laws – counterproductively increase rather than decrease the likelihood that registrants will commit future sex crimes. While this possibility may seem counterintuitive, it emerges naturally from a comprehensive model of offending behavior. Sex offender registration and notification burdens can themselves be criminogenic in their effects, and unless the monitoring and precaution-taking benefits of information-sharing more than offset these negative consequences, we should expect to observe no change or perhaps even increases in re-offending rates.

7.3.1 *SORN Recidivism Effects: Evidence from Federal Crime Reports*

The two largest studies of the effects of SORN laws to date are Agan (2011) and Prescott and Rockoff (2011). Both studies use data from many states over many years and take into account offense- or offender-level information in at least some of their analyses. Both sets of authors explore the robustness of their findings and investigate the plausibility of various alternative interpretations of the patterns they identify in the data. Both pay careful attention to the differences in SORN laws across states and over time. In the end, neither study detects evidence that community notification (as opposed to registration alone) reduces sex offense recidivism. However, Prescott and Rockoff find some evidence that registration alone may reduce registrant recidivism and that community notification may actually increase registrant recidivism (with the two effects offsetting each other in states with relatively small registries).[11] To

---

[11] Agan (2011) and Prescott and Rockoff (2011) are seemingly the only studies to evaluate the independent effect of registration *alone* on registrant recidivism before Bouffard and Askew's (2019) Texas-based study, which we discuss later in this chapter. Recent work by Bierie and Budd (2020) examines the effect of registration alone on the closure speed of sex offense incidents reported as involving stranger perpetrators using incident-level data from six states. The authors present evidence that law enforcement use of registration databases is associated with a reduction in the time to case closure.

better explain the admittedly nuanced findings of Prescott and Rockoff's work, we describe their empirical approach and conclusions in more detail.

Prescott and Rockoff evaluate the implementation of SORN laws in fifteen states using data from the National Incident-Based Reporting System (NIBRS), the same data the FBI use to construct Uniform Crime Reporting (UCR) Program statistics. The authors separately collect and catalog the enactment and effective dates of both registration and notification laws (including various types of notification laws) to identify their possibly distinct effects on criminal behavior.[12] Prescott and Rockoff study offense reports to law enforcement agencies, which allows them to abstract away from any independent effects SORN laws may have on case processing.[13] Because NIBRS includes information on the reported relationship between the offender and any victim, Prescott and Rockoff can assess SORN-induced changes in victim-type composition. Unfortunately, NIBRS data do not indicate whether an offender is a recidivist. Thus, to identify SORN effects on recidivism, Prescott and Rockoff incorporate registry size data by state over time as well as any retroactivity provisions affecting the scope of SORN coverage into their analysis. They reason that SORN laws cannot reduce recidivism in the immediate aftermath of their implementation when the provisions only apply prospectively to convicted or released individuals because the registry would be effectively empty on day one. They further assume that the relative importance of any recidivism effect grows with the size of the registry since any deterrence effect would at least plausibly remain constant over time.[14] (We discuss the potential for SORN-law deterrence of non-registrants later in this chapter.)

Prescott and Rockoff find that registration alone appears to reduce registrant recidivism. They report that private registration laws are associated with an average

---

[12] Agan (2011) also recognizes the important distinction between registration and community notification in her work, but most other studies conflate the two in their data analysis, despite their potentially disparate effects. Today, all states use community notification, so it is understandable that most research has concentrated on the consequences of the public release of registrant information, but at the outset of the SORN era many states employed registration alone.

[13] One perennial issue in crime research is the potentially distorting role of sharp changes or even trends over time in victim reporting behavior. Victims must report a sex offense to law enforcement for it to be recorded as an incident in federal crime data, for it to result in arrest and prosecution, and for it to be reflected on an individual's criminal record. Therefore, any measured change in the frequency of reported incidents will actually be the combination of any change in victim reporting propensity and any change in offending behavior. According to National Crime Victimization Survey data (Bureau of Justice Statistics, 2018), victim reporting propensity for sex offenses appears to have declined over the last twenty years, potentially as a consequence of SORN laws. Although this apparent trend may have other explanations, lower reporting rates would imply that any measured reduction in sex offense frequency might be the spurious result of fewer reports, not fewer crimes. By the same logic, evidence of SORN-caused increases in crime frequency may be biased downward (meaning increases in recidivism may be greater than measured) and a lack of evidence of any effect of SORN laws would presumably be consistent with higher offending rates.

[14] This assumption is admittedly nontrivial because registry size may affect nonregistrant awareness of the registry and its effects. This might cut both ways; as a registry grows, it might become better known but also be considered less severe by potential registrants.

reduction in the reported sex offense rate of approximately 1.1 percent for each additional registrant per 10,000 people.[15] Because registration laws require that any registry information be kept confidential, public monitoring and potential victim precaution-taking cannot explain this reduction in offense frequency. Given that there is little other rigorous work on the effects of registration alone, it is difficult to describe the study's result as a consensus finding.[16] Moreover, because private registration without notification was in effect for only a short span of years at the dawn of the SORN era, relatively less information stands behind their conclusion. It is also impossible to know whether the detected reduction in recidivism was simply a temporary response to a new, untested form of police monitoring.

Using a similar empirical strategy, Prescott and Rockoff also evaluate the *marginal* effect on recidivism of sharing registry information with the broader public – that is, the added value of community notification. They find that notification appears to *increase* registrant recidivism (in terms of reported sex offense incidents) by about the same amount that registration alone appears to reduce recidivism, such that the two effects, operating together on the same registrants, roughly offset each other.[17] Assuming that making registry information public neither *inhibits* victim precautionary behavior nor *reduces* the total monitoring level,[18] the model suggests that notification laws may increase recidivism by increasing traditional risk factors, such as unemployment, unstable housing, and social isolation (reducing u_i). As we indicate in various places below, there is significant evidence that community notification effectively reduces the benefits of law-abiding behavior for registrants and thus may make recidivism relatively more likely.

Agan (2011) offers a useful comparison to Prescott and Rockoff (2011). The two analyses are complementary and mutually reinforcing because they study different states, use different data sources, and incorporate independently collected law and registry information yet draw the same basic conclusions about the effects of SORN laws on sexual offending. Agan relies on UCR data, allowing her to study a longer time period and almost all states, but her analysis is limited to the state-year level. By

---

[15] But see note 13 on the role of changes in reporting propensities.

[16] To our knowledge, one of the very few other studies on the effects of registration alone on recidivism is Bouffard and Askew (2019). They specifically study the effects on recidivism of Texas's private registration law in 1991 (notification did not arrive until 1995) using data only from Harris County, Texas. They find no evidence of private registration reducing recidivism. It is also worth mentioning recent NIBRS-based work by Bierie and Budd (2020), which focuses on identifying the effects of registration alone on the time it takes for law enforcement to close a case involving a stranger perpetrator. The authors' evidence that, conditional on the occurrence of a sex offense involving a stranger, registration alone may speed apprehension is distinct from evidence that registration reduces recidivism in the first instance, and indeed could be explained by higher recidivism levels among less careful sex offenders, but both outcomes are admittedly policy relevant.

[17] Importantly, this makes Prescott and Rockoff's results consistent with other work that treats registration and notification as a single policy.

[18] Notification might have this latter repercussion, for example, if the release of registry information causes law enforcement to rely on the public to look out for itself, which it might do poorly.

contrast, Prescott and Rockoff parse their NIBRS data by month, county, and even reporting agency, but they analyze a shorter sample period and must work with data from many fewer states. Agan also codes registration and notification laws differently; she treats registration law start dates much as Prescott and Rockoff do, but she considers community notification to begin in earnest only when registry information is posted online, which, given how much easier internet registries are to access and their social salience, may be a more appropriate choice. Any earlier forms of notification are commingled with the use of registration alone, and later forms of more active notification (e.g., receiving a postcard indicating that a new neighbor is a registrant) are not treated separately, but Agan also avoids any bias that may result from misattributing laws to the fastidious categories Prescott and Rockoff employ.

In her UCR-based research, Agan principally studies the overall effect of registration and notification (via the internet) on total offense frequency rather than their effect on recidivism specifically. She finds no evidence that registration and internet notification reduce the total frequency of reported rape incidents; if anything, the data Agan studies suggest that SORN laws are associated with more reported rape. Unfortunately, UCR data only contain incident-level information for rape, which is underinclusive of all registerable sex offenses. Agan addresses this data limitation by also studying UCR arrest reports for a broader category of sex offenses and finds some evidence that internet notification reduces the number of sex offense arrests. But this result is difficult to interpret because the relationship may capture only a reduction in the arrest rate and not in the number of underlying incidents. More importantly, the reduction in arrests might simply capture the deterrence of nonregistered potential offenders. Indeed, when Agan attempts to distinguish recidivism effects from deterrence effects in her work (using the same strategy, although not the same data, as Prescott and Rockoff), the reduction in arrests disappears, leaving a positive, statistically significant effect on recidivism.[19] Although Prescott and Rockoff focus primarily on offense rates, when they conduct a similar analysis of sex offense arrest rates, their results are similar to Agan's arrest-rate findings.

There are a handful of other multistate studies that examine the effects of SORN laws using federal data like the UCR and NIBRS, but none of them raises serious questions about the reliability of the conclusions in either Agan (2011) or Prescott and Rockoff (2011). Vasquez, Maddan, and Walker (2008) is the earliest of these other studies.[20] The

[19] Although much of the research on SORN laws studies the effects of the laws on arrest and conviction rates, these outcomes are less attractive in some sense because any measured effect also captures any behavioral changes by police, prosecutors, and other criminal justice actors.

[20] Zgoba, Witt, Dalessandro, and Veysey (2008) is a single-state study, but it uses time-series methods like Vasquez, Maddan, and Walker (2008) to examine trends in UCR offense reports in New Jersey counties. The authors conclude that 1994, the year New Jersey enacted the original Megan's Law, is the statewide change point in sex offense trends (with offense rates going down after 1994). This appears to be a coincidence, though, with only two counties actually showing 1994 as the peak in offenses (and only three other counties showing 1993 or 1995). Other factors may therefore account for the changes, and the authors do not control for other differences across counties. Moreover, the authors cannot distinguish between changes in recidivism and changes in deterrence.

authors evaluate the effect of "registration and notification laws" on UCR rape reports from 1990 to 2000 (at the state-year level) using time-series methods. Their evidence is mixed at best. For most of the states they evaluate, they detect no impact of SORN on reports of rape, though they do observe some evidence that SORN may have led to fewer offenses in three states. However, their analysis conflates registration and notification laws and does not separately consider the recidivism of registrants and the deterrence of nonregistrants. In addition, their coding of SORN laws does not appear to be congruent with the timing and scope of actual state enactments.[21]

Ackerman, Sacks, and Greenberg (2012) conduct an analysis similar to Agan (2011) for UCR-reported incidents of rape, though they do not distinguish between registration and notification for at least some states and they do not account for any deterrence effects on nonregistrant behavior. They do, however, control for other changes in relevant criminal justice policies, including the rather common implementation of sexually violent predator commitment laws at the state level. They similarly find no effect of SORN laws on reported rape. Most recently, Sandler, Letourneau, Vandiver, Shields, and Chaffin (2017) study the effects of SORN laws on juvenile offense counts using time-series methods and NIBRS data from four states. Their study also finds no evidence of any effects on sexual offending.[22]

To reiterate, none of these studies – despite different methods, data, and assumptions – detect any reliable reduction in sex offense recidivism as a result of SORN

---

[21] For instance, Vasquez, Maddan, and Walker (2008) treat Idaho's intervention as occurring in 1993, but registration also became effective at this time, and public access to registrant information was only available upon written request. Thus, Vasquez, Maddan, and Walker's findings may speak more directly to the effects of registration alone on recidivism. They also treat Ohio's and Hawaii's "registry" interventions as occurring in 1998, but notification in those states was limited in its coverage and actually became effective in the middle of 1997, not 1998. Maurelli and Ronan (2013) also employ this strategy, using a longer time series (UCR data from 1960 to 2008). They find quite different results. In particular, after correcting the dates for Ohio, Idaho, and Hawaii, the findings of fewer sex offenses in these states disappear. However, the larger data set allows them to conduct a similar analysis for forty-nine states, and they claim to offer other evidence that SORN laws reduce the frequency of forcible rape. While they do not conclude that notification laws necessarily reduce sex offense frequency across all states, they contend that seventeen states out of forty-nine show some evidence of a reduction. Yet, like Vasquez, Madden, and Walker (2008), Maurelli and Ronan's results *also* commingle recidivism and first-time deterrence effects. There may also be mistakes in their coding of state laws. For instance, among the states for which they find reductions in forcible rape rates, which they specifically attribute to notification laws, they record Virginia's SORN law as beginning in 1994, but public access did not commence in that state until 1998. Likewise, they combine private registration and notification, recording Delaware, Michigan, Missouri, and South Carolina as beginning notification in 1994, 1995, 1995, and 1994, respectively, instead of 1999, 1997, 1999, and 1996. Texas is miscoded in the opposite way: Maurelli and Ronan code Texas as beginning its intervention in 1995. This is when notification began, but registration started in 1991. And they code Florida as 1997 instead of 1995.

[22] A working paper by Shao and Li (2006) using UCR data to study the effect of registries on the frequency of sex offenses was never published and is no longer easy to locate (and so we do not describe its findings, which are subject to criticism). The working paper is cited often in the early literature, however, so we include it here for completeness. Shao and Li's draft is cited and discussed in Prescott and Rockoff (2011, pp. 163–65, note 2, 4, 5).

laws, either when evaluating registration and notification *combined* or when evaluating community notification on its own. Importantly, none of these multistate federal crime data studies – other than Agan (2011) and Prescott and Rockoff (2011) – attempt to separately identify the effects of SORN laws on registrant recidivism versus the laws' potential to deter nonregistrants. Because these two effects may point in opposite directions, undifferentiated results are consistent both with (1) neither registration nor notification having any effect on offense frequency and with (2) their just having no *net* effect when their individual effects are aggregated. In other words, any crime-reducing effects of registration alone may be offset by the plausible criminogenic effects of notification, as found by Prescott and Rockoff (2011). In that sense, all the studies are consistent with each other.

7.3.2 *SORN Recidivism Effects: Evidence from Criminal History Data*

Another way to assess the effects of SORN laws on recidivism is to study individual-level criminal histories — that is, assemble the subsequent criminal behavior of individuals previously convicted of sex offenses and compare the future offense trajectories of those actually subject to SORN to the trajectories of a control group of individuals not subject to SORN. Most papers studying the effects of registration and notification on sex offense recidivism rely on this empirical strategy. This is not surprising, given that it may be the most direct, natural, and intuitive way to evaluate the effects of SORN on sex offense recidivism levels.

From the perspective of policy makers, however, this approach has significant limitations. One drawback of focusing exclusively on individuals with registration-qualifying sex offense *convictions* is that the analysis discounts any behavioral effects the laws might have on nonregistrants. Another is that it is unable to isolate the impact of SORN on all reported sex offense incidents; the approach can only analyze detected criminal behavior that is also linked to a particular offender (e.g., an incident resulting in an arrest). Criminal records only contain data on arrests, charges, convictions, and sentences. Thus, any measure of the "effect" of SORN laws using this approach is actually an aggregate of effects on offender behavior, law enforcement success in apprehension, and case processing efficiency and accuracy. An increase in sex crime arrests following the enactment of SORN laws could imply *greater* levels of recidivism caused by the burdens SORN imposes (reducing u_i), or it could signify improved law enforcement ability to detect and apprehend recidivists (increasing p_{ijl}). Still, for better or worse, researchers have not faced this dilemma in practice in light of their findings: the dozen-plus studies in this category all essentially conclude that SORN laws have no effect on the likelihood that a registrant recidivates, regardless of the recidivism measure one prefers.

Agan (2011) includes the largest analysis of this sort. She leverages Bureau of Justice Statistics (BJS) data that follow all individuals imprisoned for a sex offense *and* who were released from state prisons in 1994 in fifteen states (Langan, Schmitt, and Durose, 2003). Agan takes advantage of the fact that some individuals were released in states where SORN laws were already in effect (and were therefore required to comply with SORN) while others were released at the same time but were not subject to SORN because such laws were not yet enacted where they were released. Agan examines any differences in the likelihood and timing of rearrest for rape, rearrest for any sex offense, and reconviction for any sex offense. Despite her large sample size, Agan finds no statistically significant difference between the two groups of releasees on any of these measures. If anything, the results hint at *higher* arrest and conviction rates for those subject to SORN laws. Importantly, this post-SORN increase in "recidivism" outcomes is more consistent with registrants committing additional sex crimes than with better police monitoring leading to more arrests per incident (but fewer incidents overall) because in Agan's analysis the individuals subject to SORN laws also appear more likely to be arrested for non-sex offenses (i.e., pointing to SORN being generally criminogenic). On the other hand, the timing of Agan's analysis (the offenders in the study were released circa 1994) means that the implicated SORN laws mostly entailed registration alone, at least at the inception of the recidivism window. Thus, any increase in arrest or conviction rates is also consistent with Prescott and Rockoff's (2011) finding that registration alone may have public safety benefits via improved law enforcement monitoring and apprehension effectiveness.[23]

Other studies using individual criminal histories to examine recidivism effects analyze data (and laws) from just one or two states and typically rely on a pre- and post-implementation comparison strategy. By and large, these studies address the effects of notification, not registration. The authors in these papers essentially compare the offending trajectories of those subject to notification laws to the trajectories of those not subject to them, using various methods to try to make these different groups otherwise comparable. Most of these studies have small sample sizes and assume away the possibility of other confounders. This latter assumption is troublesome in a single-state scenario because the comparison-group members usually committed crimes, were convicted, or were released at a different point in time. This is particularly problematic in single-state settings when other policy interventions in the jurisdiction accompany the introduction of notification. But, despite their potential shortcomings, these empirical studies still tell the same consistent and mutually reinforcing story: they find no evidence that notification has any effect on recidivism.[24] Where there is any glimmer of evidence in one direction or another, it is consistent either with an increase in recidivism or

---

[23] Again, Agan's sample of potential recidivists includes only individuals released from prison, so one must take into account the fact that individuals who serve a prison sentence following a sex offense conviction are only a subset – admittedly, surely a very large subset – of all registrants and were probably convicted of more serious crimes on average. Some number of registrants may spend time only in jail and still others may never be incarcerated for their crimes. Therefore, to be more precise, SORN laws do not appear to reduce the probability of re-offending at least for state prison releasees.

[24] None of these studies are able to examine the deterrence effects of SORN laws on nonregistrant behavior. We discuss the smaller body of research on this question later, in Section 7.3.5.

with the idea that only narrow, risk-based public notification regimes are effective (as in Minnesota, see below).

Schram and Milloy's (1995) work appears to be the first empirical study to evaluate the effects of notification on recidivism using criminal history records. They study a small sample of public registrants (n = 125) from one state – Washington, one of the earliest adopters of community notification, which at the time subjected only high-risk registrants (approximately 20 percent of all registrants) to notification.[25] They detect no difference in sex offense rearrest rates for those subject to SORN laws as compared to similar individuals convicted of a sex offense and released prior to the implementation of Washington's SORN law.[26] Adkins, Huff, and Stageberg (2000) similarly compare recidivism outcomes of 233 registrants to those of 201 individuals convicted of a sex offense prior to the implementation of the registry law and find no evidence of any effect on their measures of recidivism over an average of 4.3 years. Zevitz (2006) uses plausibly exogenous variation in local policies to study the effect of "extensive" notification relative to more limited forms of information disclosure in Wisconsin (n = 213). Like others, he finds no differences in arrest or reconviction rates across the groups. Maddan (2005; 2008) and Maddan, Miller, Walker, and Marshall (2011) investigate the potential effects of notification in Arkansas on almost 3,000 registrants over 5 years. They, too, find no effect of that state's SORN law on the likelihood of rearrest or reconviction for a sex offense.[27]

In an important and well-known study, Sandler, Freeman, and Socia (2008) evaluate the effects of New York's SORN laws on sex offense recidivism by tracking the behavior over time of all individuals convicted of registerable sex offenses. They capitalize on the fact that only those convicted or released post-1996 would be subject to the state's registration and notification laws. The authors are able to

---

[25] Barnoski (2005) revisits data from Washington. He examines whether there had been a change in sex offense recidivism (measured by a new conviction) over time (during which a SORN law had been implemented), but he does not explicitly study the role of an individual's notification status. He also admits that any reduction in sex offense recidivism over time may have many causes, including presumably lower enforcement levels or other secular trends in offending behavior.

[26] But Schram and Milloy (1995) do detect some evidence suggesting that registrants subject to notification were more likely to be rearrested for *non*-sex offenses. There are two potential interpretations of these findings. The first is that those subject to notification were disproportionately burdened by SORN publicity (through, e.g., unemployment and housing difficulties) and therefore became more at risk of committing non-sex crime – possibly property, auto theft, or other "profitable" crimes (consistent with a lower u_i in our model). The second is that non-sex recidivism patterns provide a baseline for what we should expect to occur with sex offense recidivism absent notification. With this interpretation, their finding implies that SORN laws effectively produced lower sex offense recidivism rates. Schram and Milloy give us no good reason to believe this interpretation, however, and one might *also* expect SORN-related monitoring by police to have effects on non-sex recidivism. Perhaps a more important limitation of the study is the narrow use of notification in this early Washington State SORN law, targeting only the 20 percent of registrants deemed particularly high risk.

[27] Like Schram and Milloy (1995), these two studies find some evidence that notification is associated with an increase in non-sex crime recidivism, a pattern consistent with its burdens being crimino-genic. Letourneau and Armstrong (2008) find something substantively similar using data from South Carolina in the juvenile SORN context.

examine the role that registrants play in all sex offenses for which there is a recorded arrest (an important caveat) and test whether the relative significance of recidivism in accounting for all cleared sex offenses changed after community notification went into effect. They find no evidence that SORN laws affect recidivism levels (if anything, their findings indicate that SORN laws increase sex offense recidivism). Crucially, their study also reveals little room for potential improvement on this dimension. Specifically, reducing recidivism can only make a small contribution to reducing total victimization levels in their data because approximately 95 percent of sex offense arrests in New York involved individuals with no sex offense-related criminal history (and who were thus not subject to registration).

Subsequent studies – using an assortment of methods and criminal history data – also determine that SORN laws (particularly notification) have essentially no effect on recidivism. For example, Letourneau, Levenson, Bandyopadhyay, Armstrong, and Sinha (2010) use a survival analysis framework and data from South Carolina in the 1990s and 2000s to assess whether SORN laws influence recidivism rates. The authors argue that, unlike other traditional predictors of criminal recidivism risk (e.g., age and criminal history), registration status does not affect the likelihood or timing of another sex crime arrest or conviction.

Other studies arrive at the same verdict. Tewksbury and Jennings (2010) consider a large, matched sample of pre- and post-SORN individuals convicted of a sex offense in Iowa. Because notification laws may affect the behavior of different types of potential re-offenders (e.g., high risk v. low risk) differently, Tewksbury and Jennings sort everyone into a risk group based on their future offense trajectory and then they compare and contrast the composition of the risk groups pre- and post-SORN. They show that SORN laws have no apparent effect on any group's recidivism risk nor do they seem to alter the composition of the groups. Zgoba, Veysey, and Dalessandro (2010) test for differences in recidivism behavior (using arrest, conviction, and incarceration measures) in New Jersey ($n = 550$) according to notification status. They find no differences with respect to sex offense recidivism. Tewksbury, Jennings, and Zgoba (2012) apply the methods of Tewksbury and Jennings (2010) to the New Jersey data studied in Zgoba, Veysey, and Dalessandro (2010), again finding no evidence that SORN affects recidivism patterns either on average or for particular groups of potential offenders.[28]

Reaching the same conclusion by a slightly different inferential path, Freeman (2012) examines pre- and post-notification recidivism patterns over time for New York registrants and finds that those subject to community notification (i.e., high-risk registrants) were likely to be arrested twice as quickly as comparable individuals who – because they committed their registerable sex offenses prior to

---

[28] Zgoba, Jennings, and Salerno (2018) return to this New Jersey criminal history data, using a similar methodology on a longer trajectory period – 15 years (sample size = 547). The authors uncover no evidence that SORN laws have any effect on recidivism, even when they assume there might be heterogeneous responses, with SORN effects perhaps emerging for only a particular subgroup.

the law's effective date – were not subject to notification.[29] Freeman acknowledges that this finding could be read to be inconsistent with the consensus of the foregoing scholarship: even if community notification does not reduce sex offense recidivism (as measured by arrests), it might nevertheless improve law enforcement *detection* of sex offense recidivism, which would presumably reduce harm in the future. But Freeman also posits other interpretations that are equally consistent with these patterns in the data, including that notification may either lull potential victims into a false sense of security (reducing p_{ijl}) or exacerbate recidivism risk factors (reducing u_i), or both. These scenarios would lead to additional *incidents* for which a registrant is at risk of being arrested (if these are marginal crimes – and therefore more risky on average – it would make even more sense that arrest would typically occur earlier under notification). Bolstering this latter reading, Freeman's research also indicates that being subject to notification is associated (albeit imprecisely) with higher non-sex offense recidivism as well, so more recidivism leading to earlier arrests on average seems most likely to be the correct explanation, which Freeman readily accepts.

Levenson and Zgoba (2016) examine sex offense rearrest rates in Florida, deploying an approach somewhat similar to that of Sandler, Freeman, and Socia (2008). Levenson and Zgoba use the aggregate fraction of rearrests (for the same type of crime as an earlier conviction) over total arrests in a given crime category as a recidivism index. They investigate whether SORN laws cause the index for sex offenses to decline relative to the indexes for other crimes between 1990 and 2010. They uncover no evidence to support this possibility – in fact, they find that sex offense rearrest rates increase, although the rate of increase post-SORN was not statistically different from the comparable rate of increase for other crimes. Bouffard and Askew (2019) follow in Levenson and Zgoba's footsteps by conducting a time-series analysis (1977–2012) of recidivism in Harris County, Texas. They find that, while the total number of sex offense charges increased absolutely over time, interrupted time-series methods indicate that SORN-law enactments and amendments played no role in this increase. Specifically, Bouffard and Askew detect no change in the number of charges against repeat offenders, against first-time offenders, for all offenses against children, or for all sexual assaults.

Duwe and Donnay (2008) provide the only potentially probative evidence in support of notification-induced recidivism reduction. They study Minnesota's early, highly targeted notification regime (covering only 10 percent of all individuals convicted of a sex offense) using a small sample ($n = 155$) of high-risk registrants. With these caveats, and after matching these high-risk potential recidivists to arguably comparable sets of pre-notification and lower-risk non-notification individuals, the authors conclude that notification is associated with lower sex offense recidivism. Duwe and Donnay also present evidence suggesting that re-offenders covered by notification are arrested and reconvicted sooner.

[29] Using New York data, Freeman and Sandler (2010) examine whether male recidivism rates differ across Adam Walsh Act risk tiers. They find that they do not but leave open the possibility that better risk-tiering could be used to target those most likely to recidivate, possibly with positive results.

To our knowledge, Duwe and Donnay's 2008 work is the only plausibly credible evidence that – under some circumstances – notification may reduce recidivism. However, context and lack of data reduce the salience and significance of the paper's findings. For instance, all potential re-offenders in Minnesota during the study's "post period" (both treatment and control groups) were subject to active notification provisions of some sort, and the pre-notification comparison group's behavior came earlier in time and so these individuals may have faced a very different environment. Furthermore, significant discretion existed under Minnesota law in how registrants were assigned to notification during the study period, which may interfere with control-group comparability. In addition, the substantive requirements of Minnesota's SORN laws changed between 1997 and 2000; these changes, which include the launch of an internet registry in 2000, may contaminate Duwe and Donnay's inferences. Finally, Duwe and Donnay are unable to offer evidence on the relationship, if any, between notification and total sex offense frequency, which opens up their results to alternative interpretations.[30]

7.3.3 *SORN Recidivism Effects: Alternative Approaches*

Agan and Prescott (2014) adopt a new approach to identifying notification's effects on recidivism using the preexisting variation in where registrants live in Baltimore County, Maryland, and the area's sex offense incident report data.[31] They find that, on average, reported sex offenses rise in neighborhoods with more registrants relative to neighborhoods with fewer registrants following the implementation of Maryland's notification regime. This result is at a minimum consistent with the idea that community notification leads to greater levels of recidivism.

Agan and Prescott include two crucial caveats in their work. First, while the average number of reported sex offenses increases post-notification in neighborhoods that are dense with registrants, the number of reported adult rapes and sex offenses against children *falls* with notification in those neighborhoods relative to other neighborhoods. This pattern could indicate either a reduction in recidivism or displacement (in which registrants travel to other neighborhoods where they remain unknown in order to commit crimes). Second, because Agan and Prescott investigate *reported* incidents, they cannot exclude the possibility that nonregistered potential offenders seek out neighborhoods with many registrants to commit crimes (assuming they will be more likely to evade detection as not the "usual suspects" in those neighborhoods). In the end, the authors concede that the ability of

---

[30] One alternative interpretation of these findings is that certain potential recidivists subject to notification became better able to avoid detection (perhaps by offending outside of their neighborhood), in which case Duwe and Donnay's findings of "reduced recidivism" would actually represent just a reduction in law enforcement detection.

[31] Agan and Prescott's (2014) identifying assumption is that any difference in sex offense frequency between neighborhoods where registrants live relative to the frequency in neighborhoods where they do not live can be taken as a proxy for registrant recidivism.

nonregistrants to react to a notification regime makes it difficult to draw strong inferences about the effects of online notification on recidivism levels using their approach; however, their findings do allow them to say something precise about overall risk levels in registrant-heavy neighborhoods.[32]

Also taking a different approach, Carr (2019) uses plausibly exogenous variation in the duration of registration to study the effect of SORN laws on recidivism. In 2006, North Carolina extended the length of its registration requirement for anyone who was *currently* registered as of December 1, 2006, which effectively randomly kept a group of slightly more recently registered individuals on the registry for an additional 20 years. Using sex offender criminal history data, Carr finds no evidence of any difference in the likelihood of sex offense recidivism (after 10 years) between those required to register for 10 years versus those who remained subject to SORN for many more years. Her work suggests that applying SORN requirements more than 10 years following release has no public safety payoff.

7.3.4 *SORN Recidivism Effects: Summary*

Dozens of studies to date have sought to assess whether and how SORN laws affect sex offense recidivism. Multistate studies – some national in scope – using federal crime data and deploying panel data methods or time-series approaches have found no evidence that notification reduces recidivism and some evidence that it may increase recidivism. In single-state studies, using many different empirical research tools and data sources and examining different measures of sex offense recidivism in different jurisdictions (including Arkansas, DC, Florida, Iowa, Maryland, Minnesota, New Jersey, New York, North Carolina, South Carolina, Texas, and Wisconsin), researchers from different disciplines, working independently, have essentially all failed to detect any evidence that notification reduces recidivism. The sole exception to this scholarly consensus is Duwe and Donnay (2008), who, using a small sample of potential recidivists, in a jurisdiction (Minnesota) employing an atypical, narrow, individual risk-based approach, find at least some nontrivial evidence that notification may reduce recidivism.

By contrast, evidence on the effects on recidivism of registration alone is more mixed. Although Prescott and Rockoff's (2011) results indicate that registration may reduce registrant recidivism, Agan's (2011) analysis of mostly private registration laws does not detect any effects worthy of comment. Some support for registration alone can also be gleaned from the studies that conflate registration and notification (e.g., Vasquez, Madden, and Walker, 2008). But generally we have far less evidence on registration's efficacy at reducing recidivism than we do on the recidivism-reducing

---

[32] See also Agan (2011), who conducts a similar type of study in Washington, DC, although she only has information on registrants' current addresses and therefore has to assume registrants do not move very often over time. Agan finds no evidence that the risk of victimization changes near where registrants live when the city implemented community notification.

effectiveness of notification, and there are decent reasons to surmise that the former might succeed where the latter fails. We need more research.

7.3.5 *SORN Effects on Nonregistrant Criminal Behavior*

Perhaps because the principal aim of SORN laws is to reduce sex offense *recidivism* by registrants, there is much less work on the deterrence effects of SORN laws on *non*registrants – that is, whether the threat of becoming subject to registration and notification upon conviction for a sex crime might cause potential sex offenders who have never been convicted (or are at least not currently registered) to offend less often on average. In theory, SORN laws might discourage potential "first-time" sex offenders from ever offending in the first place, which would be important because the overwhelming number of sex offenses are committed by first-time sex offenders (Sandler, Freeman, and Socia, 2008).

However, it is appropriate to be skeptical of this possibility. Evidence is very thin that *lengthening* already long prison sentences improves deterrence (see, e.g., the review in Durlauf and Nagin (2011)), and sex offense sentences are generally long. Because the burdens of SORN laws on those newly convicted of sex offenses would come *after* any prison sentence (potentially many years in the future), any deterrence gains appear likely to be second-order. This seems especially true for any threatened use of registration alone, which potential offenders may not distinguish from parole and supervision conditions generally (if indeed they are aware of the requirement at all prior to their first sex offense conviction). But notification has greater potential to change nonregistrant behavior. The prospect of being listed publicly on a registry as a sex offender is quite salient. A potential offender may not distinguish between prison sentences of say 10 and 12 years but may very well view at least 10 years of notification – and the public pariah status it carries – as a much worse consequence than two additional years of prison.

While relatively little evidence exists on the deterrence effects of registration alone, available data indicate that any beneficial consequences are trivial at best. Prescott and Rockoff (2011) consider the possibility, using NIBRS data from a dozen states, but they find no evidence of any first-time offense deterrence effect. Using a similar approach and data from UCR states, Agan (2011) also fails to uncover any evidence that the threat of early, pre-internet SORN laws deters potential first-time sex offenses. Bouffard and Askew (2019) examine the impact of a registration law implemented in Harris County, Texas, in 1991 using interrupted time-series methods (notification did not commence until sometime in 1995) and similarly detect no evidence of any effect on the number of first-time offenses. Other studies of registration either do not address first-time offense deterrence (focusing only on recidivism) or actually speak only to the deterrence effects of notification policies.

More research exists on the first-time deterrence effects of community notification (or a combined measure of registration and notification). The evidence that notification deters first-time offenses is best characterized as mixed, but unlike the less-than-negligible possibility that community notification may reduce sex offense recidivism, there is enough evidence of socially beneficial deterrence effects resulting from notification to take the idea seriously. Importantly, studying first-time offense deterrence questions requires data on the total number of sex offense incidents committed, reported, charged, or resulting in conviction, not just instances of sex offender recidivism. There are at least two strategies by which one could draw inferences about the effects of SORN laws on the criminal behavior of nonregistrants. Both approaches require assumptions, so they are usefully juxtaposed.

First, one could start with data on all sex offenses that include an indication of whether the offender in question was previously convicted of a qualifying sex offense (as in, e.g., Sandler, Freeman, and Socia (2008)). With these data, one can essentially track the number of offenses committed by *nonregistrants* during any period of time. One can then evaluate whether SORN implementation changes this number (or the relative importance of this number). Unfortunately, data sets like these are rare.[33] Perhaps the first study to use this strategy to focus significant attention on first-time sex offense behavior is Sandler, Freeman, and Socia (2008), which relies on criminal history data from New York. Besides calculating that over 95 percent of sex offenses in New York are committed by first-time offenders (again, making clear the importance of inhibiting first-time offending), they find no evidence to support the claim that SORN laws reduce the total number of first-time offenses. But the study's results do reveal some heterogeneity across types of crimes. In particular, the authors estimate a large negative effect of notification for first-time child molestation offenses. The coefficient, which is only borderline statistically significant (*t-stat* = –1.81), offers at a minimum tepid support for notification's deterrence effects, at least with respect to these particular crimes.

Building on this research, Letourneau, Levenson, Bandyopadhyay, Armstrong, and Sinha (2010) examine similarly structured South Carolina data. They identify 1995 as the year that South Carolina implemented a public sex offender registry (via mandatory public access to paper-based registry information). Unlike Sandler, Freeman, and Socia (2008), these authors present more consistent evidence that notification results in fewer first-time offenses. The authors report that first-time arrests – not incidents[34] – drop by 11 percent relative to the pre-notification era.

---

[33] To our knowledge, researchers to date have only been able to acquire data of this sort for a single state at a time. Moreover, an additional limitation of this approach – a limitation that runs throughout empirical work on criminal behavior – is that it can only account for changes in the number of first-time offenses *resulting in an arrest*. After all, apprehension (and possibly conviction) is necessary for the researcher to be able to discern whether the offense in question was committed by a first-time offender. If many sex offenses do not result in (accurate) arrests or convictions, the researcher is forced to make assumptions about the stability over time of sex offense clearance rates.

[34] It is worth remembering that the number of arrests for sex offenses can drop post-SORN whether or not the number of actual offenses drops, such as when there are SORN-induced reductions in sex offense reporting by victims or less effective police investigation of reported crimes or apprehension of suspects. See note 13.

However, they fail to observe any incremental reduction in first-time offenses from the launch of an online registry in 1999, which one might have expected to generate the largest impact given the salience of internet registries and the publicity surrounding their launches.[35] This inconsistency may imply either that some early versions of public access laws are equal to internet registries in their deterrence potential or that the drop in first-time offenses post-1995 was due primarily to chance. To explore these possibilities further, Park, Bandyopadhyay, and Letourneau (2014) return to these South Carolina data with new methods and find more convincing evidence in favor of deterrence of first-time offenses following the launch of the state's online registry in 1999. In any event, whether we read these three papers together as presenting conflicting evidence or as reinforcing the idea that notification laws may be able to deter potential first-time sex offenders, this research is only able to speak to the laws' effects on the frequency of sex offenses that lead to *arrests* because they all rely on criminal history data.

A second approach to examining first-time deterrence effects is to use data on all reported sex offenses in a particular jurisdiction and leverage the number of individuals listed on the relevant sex offender registry to isolate any SORN effects on first-time offenses. In essence, this empirical strategy assumes that any SORN effects on sexual offending that vary with registry size (whether private or public) over time and across jurisdictions (controlling for other potential confounders) are attributable to changes in levels of sex offense *recidivism*. In other words, this research design assumes that the size of the registry does not predictably affect nonregistrant behavior.[36] If this assumption is approximately correct or if any departures are likely to offset each other, the residual – what stays constant across registries of different sizes at different times – captures the fixed "threat" of future SORN burdens (deterrence) if one is convicted of a sex offense.

Prescott and Rockoff (2011) use NIBRS data on all reported incidents from fifteen states – exploiting the variation in registry sizes over time and across states – to test for

---

[35] Letourneau, Levenson, Bandyopadhyay, Armstrong, and Sinha (2010) find no independent reduction in sex offense arrests beginning in 1994 (p. 547), the year in which private registration began (in July) in South Carolina, adding another attempt to test for first-time deterrence effects of registration alone to Prescott and Rockoff (2011) and Agan (2011). Separately, Letourneau, Bandyopadhyay, Armstrong, and Sinha (2010) study first-time deterrence effects of community notification in the context of potential first-time *juvenile* offenders. They conclude there is little evidence that notification reduces first-time juvenile arrests for sex offenses, especially in light of other procedural changes affecting juvenile prosecutions in South Carolina around that time that make it difficult to draw reliable inferences from their data about notification specifically. More recently, Letourneau, Shields, Nair, Kahn, Sandler, and Vandiver (2018) study juvenile charges and adjudications in Maryland and Oregon and find no evidence of SORN-related first-time deterrence effects.

[36] Prescott and Rockoff (2011, p. 170, n. 17) acknowledge that this assumption may not hold. For instance, large public registries may be more salient to the public – i.e., nonregistrants – in some way. Or large registries may instead lead to registry fatigue, habituating the public to the existence of known registrants. In either case, we might expect any deterrence of first-time offenses to vary with the size of the registry. Even so, the latter possibility does not appear to have occurred yet, and it is certainly unclear whether an individual (especially someone at risk of committing a sex crime in the future) is more (or less) likely to be aware of SORN obligations if the registry is larger or smaller given the public fanfare around sex offender laws and particularly the implementation of notification policies.

the existence of notification effects on the frequency of first-time offenses. They unearth sizeable effects (a 12.8 percent reduction), surprisingly close to Letourneau, Levenson, Bandyopadhyay, Armstrong, and Sinha's (2010) finding of an approximately 11 percent reduction. Prescott and Rockoff's results remain intact even when they focus only on the number of sex offense arrests. Agan (2011), employing the same identification strategy to examine sex offense trends in UCR states, also finds statistically significant evidence of first-time deterrence effects from the implementation of notification (specifically, internet registries). This finding is not inconsistent with Letourneau, Levenson, Bandyopadhyay, Armstrong, and Sinha's (2010) failure to discern internet-registry deterrence effects in light of Park et al.'s (2014) alternative results but also because internet registries in many states significantly increased the public availability of registry information and were more likely to be implemented concurrently with paper-based forms of notification in contrast to the timing in South Carolina.

Importantly, evidence of notification's beneficial effects on deterring first-time offenses cannot be viewed in isolation. There is little evidence that notification reduces recidivism and some evidence that it actually increases recidivism by exacerbating risk factors; meanwhile, very large numbers of people continue to commit first-time sex crimes, despite the threat of being subject to notification. Moreover, notification is financially costly to maintain and burdensome to many third parties, including registrants' families, employers, and landlords. In light of the foregoing, any first-time deterrence effect may not be worth the candle. Making simple calculations from their results, Prescott and Rockoff (2011) argue that the deterrence benefits of notification are likely offset by its criminogenic effects, even when notification applies to a relatively small population of registrants – specifically, to a registry that was below average in size in the United States around the year 2000 – far smaller than the public registries in almost every state today.

7.3.6 *SORN Effects on Geographic and Victim Incidence*

In the behavioral model we introduce in Section 7.2, we describe potential offender i's decision to commit a sex offense not as something abstract but instead as a decision to commit a particular type of crime against a particular type of victim (j) in a particular location (l). Offenders may be willing to commit some crimes under certain circumstances (a combination of the offense type, the victim type, and the location) but not others depending on the probability of punishment (p_{ijl}), the level of punishment (f_{ijl}), the cost of carrying out the crime (c_{ijl}), and the utility (benefit) of lawful behavior relative to sexual offending (u_i).

A critical but relatively understudied implication of this framework is that SORN laws may change *how* registrants (and nonregistrants) offend – which sex crimes, where, and against whom – without necessarily changing the overall frequency of sex offenses. While policy makers might be primarily interested in reducing the total number of offenses, investigating these distributional consequences of SORN laws is important because – like any law with consequences that vary across people – these policies will create winners and losers.[37] Moreover, because potential offenders will likely respond to their legal and social environment in ways both expected and unexpected, policy makers ought to probe potential behavioral responses comprehensively and try to anticipate unintended consequences of SORN laws.

Agan and Prescott (2014) analyze whether SORN (and particularly notification) laws produce geographic shifts in where sex offenses occur and whether any such effects depend on the specific type of sex offense. They use historical data on registrants' residences, the locations of reported sex offenses (of different types), and the implementation timing of online notification in Maryland to study these questions. In particular, the authors match reported crime incidents to neighborhoods to observe whether neighborhoods with more registrants at a given time have more or less sex crime in subsequent periods.[38]

Complex behavioral predictions emerge from a model like the one outlined in Section 7.2 of this chapter. With registration alone (marked by increased police but not public monitoring), we might expect fewer sex offenses to occur (on average and controlling for other differences) in neighborhoods with more registrants (relative to a world without registration – see Bernasco (2010)). In effect, registration makes it relatively less likely that registrants will be detected if they offend farther away from home where they remain unknown to law enforcement. Thus, assuming private registration does not affect where first-time offenses occur, sex offense victimization risk should be *lower* where there are relatively *more* registrants under registration alone. Essentially, registrants have incentives to avoid police detection by offending elsewhere (when it is not too costly to travel to another neighborhood), so high-density registrant neighborhoods should be safer all else equal.

Agan and Prescott (2014) find evidence consistent with this prediction in their data – indeed, using various neighborhood definitions, each additional registrant in a neighborhood appears to be associated with 7.5 percent fewer reported sex offenses in that neighborhood. This finding is consistent with both recidivism reduction (Prescott and Rockoff, 2011) and displacement of recidivism to other neighborhoods (Barr and Pease, 1990; Canter, 1996) as well as potentially non-SORN related explanations, such as the possibility that registrants are disproportionately more

---

[37] See, for example, Linden and Rockoff (2008), which identifies the negative home value consequences of community notification when a registrant lives nearby.

[38] Agan (2011) and Stucky and Ottensmann (2016) also address this descriptive question – whether, after taking into account other features of neighborhoods and their residents, it is accurate to assume that victimization risk is higher in areas closer to where registrants live – for Washington, DC, and Indianapolis, Indiana, respectively. Agan exploits changes in the community notification regime, but she has to make strong assumptions about residential continuity because of her fixed "snapshot" data on registrant addresses. She analyzes data on crimes from both before and after DC implemented online public notification. By contrast, Stucky and Ottensmann study a period in which registration and notification (but not yet residency restrictions) were already in place in Indiana, so they cannot speak to the *changes* in behavior resulting from implementing SORN laws.

likely to live in safer neighborhoods. Agan and Prescott's research accounts for some of the more likely alternative possibilities, such as the notion that neighborhoods with more registrants may contain fewer potential victims (such as children). They also investigate whether their estimates vary across different types of sex crimes (including forcible rape; other sex offenses against adults; peeping, prostitution, and pornography; and sex offenses against children). They find a lower frequency for all types of offenses in registrant neighborhoods, with the largest differences in their data emerging from peeping, prostitution, and pornography.

Agan and Prescott (2014) next evaluate how the relationship between victimization risk (based on reported sex offenses) and registrant density in a neighborhood changes when a jurisdiction implements community notification – in their case, Maryland's launch of its online registry. Their focus is less on how total offense frequency changes than on how the geographic distribution of offenses and, thus, the geography of victimization risk change in response to notification. Because notification makes registrant information available to the public (including to all prospective first-time offenders – that is, nonregistrants – whose sex offense behavior may also change in response to registry information and the threat of being subject to notification), the behavioral model's predictions are ambiguous.

If notification informs the public of the identities of nearby registrants (e.g., neighbors), making it easier to monitor and avoid them, one might expect registrants to be more likely to recidivate away from home, all else equal, because the likelihood of their crimes being detected (p_{ijl}) near home and the difficulty of committing crime locally due to SORN-generated victim precaution-taking (c_{ijl}) would be higher. Offsetting considerations include notification-driven increases in recidivism risk factors (u_i), which might be powerful enough to produce higher victimization levels in registrant neighborhoods. Then again, these risk factors may produce even higher levels in other neighborhoods. As always, any local reduction in sex offense frequency may be partially offset by crimes displaced to other neighborhoods.

Unexpectedly, depending on whether and how the law's potential beneficiaries use the registry's information, potential first-time offenders may find it either more or less attractive to offend in registrant-filled neighborhoods under a community notification regime (e.g., Kernsmith, Comartin, Craun, and Kernsmith, 2009). If the police and public focus on registrants and otherwise let their guard down, committing a first-time offense in a registrant-dense neighborhood might become more attractive. Alternatively, if monitoring and precaution-taking make all sex offenses harder to commit, potential first-time offenders might avoid places with more registrants, driving risk down in those areas. The geographic offending behavior of nonregistrants is particularly important because, as we note above, first-time offenders commit a very large percentage of sex crimes (Sandler, Freeman, and Socia, 2008).

Agan and Prescott (2014) analyze reported crime incidents, not criminal history information that would allow them to determine where recidivists and first-time offenders actually commit their crimes. Nevertheless, they are still able to conclude that online notification moderately increases the total number of sex offenses in registrant neighborhoods (albeit not by enough to make those neighborhoods more risky than other neighborhoods on balance).[39] They acknowledge, however, that their estimates may be distorted somewhat by any effect online public registries have on victim reporting behavior, a recurrent problem in the study of sexual offending.

Agan and Prescott (2014) also investigate whether notification's effects on the geography of risk vary by sex offense type. They find that online registries seem to reduce the number of adult rape and child molestation incidents in registrant neighborhoods but perhaps by displacing them elsewhere – the number of rape and molestation incidents grows post-notification in other, less registrant-dense neighborhoods (consistent with Yeh (2015)). These findings counter alternative theories that rely on shifting victim reporting behavior. By contrast, other sex offenses, including peeping, prostitution, and pornography, tend to increase in registrant-dense neighborhoods following notification. This pattern may be a function of reporting-behavior changes, but Agan and Prescott (2014, p. 812) observe that notification really ought to affect the frequency and geography of different sex offenses differently: "[S]ex offenses are diverse. Some require planning or involve money; others are impulse crimes or involve intimidation or violence." Perhaps because it implies inherent trade-offs between types of victims, this heterogeneity of effects has received little treatment in the literature. But the possibility that SORN laws may affect *where* offenders commit sex crimes as well as *whether* they commit a sex offense at all is too important for academics and policy makers to ignore.

Sex offender registration and notification laws may also affect whom offenders victimize. The laws were specifically designed to provide local law enforcement and community members with actionable information on registrants living or working nearby. Implicit in this policy approach are the ideas that (1) some people (e.g., family members) will already know of a potential recidivist's past crimes even without notification and (2) some people (e.g., strangers living in other neighborhoods) will be too far removed from a particular registrant to make effective precautionary use of registry information. If SORN laws work as intended, by influencing the behavior of police and potential victims thought likely to benefit from registry information, we should expect to observe disproportionately less recidivism occurring against victims in the target category – otherwise unknowing neighbors and acquaintances – than against family members and strangers.

Prescott and Rockoff (2011) explore this idea using the offender–victim relationship information recorded in NIBRS to determine whether there are heterogeneous effects of registration and notification across offender–victim relationship types. Specifically, they test whether SORN laws affect the frequency of sex offenses

---

[39] Yeh (2015) corroborates this basic finding using a similar approach with crime data and registrant address information in Lincoln, Nebraska.

against people likely to already be aware of a prospective registrant's criminal history (e.g., family, significant others, and friends), against those who could theoretically benefit from the information (e.g., neighbors, acquaintances, and otherwise known persons), and against individuals who are unlikely to be able to efficiently access or use a registrant's registry information (e.g., strangers). By allowing better local law enforcement monitoring and apprehension, and by informing those who can actually use registry information, SORN laws – if they operate as proponents argue they do – should reduce offense frequency against primarily the second set.

Prescott and Rockoff find evidence that registration alone reduces recidivism against acquaintances and neighbors, but it does not appear to reduce recidivism against either family members and friends or strangers.[40] Their results do not support the idea that registration displaces crime from acquaintances and neighbors to other victims such as strangers: while the estimated effect on stranger-crime frequency is positive, it is close to zero and not statistically significant. By contrast, they uncover no evidence that notification reduces recidivism against any group of victims. Instead, recidivism appears to increase across all groups of victims following notification's implementation, a finding coinciding with the supposition that the heavy burdens of notification render it criminogenic on the whole (reducing u_i). As the behavioral model predicts, the effects of notification on first-time offenses appear to be similar across relationship groups. Prescott and Rockoff argue these results bolster the causal interpretation of their findings on the overall effects of registration and notification on first-time offenses and recidivism. Their victim-type findings, moreover, are independently important because they constitute some of the only evidence on SORN laws' distributional consequences.

7.3.7 SORN and Failure to Register

A modest body of research has assessed the recidivism consequences of an individual's failure to register (FTR) upon release or to verify or update registry information at a later time, a serious crime under all SORN laws. It is often hard to find statistics on FTR offenses. In 2008, nationwide, an estimated 16 percent of individuals required to register were not in compliance with their registration obligations (Levenson, Letourneau, Armstrong, and Zgoba, 2010). When considering this estimate, it is important to recognize that many individuals who fail to register are not "absconders" running from the law or committing new crimes (Bierie and Detar, 2016). Indeed, because noncompliance is often unintentional, and only a paucity of

---

[40] This particular result seems to be in tension with recent evidence assembled by Bierie and Budd (2020) that registration alone reduces the time to closure in cases involving strangers. However, if the sole effect of registration is to reduce closure times by a day or two (in line with Bierie and Budd's estimates), it may have little effect on offender behavior. Indeed, their findings are even consistent with higher recidivism levels, if the additional offenses committed by stranger offenders are more marginal and therefore easier for law enforcement to detect.

research supports the claim that public notification reduces recidivism in the first place (and may in fact increase it), it is unclear whether FTR offenses should be an important public policy concern. Failure-to-register violations can be explained by the many burdens of satisfying registration requirements and the life circumstances of many registrants. Registrants move a lot (Yeh, 2015) and are more likely to live in poor, socially disorganized neighborhoods than nonregistrants (Mustaine, Tewksbury, and Stengel, 2006). All of these considerations suggest that failing to register may signal many things about those who are subject to SORN, but not necessarily that they are relatively more likely to recidivate.

Is there an empirical relationship between failing to register under SORN laws and recidivism? Does failing to register actually increase a potential offender's likelihood of recidivating? Put another way, can law enforcement use FTR violations to identify the registrants who are most likely to commit additional sex crimes in the future? The research presents a mixed picture. There is some evidence that failing to register increases recidivism risk, but it may signify that an offender is more likely to engage in crime generally rather than sex crime specifically. Unfortunately, there is little work on the recidivism effects of absconding, which only becomes an FTR conviction if the individual is later caught.

Barnoski (2006) examines FTR convictions in Washington State. Although details in the report are thin, Barnoski documents that FTR convictions are common, that it is difficult to predict from simple demographic characteristics who is likely to commit an FTR offense, and that FTR convictions are associated with higher felony, violent felony, and sex offense recidivism, at least in his sample (which exceeds 10,000 individuals). At odds with this research is Duwe and Donnay (2010), who use propensity score matching to contrast comparable FTR and non-FTR potential recidivists in Minnesota ($n = 1{,}561$). They find that FTR status is not predictive of recidivism except with respect to the crime of failing to register again. Failure-to-register risk grows with a prior FTR – a finding that is at odds with the conjecture that FTR occurs as a result of confusion about the process (i.e., lack of experience or sophistication) rather than a registrant's inattentiveness, challenging life circumstances, or intentional noncompliance.

Levenson, Letourneau, Armstrong, and Zgoba (2010) study the consequences of an FTR conviction for registrants (relative to compliant registrants) in South Carolina ($n = 2{,}970$). Their data show that an FTR conviction is predictive of general recidivism, but they find no evidence of any statistically significant difference in sex offense recidivism risk between the groups. The authors also use the time to re-offense to estimate survival models, and they find no difference in the timing of sex offense recidivism with this approach either.

Levenson, Sandler, and Freeman (2012) address essentially the same question using New York data ($n = 7{,}055$) and come to somewhat different conclusions. In their data, an FTR "charge" (presumably highly correlated with an FTR conviction) is associated with both general recidivism and sex offense recidivism, but the latter relationship is much weaker. And when sex offense recidivism is broken down into new crimes against adult victims and new crimes against child victims, an FTR charge is only predictive of recidivism against adults. The authors maintain that FTR charges appear to be more indicative of general criminality than of sexual deviancy; they note that no element of an FTR charge is sexual in nature, and FTR charges are generally more common among registrants who are more likely to commit crime as a general matter. Socia, Levenson, Ackerman, and Harris (2015) develop empirical support for this idea by using Florida data to demonstrate that FTR convictions are associated with registrant transience, which they describe as a "major impediment to reentry success" (p. 559).

Finally, Zgoba and Levenson (2012) investigate FTR offenses using data from New Jersey. In a somewhat small sample ($n = 1,125$), they find no evidence that FTR predicts sex offense recidivism. They also observe that those who fail to register are more likely to have targeted adult female victims and are less likely to have been convicted of offenses against minors. This is consistent with Levenson, Sandler, and Freeman's (2012) conclusion that FTR is predictive of sex crimes against adults but not against children.

7.3.8 Concluding Thoughts on Empirical Evidence on the Effects of SORN Laws

In this section, we have sought to summarize and integrate the empirical evidence on the effects of SORN laws on objective measures of sexual offending: either incident report data (usually multistate federal data such as UCR or NIBRS) or data coming from criminal history records at the state level (and in a few cases – e.g., Agan (2011) – from federal sources). Many researchers from different academic fields have deployed many empirical tools and sources of data from different jurisdictions for many years. And, at least with respect to community notification's potential effects on recidivism, researchers have arrived at a consensus.

In a nutshell, while there is some tentative evidence that registration alone might reduce sex offense recidivism, there is almost no evidence that notification laws (of various sorts: online registries, active notification, etc.) reduce recidivism, despite many attempts to find support for the proposition. The one potential exception may be narrowly defined notification laws that operate only on high-risk registrants (for example, the top decile). Instead, in alignment with reentry theory and research more generally, the data indicate that the common and acute burdens of SORN regimes increase recidivism by exacerbating criminogenic risk factors and by reducing the comparative harshness of reconviction and incarceration. Notification may deter potential first-time offenders; becoming a "known sex offender" these days is tantamount to entering a pariah caste. But this ancillary upside is cold comfort: using notification to regulate those who are not deterred in the first place is costly, onerous, and may make potential recidivists more dangerous.

Sex offender registration and notification laws also influence behavior beyond simply increasing or decreasing sex offense frequencies. They likely alter how, where, and against whom registrants and nonregistrants commit crimes. There is less work in this area, but extant evidence clarifies the importance of these distributional ramifications. And because these findings cohere with the basic findings on SORN frequency effects, they are a basic robustness check on the idea that, for instance, registration alone — but not notification — reduces recidivism in the way SORN proponents expect. Finally, FTR research shows, somewhat surprisingly, that FTR has little association with sex offense recidivism. Failure-to-register may be better characterized as a signal of general criminal tendencies or perhaps the common disorganized life conditions experienced by registrants. In any event, it does not mesh well with the all-too-common assumption that those who do not comply with SORN laws are necessarily incorrigible rapists or child molesters.

7.4 REGISTRANT BELIEFS ABOUT THE EFFECTS OF SORN LAWS

Another plausible way to explore whether SORN laws influence criminal behavior (and specifically recidivism) is to ask registrants directly for their views on this question. A fairly large literature taking this approach now exists, but the findings that emerge from this body of work are mixed. They are also subject to respondents' various cognitive and self-serving biases, and they often reflect inconsistencies even within the same study, undercutting their utility. In the end, however, such beliefs can affect behavior and may provide a lens through which we can better understand the research laid out in this chapter.

Perhaps surprisingly, a number of these studies document that at least some registrants believe that SORN laws can encourage offender desistence and enhance public safety. In an important sense, however, this apparent concession is fairly predictable. A large fraction of registrants reject the label "sex offender" as inappropriate when it is applied to them (ten Bensel and Sample, 2017), perhaps especially when they consider themselves wrongly convicted, not dangerous, or not "really" a sex offender (Tewksbury and Lees, 2007). Individuals convicted of sex offenses are also members of society and potential victims – and they harbor the same illusory "stranger danger" angst causing a panic response in the general public.

Accordingly, registrant beliefs may mirror common (and often unfounded) societal opinions and fears about (other) people convicted of sex offenses. Indeed, registrants, like others, may view helpful aspects of SORN laws in isolation – that is, from a static perspective, ignoring the fact that SORN may also exacerbate recidivism risk factors (Prescott, 2016). In fact, the data provide good reason to believe that registrants might be evaluating the wrong counterfactual when considering the benefits of SORN: The minority of registrants with positive views about SORN's potential to reduce recidivism also appear to express strongly held and pervasive beliefs that SORN laws are unfair (e.g., Lasher and McGrath, 2012) and produce serious collateral consequences, including unemployment and financial difficulties, housing instability, loneliness, and stigmatization (e.g., Levenson and

Cotter, 2005). Both have been shown to lead to greater recidivism risk.[41] Thus, even if many registrants were to believe that SORN laws can be helpful *given* existing levels of registrant unemployment, poverty, homelessness, and isolation, the research does not tell us whether these public safety upsides in the eyes of registrants entirely offset the significant criminogenic consequences of SORN laws.

The foregoing notwithstanding, in what follows, we summarize the corpus of research on registrant views of the relationship between SORN laws and public safety. Because no work to our knowledge explores registrant beliefs about the possible deterrence impact of SORN laws on first-time offenses or geographic or victim-type offense patterns, we concentrate on whether registrants believe SORN laws reduce recidivism risk, either their own or that of registrants generally. We do not describe the very large literature on the negative collateral consequences of SORN laws – much of which also builds on survey and interview data – nor related views about whether SORN laws are "fair."

Researchers in this domain use either survey or interview methods. All subjects are registrants (or individuals convicted of a sex offense), but they vary along many demographic dimensions (age, race, type of crime, treatment status, etc.). Moreover, some subjects are in open communities while others are receiving residential treatment (and are thus less familiar with how SORN laws work "on the outside"). We mostly take the work on its own methodological terms, despite the fact that most analysis samples are neither random, nor representative, nor large, and virtually all have low response and participation rates. Some jurisdictions figure repeatedly in these studies, and some survey questions also appear repeatedly, as researchers build on previous work. We also put to one side the set of self-serving biases that can lead respondents to downplay the magnitude of their own criminal histories and that cause some of them to consider only whether SORN laws will reduce recidivism for "real" sex offenders (i.e., not them).

* * *

Zevitz and Farkas (2000) present some of the earliest work on registrant beliefs about the public safety consequences of SORN laws. Using interview data from thirty registrants from Wisconsin, the authors find that "[o]nly a few" subjects thought community notification was likely to "prevent reoffending" (p. 387). While two respondents in the study indicated that they felt that full disclosure made their treatment more effective, more viewed notification as counterproductive, likely to "drive many back to prison" (p. 388).[42]

---

[41] In our model, the burdens imposed by SORN laws on registrants (i.e., reducing u_i) are likely to increase recidivism all else equal, and procedural justice theories imply that compliance and law-abiding behavior turn significantly on whether SORN laws as they are applied are considered fair and appropriate by the registrant (Tewksbury and Lees 2007). Many chapters in this volume touch on these issues.

[42] Elborgan, Patry, and Scalora (2003) survey forty registrants receiving residential treatment in Nebraska. Their sample is atypical – 48 percent of the participants were unfamiliar with notification and how it would work. Their offenses were serious, and it is unclear how many, if any, had lived under notification requirements. With these important caveats in mind, the authors find that a majority of participants (72 percent) viewed notification laws as providing them with an incentive

Tewksbury (2004) surveys forty female registrants in Indiana and Kentucky, asking them both about SORN's collateral consequences and notification's potential effect on their likelihood of re-offending. While "nearly two-thirds" of respondents agreed that community notification made it "less likely" that they would commit another sex offense, even more felt ashamed and "unfairly punished" by being listed on a registry. When respondents were asked whether the registry was a "good thing," responses averaged to 6.45 on a scale from 1 (strongly disagree) to 10 (strongly agree). They also claimed to "understand" why society wants registries. Tewksbury (2005) surveys 121 registrants in Kentucky, mostly men, with similar questions. He finds a more mixed reaction from these male registrants on whether notification is a good thing (5.75 on a 1–10 scale) and on whether SORN would reduce their likelihood of recidivating (5.60), with 37.9 percent completely disagreeing and 43.2 percent completely agreeing. In concluding, Tewksbury (2004) intimates that the serious collateral consequences reported are more likely to result in higher recidivism notwithstanding some of the positive reactions to notification.

Levenson and Cotter (2005) is typically cited for the proposition that SORN laws produce very serious collateral consequences for registrants, but the study also directly analyzes registrants' beliefs about the effects of notification on registrant behavior. Using survey data from a nonrandom sample of 183 registrants in Florida, Levenson and Cotter find that 36 percent of respondents attested to being more willing to "manage [their] risk factors" because they know their "neighbors are watching," 66 percent reported being "more motivated to prevent reoffense" to prove they are not "a bad person," and 22 percent indicated a belief that registration and notification help them "prevent reoffending." In addition, 26 percent reported that they have less access to victims because they are known sex offenders, and 32 percent agreed that "communities are safer when they know where sex offenders live."[43] As a point of comparison, however, these respondents simultaneously revealed significantly stronger beliefs in the criminogenic consequences of notification, including 71 percent agreeing that SORN interferes with recovery by "causing more stress," 72 percent reporting "less hope for the future," and 49 percent admitting feelings of hopelessness, ominously agreeing to the statement "[no] one believes

---

not to re-offend (an opinion that was correlated with their viewing the laws as relatively fair). A significant percentage also felt notification had a positive impact on their willingness and motivation for treatment, although the study also revealed many negative assessments of notification, including its many unfair requirements and the embarrassment resulting from being publicly listed.

[43] Interestingly, family members appear less likely to agree with this last estimate. In Levenson and Tewksbury (2009), which studies a nonrandom national sample of family members of registrants using an online survey, only 9 percent of family members agreed with the statement "communities are safer when they know where registrants live." Somewhat similarly, Burchfield and Mingus (2008), in a small interview study ($n = 23$), report that two (or "a few" – thus, roughly 10 percent) of their subjects indicated positive effects of notification publicity, including "public safety and awareness, as well as incentive for the registrants themselves to be accountable for their behavior" (p. 366).

I can change so why even try?" A number of other studies have subsequently replicated these qualitative findings with other samples in other states.[44]

Tewksbury and Lees (2007) catalog registrant perceptions of SORN's ability to "enhance community awareness and promote public safety" using interview data from twenty-two Kentucky registrants (p. 380), including their views on how to improve registration and notification. The authors conclude that many registrants view registries positively in the abstract (i.e., leaving themselves out of the picture), noting that, by their lights, a properly designed registry "makes sense" (p. 392). However, registrants offer "mixed views" on whether community members can use the information effectively (e.g., because there might be too many registrants on registries) and are of "varying mind-sets" on whether notification is likely to reduce recidivism risk (p. 392). Specifically, Tewksbury and Lees conclude that only a "minority" of registrants in their data indicated that registries as currently constructed are able to reduce recidivism (p. 402).

Brannon, Levenson, Fortney, and Baker (2007) surveyed 125 registrants in outpatient treatment in Florida and compare their responses to those of 193 nonregistrants (i.e., the public). Registrant respondents were four times as likely as the public to view community notification as ineffective in reducing the number of sex offenses (41.6 percent v. 10.4 percent). Moreover, 70 percent of registrants viewed notification laws as somewhat unfair or unfair (relative to 22 percent of the public). Although these results establish that at least some registrants believe community notification

---

[44] Levenson, D'Amora, and Hern (2007) replicate this survey using 239 registrants in treatment programs in Connecticut and Indiana. While their numbers are not identical to those in Levenson and Cotter (2005), the qualitative results about both the positive and negative recidivism-related effects of SORN are very similar (both in magnitude and in the order of relative agreement across the relevant survey statements). With respect to respondent views about whether SORN laws help them to "prevent reoffending," the estimate is identical, with 22 percent of the sample agreeing or strongly agreeing with this statement. Mercado, Alvarez, and Levenson (2008) use a modified version of the Levenson and Cotter (2005) survey instrument to study 138 community registrants in New Jersey. The results of this study are not reported in a way that makes them directly comparable to the earlier studies, but the substance of the results appears similar, with the authors interpreting the data as showing that respondents "clearly disagreed with the notion that notification helped them prevent reoffending" (p. 196). Of course, not every respondent strongly disagreed with the idea that community notification can be effective. McGrath, Cumming and Lasher (2009) also use the Levenson and Cotter (2005) instrument to explore the views of 515 adult males in treatment programs in Vermont, some surveyed in 2004 shortly before internet notification began and some in 2008. Again, the results track with earlier studies, with a few exceptions, and with SORN laws generally faring better in the eyes of registrants. Importantly, roughly 34 percent (v. 22 percent) viewed notification as helping them avoid re-offending, higher than in earlier studies, although this was a group of respondents in treatment in a small, relatively liberal state. The implementation of online notification does not change registrant beliefs all that much (perhaps because less than a quarter of respondents were listed online in 2008), although it does seem to improve a respondent's reported motivation to prevent re-offense so as to "prove to others" that they are "not a bad person." Lasher and McGrath (2012) compare and contrast the results of these studies (see table 4, p. 17) and conclude that "[a]bout one third (37 percent) of all participants agreed that communities were safer when they know where registrants live and almost three quarters (74 percent) opined that community notification made them more motivated to prevent themselves from re-offending [to prove others wrong]" (p. 20).

has public safety benefits, the survey question appears to refer to SORN effectiveness with respect to sexual re-offending of registrants generally. In other words, this objective phrasing seems likely to be taken to refer to the probable response of "other" registrants and not to the respondents' views of SORN effects on their own likelihood of re-offending.

Ackerman and Sacks (2012) sent surveys to a large number ($n = 3,506$) of registrants in Nebraska, Montana, and Kansas, and they use their sample ($n = 246$; response rate = 7 percent) to relate the "strain" registrants experience from being subject to SORN laws to self-reported recidivism.[45] While they do not explicitly address registrants' views on whether SORN is likely to reduce recidivism, they do so indirectly by connecting registrants' subjective views of how much they are affected by SORN to whether they self-reported having returned to crime. The authors find that SORN-associated strain is positively linked to sex offense recidivism (albeit weakly in some models), consistent with the idea that SORN laws reduce u_i – that is, SORN exacerbates risk factors and/or reduces the deterrence effects of criminal law. They also report that SORN-caused collateral consequences are correlated with general recidivism, including violent and drug crimes. Ackerman, Sacks, and Osier (2013) examine sixty-six unsolicited responses/ comments received from this same survey, analyzing any proffered respondent statements on SORN ineffectiveness. The authors report that "most offenders state emphatically that it is ineffective" (p. 36), although their reported data (Table 3) better support a later conclusion: "[h]alf of the participants acknowledge that registration does not work in its current form" (p. 39). Respondent opinions seem to indicate a view that registration *could* work if it were implemented differently (e.g., made available only to law enforcement or if it included only high-risk or repeat offenders), but at least some respondents argue that it only works "in theory not in practice" (p. 39) and that registration is more likely to generate crime than to deter it.

Bowen, Frenzel, and Spraitz (2016) analyze 286 surveys from registrants in Pennsylvania, Texas, and Wisconsin, asking them whether they were less likely to commit another sex offense "because of the registry." On a scale from 1 to 10, respondents on average reported 5.26. The authors do not indicate the distribution of answers to this question nor whether responses were symmetrical around the mean, which matters for interpretation. For example, a mean of 5.26 is consistent with roughly 15 percent responding 1 (disagree strongly) and 85 percent responding 6 (agree slightly) but also with roughly 20 percent responding 10 (agree strongly) and 80 percent responding 4 (disagree slightly). At a minimum, however, a nontrivial share of respondents agreed with the idea that the registry was helpful to them in

---

[45] The authors define "strain" as "the removal of positive stimuli, the imposition of negative stimuli, or the failure to achieve personal goals" (p. 189). They proxy for SORN-related strain by creating a 25-item additive variable with each item linked to a known collateral consequence of SORN laws (e.g., "I have lost a job" and "I have been threatened or harried by neighbors"). In other words, the strain variable seeks to capture the burden of registration and notification – that is, "negative experiences they endured after inclusion on the sex offender registry" (p. 189).

reducing their likelihood of recidivating. To better understand this finding, the authors also examine whether registrant experiences under SORN were associated with their view of SORN effectiveness. Consistent with our model, they find that (1) never being contacted by the police (less monitoring – i.e., lower p_{ijl}) and (2) having a family member suffer negative consequences as a result of their registrant status (exacerbated recidivism risk factors – i.e., lower u_i) are associated with less agreement with the notion that SORN reduces recidivism.

Cooley, Moore, and Sample (2017) study seventy-seven registrants (who averaged 8.2 years out of correctional control with no self-reported re-offending) using informal conversational interviewing techniques. With respect to the act of registering (and other compliance-related obligations), the authors state that "registrants noted that SORN was more of an inconvenience; however, those with predatory contact offenses appreciated registration because it reminded them that they have a problem they need to control" (p. 148). Also, "[r]espondents' comments infer the registry did not deter their behavior and does not play a role in their desistance, yet almost all of them (73 percent) mentioned how they recognize its value for perceptions of public safety, regardless of its inconveniences or inapplicability to them being a threat" (p. 148). Finally, focusing on notification, the authors report that "[n]o participants suggested that public notification deterred them from reoffending" (p. 149) whereas "[f]ifty-one percent of participants suggested notification created stress and strain among registrants and their family members in a way that may inhibit the desistence process" (p. 150). Cooley, Moore, and Sample's work indicates that registration and notification may have different – even offsetting – effects on recidivism, consistent with the evidence in Section 7.3.[46]

* * *

In our view, the evidence we assemble in this section complements the research we catalog in Section 7.2. There are tensions between the two sections, but we believe a consistent empirical story knits them together – one largely critical of SORN

---

[46] All of this work suggests that registration alone may be relatively more effective than community notification at inhibiting re-offending. Relevant to this possibility, Murphy and Federoff (2013) use open-ended questionnaires to study thirty registrants in Canada – where registration is non-public. Apparently, 9 (39 percent of the 23 who responded) felt that the registry "acted as a deterrent to reoffending" (p. 244). Perhaps more importantly, because of its significantly reduced burden, registration alone may not increase recidivism risk levels. Roughly two-thirds of the participants indicated that being privately registered "has little or no impact on their ability to successfully reintegrate into the community" (p. 244). This somewhat unusual sentiment may be the result of the applicable registration process being comparatively easy to navigate – just a yearly check-in that registrants analogized to updating their driver's license. On the other hand, looking to Australia, Seidler (2010) finds that registrants do not believe registration alone is effective at reducing re-offense rates. Seidler interviewed registrants in New South Wales (which employed a non-public registry at the time of the study), orienting in part around the question: "Do you think the register is helpful or unhelpful in assisting you to manage your risk?" (p. 67). Seidler concludes that registrants view private registration as merely window dressing designed to satisfy the public, unlikely to deter anyone from re-offending and just another form of punishment. However, the author acknowledges that some registrants indicated that they "might think twice" before re-offending (p. 74).

legislation. The fundamental tension is that the large body of research finding no support for the idea that notification reduces registrant recidivism is at odds with the minority of registrants who claim to believe that SORN has some positive effect on reducing recidivism. Surely part of this assessment stems from registrants being people like everyone else who find the conventional wisdom about SORN laws convincing about *other* sex offenders, but even when they speak of effects on their own behavior, not all registrants view SORN laws entirely negatively.

One plausible answer to this contradiction springs from the apparent internal inconsistencies of registrant views contained within the belief studies. For example, registrants report feeling more motivated to avoid re-offending by SORN monitoring but also much more stressed, isolated, and hopeless. These registrant responses reveal the basic trade-off inherent in attempting to use community notification to reduce sex offense recidivism: while notification probably at least minimally improves monitoring and victim precaution-taking (making it at least not any easier for a registrant to re-offend without getting caught), the negative effects of notification (i.e., the significant economic, psychological, and social burdens, etc.) may render registrants much less capable of resisting any of the many pressures impelling them toward re-offending, including the possibility that the well-documented difficulties notification creates for registrants' lives "on the outside" simply cause them to care much less about the prospect of returning to prison if they are caught and convicted for a subsequent crime.

If the latter effects outweigh the former, we should expect SORN laws (or at least community notification) to result in more recidivism on average, not less. Thus, even if registrants acknowledge that SORN laws offer them something beneficial, it is another thing altogether to claim that notification's positive aspects more than offset its criminogenic features. We have reviewed the empirical research on the net effects of notification on criminal behavior at length, but in this chapter we do not review the very large literature on SORN's negative collateral consequences – nor the emerging evidence on the limited practical usefulness of providing notification information to potential victims. We hope it suffices to say that what we know about both topics may well identify the key mechanisms accounting for SORN's failure.[47]

7.5 CONCLUSION

This chapter has sought to summarize and carefully review the existing empirical evidence evaluating SORN's effects on criminal behavior, broadly construed. The

---

[47] A few of the studies that document the criminogenic collateral consequences of community notification in particular include Ackerman and Sacks (2012), Bailey and Klein (2018), Bowen et al. (2014), Burchfield and Mingus (2008, 2014), Hanson and Morton-Bourgon (2005), Jeglic, Mercado, and Levenson (2012), Kilmer and Leon (2017), Klein, Tolson, and Collins (2014), Lasher and McGrath (2012), Levenson and Cotter (2005), Levenson, D'Amora, and Hern (2007), Mustaine and Tewksbury (2011), Mustaine, Tewksbury, and Stengel (2006), Robbers (2009), Socia, Levenson, Ackerman, and Harris (2015), Terry (2015), Tewksbury, Mustaine, and Rolfe (2016), Tewksbury and Lees (2007), and Tewksbury and Zgoba (2010).

accumulated evidence largely rejects the claim that SORN laws have achieved their goal of increasing public safety. This is particularly the case with the most controversial aspect of SORN laws – community notification. The jury is still out on whether notification laws deter first-time offenses by nonregistered individuals. But there is virtually no evidence that notification successfully reduces recidivism among actual registrants, the main target population, and it may increase re-offending by dramatically aggravating recognized recidivism risk factors and reducing the deterrence value of criminal punishment. Unfortunately, we know comparatively less about the effects of registration, standing alone, which may offer a plausible alternative to community notification: there is no evidence to indicate that registration deters first-time sex offenses, but it may reduce registrant recidivism by increasing actual or felt law enforcement monitoring.

Taking a broader view, the notion that government could noticeably reduce the frequency of sex offense victimization by publicly identifying individuals with any history of sex crime has always rested on shaky ground, at least here in the United States. At least 90 percent of arrests for sex offenses, if not significantly more, involve individuals who have never previously been arrested for (much less convicted of) a sex crime (Sandler, Freeman, and Socia, 2008; Levenson and Zgoba, 2016). We also know that the vast majority of sex offenses are committed by persons familiar to their victims (Prescott and Rockoff, 2011), an empirical reality that undercuts the foundational "stranger danger" premise of notification itself.

At the same time, same-crime recidivism rates for people previously convicted of sex offenses are relatively low, around 5–10 percent for those released from state prison (Langan, Schmitt, and Durose, 2003; Alper and Durose, 2019) – that is, the potential registrants who are presumably at the highest risk of re-offending. Sex offenses as a class do not appear to be driven by a small number of repeat offenders. Thus, the margin for potential improvement has always been small, and any detectable change in the sex offense rate would require a very large behavioral response from a group that already has a relatively low recidivism rate. In retrospect, it thus may not be surprising that there is little evidence that community notification reduces overall sex offense frequency – or even the likelihood of registrant recidivism (fewer than 10 percent of registrants were likely to re-offend in any event). Given that notification significantly increases recidivism risk factors even for those registrants who otherwise would have never re-offended, evidence of *increases* in recidivism risk is perhaps only slightly more surprising.

The evidence tells us, therefore, that policy makers would be wiser to focus their efforts on preventing first-time sex offenses. Importantly, the model we use to organize the potential consequences of SORN laws clarifies that registration and notification *may* impact nonregistrant behavior as well – that is, they might theoretically aid in reducing the number of first-time offenses. In line with this possibility, our summary demonstrates that there is at least some credible evidence that notification (but not registration on its own) can deter first-time offenses.

Unfortunately, the legal basis for applying SORN laws to individuals retroactively has always been their nonpunitive, regulatory character. The designation of SORN laws as civil and regulatory in nature, which frees the laws from many constitutional constraints that limit law enforcement prerogatives in the criminal domain, has relied critically on SORN laws' ostensible purpose of protecting the public by reducing individual registrants' likelihood of re-offending. Thus, the idea of explicitly justifying SORN as a punishment designed to deter first-time potential offenders presents obvious concerns. Distinguishing the burdens imposed by SORN laws from criminal punishment under the Constitution may become increasingly unworkable in any event, as it has become clear that SORN laws fail to prevent recidivism while nevertheless systematically imposing draconian burdens and disabilities on registrants. In sum, the contents of this chapter raise significant doubts about the future viability of SORN laws as a public safety strategy.

REFERENCES

Ackerman, A. R. & Sacks, M. (2012). Can General Strain Theory be Used to Explain Recidivism among Registered Sex Offenders? *Journal of Criminal Justice, 40*, 187–193.

Ackerman, A. R., Sacks M., & Greenberg, D. F. (2012). Legislation Targeting Sex Offenders: Are Recent Policies Effective in Reducing Rape? *Justice Quarterly, 29*(6), 858–885.

Ackerman, A. R., Sacks, M., & Osier, L. N. (2013). The Experiences of Registered Sex Offenders with Internet Offender Registries in Three States. *Journal of Offender Rehabilitation, 52*, 29–45. DOI: 10.1080/10509674.2012.720959.

Adkins G., Huff, D., & Stageberg, P. (2000). Iowa Sex Offender Registry and Recidivism. *Iowa Department of Human Rights Division of Criminal and Juvenile Justice Planning and Statistical Analysis Center,* 1–21. https://humanrights.iowa.gov/sites/default/files/media/SexOffenderReport%5B1%5D.pdf.

Agan, A. Y. (2011). Sex Offender Registries: Fear Without Function? *Journal of Law & Economics, 54*, 207–239.

Agan, A. Y. & Prescott, J.J. (2014). Sex Offender Law and the Geography of Victimization. *Journal of Empirical Legal Studies, 11*(4), 786–828.

Agan, A. & Prescott, J.J. (2015). Sex Offenses. *Encyclopedia of Law and Economics,* 1–15. DOI: 10.1007/978-1-4614-7883-6_579-1.

Alper, M. & Durose, M. R. (2019). Recidivism of Sex Offenders Released from State Prison: A 9 Year Follow-up (2005–14). Bureau of Justice Statistics: Special Report, U.S. Department of Justice. www.bjs.gov/content/pub/pdf/rsorsp9yfu0514.pdf.

Bailey, D. J. S. & Klein, J. L. (2018). Ashamed and Alone: Comparing Offender and Family Member Experiences with the Sex Offender Registry. *Criminal Justice Review, 43*(4), 440–457. DOI: 10.1177/0734016818756486.

Barnoski, R. (2005). Sex Offender Sentencing in Washington State: Has Community Notification Reduced Recidivism? *Washington State Institute for Public Policy.* www.wsipp.wa.gov/ReportFile/919/Wsipp_Has-Community-Notification-Reduced-Recidivism_Report.pdf.

Barnoski, R. (2006). Sex Offender Sentencing in Washington State: Failure to Register as a Sex Offender–Revised. *Washington State Institute for Public Policy.* www.wsipp.wa.gov/ReportFile/926/Wsipp_Failure-to-Register-as-a-Sex-Offender-Revised_Report.pdf.

Barr, R. & Pease, K. (1990). Crime Placement, Displacement, and Deflection. *Crime and Justice.* 12, 277–318.

ten Bensel, T. & Sample, L. L. (2017). The Influence of Sex Offender Registration and Notification Laws on Fostering Collective Identity among Offenders. *Journal of Crime and Justice,* 40(4), 497–511. DOI: 10.1080/0735648X.2015.1131184.

Bernasco, W. (2010). A Sentimental Journey to Crime: Effects of Residential History on Crime Location Choice. *American Society of Criminology,* 48(2), 389–416.

Bierie, D. M. & Detar, P. J. (2016). Geographic and Social Movement of Sex Offender Fugitives. *Crime & Delinquency,* 62(8), 983–1002. DOI: 10.1177/0011128714530658.

Bierie, D. M. & Budd, K. M. (2020). Registration and the Closure of Stranger-Perpetrated Sex Crimes Reported to Police. *Sexual Abuse.* https://doi.org/10.1177/1079063220931824.

Bouffard, J. A. & Askew, L. N. (2019). Time-Series Analyses of the Impact of Sex Offender Registration and Notification Law Implementation and Subsequent Modifications on Rates of Sexual Offenses. *Crime & Delinquency,* 1–30. DOI: 10.1177/0011128717722010.

Bowen, K., Frenzel, E., & Spraitz, J. D. (2016). Sex Offender Registration and Notification Laws: Thoughts from Registered Sex Offenders in Three States. *Safer Communities,* 15(2), 94–109. DOI: 10.1108/SC-12-2015-0040.

Brannon, Y., Levenson, J., Fortney, T., & Baker, J. (2007). Attitudes about Community Notification: A Comparison of Sexual Offenders and the Non-Offending Public. *Sexual Abuse: A Journal of Research and Treatment,* 19(4), 369–379.

Burchfield, K. B. & Mingus, W. (2008). Not in My Neighborhood: Assessing Registered Sex Offenders' Experiences with Local Social Capital and Social Control. *Criminal Justice and Behavior,* 35 (3), 356–374. DOI: 10.1177/0093854807311375.

Burchfield, K. & Mingus, W. (2014). Sex Offender Reintegration: Consequences of the Local Neighborhood Context. *American Journal of Criminal Justice,* 39, 109–124. DOI: 10.1007/s12103-012-9195-x.

Bureau of Justice Statistics (2018). Number of Rape/Sexual Assaults by Victim-Offender Relationship and Reporting to the Police, 2001–2018. Generated using the NCVS Victimization Analysis Tool (NVAT), www.bjs.gov.

Canter, D. V. (1996). The Environmental Range of Serial Rapists. *Psychology in Action,* 13(1), 217–230.

Carr, J. B. (2019). The effect of sex offender registries on recidivism: Evidence from a natural experiment. *Department of Economics, Purdue University,* 1–37.

Cooley, B. E., Moore, S. E., & Sample, L. L. (2017). The Role of Formal Social Control Mechanisms in Deterring Sex Offending as Part of the Desistance Process. *Criminal Justice Studies,* 30(2), 136–157. http://dx.doi.org/10.1080/1478601X.2017.1299335.

Durlauf, S. & Nagin, D. (2011). Imprisonment and Crime: Can Both be Reduced? *Criminology Public Policy,* 10(1), 13–54.

Duwe, G. & Donnay, W. (2008). The Impact of Megan's Law on Sex Offender Recidivism: The Minnesota Experience. *Criminology,* 46(2), 411–446.

Duwe, G. & Donnay, W. (2010). The Effects of Failure to Register on Sex Offender Recidivism. *Criminal Justice and Behavior,* 37(5), 520–536. DOI: 10.1177/0093854810364106.

Elborgan, E. B., Patry, M., & Scalora, M. J. (2003). The Impact of Community Notification Laws on Sex Offender Treatment Attitudes. *International Journal of Law and Psychiatry,* 26, 207–219.

Freeman, N. J. (2012). The Public Safety Impact of Community Notification Laws: Rearrest of Convicted Sex Offenders. *Crime & Delinquency,* 58(4), 539–564.

Freeman, N. J. & Sandler, J. C. (2010). The Adam Walsh Act: A False Sense of Security of an Effective Public Policy Initiative? *Criminal Justice Policy Review,* 21(1), 31–49.

Hanson, R. K. & Morton-Bourgon, K. E. (2005). The Characteristics of Persistent Sexual Offenders: A Meta-Analysis of Recidivism Studies. *Journal of Counseling and Clinical Psychology*, 73(6), 1154–1163. DOI: 10.1037/0022-006X.73.6.1154.

Jeglic, E. L., Mercado, C. C., & Levenson, J. S. (2012). The Prevalence and Correlates of Depression and Hopelessness among Sex Offenders Subject to Community Notification and Residence Restriction Legislation. *American Journal of Criminal Justice*, 37, 46–59. DOI: 10.1007/s12103-010-9096-9.

Kernsmith, P. D., Comartin, E., Craun, S. W., & Kernsmith, R. M. (2009). The Relationship between Sex Offender Registry Utilization and Awareness. *Sexual Abuse*, 21(2), 181–193.

Kilmer, A. & Leon, C. S. (2017). "Nobody Worries About Our Children": Unseen Impacts of Sex Offender Registration on Families with School-Age Children and Implications for Desistance. *Criminal Justice Studies*, 30(2), 181–201. http://dx.doi.org/10.1080/1478601X .2017.1299852.

Klein, J. L., Tolson, D., & Collins, C. (2014). Lamenting the List: A Partial Test of Sherman's Defiance Theory as Applied to Female Sex Offenders. *Contemporary Justice Review*, 17(3), 326–345. https://doi.org/10.1080/10282580.2014.944798.

Langan, P. A., Schmitt, E. L., & Durose, M. R. (2003). Recidivism of Sex Offenders Released from Prison in 1994. Washington, DC: U.S. *U.S. Department of Justice Office of Justice Programs Bureau of Justice Statistics*.

Lasher, M. P. & McGrath, R. J. (2012). The Impact of Community Notification on Sex Offender Reintegration: A Quantitative Review of the Research Literature. *International Journal of Offender Therapy and Comparative Criminology*, 56(1), 6–28. DOI: 0.1177/0306624X10387524.

Letourneau, E. J. & Armstrong, K. S. (2008). Recidivism Rates for Registered and Nonregistered Juvenile Sexual Offenders. *Sexual Abuse*, 20(4), 393–408.

Letourneau, E. J., Armstrong, K. S., Bandyopadhyay, D., & Sinha, D. (2012). Sex Offender Registration and Notification Policy Increases Juvenile Plea Bargains. *Sexual Abuse*, 25(2), 189–207. DOI: 10.1177/1079063212455667.

Letourneau, E. J., Bandyopadhyay, D., Armstrong, K. S., & Sinha, D. (2010). Do Sex Offender Registration and Notification Requirements Deter Juvenile Sex Crimes? *Criminal Justice and Behavior*, 37(5), 553–569. DOI: 10.1177/0093854810363562.

Letourneau, E. J., Levenson, J. S., Bandyopadhyay, D., Armstrong, K., & Sinha, D. (2010). Effects of South Carolina's Sex Offender Registration and Notification Policy on Deterrence of Adult Sex Crimes. *Criminal Justice and Behavior*, 37(5), 435–458.

Letourneau, E. J., Levenson, J. S., Bandyopadhyay, D., Sinha, D., & Armstrong, K. S. (2010). Effects of South Carolina's Sex Offender Registration and Notification Policy on Adult Recidivism. *Criminal Justice Policy Review*, 21(4), 435–458. DOI: 10.1177/0887403409353148.

Letourneau, E. J., Shields, R. T., Nair, R., Kahn, G., Sandler, J. C., & Vandiver, D. M. (2018). Juvenile Registration and Notification Policies Fail to Prevent First-Time Sexual Offenses: An Extension of Findings to Two New States. *Criminal Justice Policy Review*, 1–15. DOI: 10.1177/0887403418786783.

Levenson, J. S. & Cotter, L. P. (2005). The Effect of Megan's Law on Sex Offender Reintegration. *Journal of Contemporary Criminal Justice*, 21(1), 49–66. DOI: 10.1177/ 1043986204271676.

Levenson, J. S., D'Amora, D. A., & Hern, A. L. (2007). Megan's Law and Its Impact on Community Re-Entry for Sex Offenders. *Behavioral Sciences Law*, 25(4), 587–602. DOI: 10.1002/bsl.770.

Levenson J. S., Letourneau, E. J., Armstrong, K., & Zgoba, K. M. (2010). Failure to Register as a Sex Offender: Is it Associated with Recidivism? *Justice Quarterly*, 27(3), 305–331. DOI: 10.1080/07418820902972399.

Levenson, J. S., Sandler, J. C., & Freeman, N. J. (2012). Failure-to-Register Laws and Public Safety: An Examination of Risk Factors and Sex Offense Recidivism. *Law and Human Behavior*, 36(6), 555–565. DOI: 10.1037/b0000002.

Levenson, J. S. & Tewksbury, R. (2009). Collateral Damage: Members of Registered Sex Offenders. *American Journal of Criminal Justice*, 34, 54–68. DOI: 10.1007/s12103-008-9055-x.

Levenson, J. S. & Zgoba, K. M. (2016). Community Protection Policies and Repeat Sexual Offenses in Florida. *International Journal of Offender Therapy and Comparative Criminology*, 60(1), 1140–1158. DOI: 10.1177/0306624X15573946.

Linden, L. & Rockoff, J. E. (2008). Estimates of the Impact of Crime Risk on Property Values from Megan's Laws. *American Economic Review*, 98(3), 1103–1127. DOI: 10.1257/aer.98.3.1103.

Maddan, S. (2005). Sex Offenders as Outsiders: A Reexamination of the Labeling Perspective Utilizing Current Sex Offender Registration and Notification Policies. *University of Nebraska: Dissertation for the Degree of Doctor in Philosophy*. Omaha: Nebraska.

Maddan, S. (2008). The Labeling of Sex Offenders: The Unintended Consequences of the Best Intentioned Policies.

Maddan, S., Miller, J. M., Walker, J. T., & Marshall, I. H. (2011). Utilizing Criminal History Information to Explore the Effect of Community Notification on Sex Offender Recidivism. *Justice Quarterly*, 28(2), 303–324.

Maurelli, K. & Ronan, G. (2013). A Time-Series Analysis of the Effectiveness of Sex Offender Notification Laws in the USA. *Journal of Forensic Psychiatry & Psychology*, 24(1), 128–143.

McGrath, R. J., Cumming, G. F., & Lasher, M. P. (2009). Impact of Community Notification on Sex Offender Reintegration Before and After Passage of a Megan's Law. *Burlington: Vermont Center for the Prevention and Treatment of Sexual Abuse*. www.researchgate.net/publication/280023713_Impact_of_Community_Notification_on_Sex_Offender_Reintegration_in_Vermont_Before_and_After_Passage_of_a_Megan's_Law.

Mercado, C. C., Alvarez, S., & Levenson, J. (2008). The Impact of Specialized Sex Offender Legislation on Community Reentry. *Sexual Abuse*, 20(2), 188–205. DOI: 10.1177/1079063208317540.

Murphy, L. & Federoff J. P. (2013). Sexual Offenders' Views of Canadian Sex Offender Registries: A Survey of a Clinical Sample. *Canadian Journal of Behavioral Science*, 45(3), 238–249. DOI: 10.1037/a0033251.

Mustaine, E. E. & Tewksbury, R. (2011). Residential Relegation of Registered Sex Offenders. *American Journal of Criminal Justice*, 36, 44–57.

Mustaine, E. E., Tewksbury, R., & Stengel, K. M. (2006). Residential Location and Mobility of Registered Sex Offenders. *American Journal of Criminal Justice*, 30(2), 177–192.

Mustaine, E. E., Tewksbury, R., & Stengel, K. M. (2006). Social Disorganization and Residential Locations of Registered Sex Offenders: Is This a Collateral Consequence? *Deviant Behavior*, 27, 329–350. DOI: 10.1080/01639620600605606.

Nagin, D. S. (2013). Deterrence in the Twenty-First Century. *Crime and Justice*, 42(1), 199–263.

Park, J. H., Bandyopadhyay, D., & Letourneau E. (2014). Examining Deterrence of Adult Sex Crimes: A Semi-parametric Intervention Time Series Approach. *Computational Statistics & Data Analysis*, 69, 198–207. DOI: 10.1016/j.csda.2013.08.004. PMID: 24795489; PMCID: PMC4002981. https://pubmed.ncbi.nlm.nih.gov/24795489/.

Prescott, J.J. (2016). Portmanteau Ascendant: Post-Release Regulations and Sex Offender Recidivism. *Connecticut Law Review*, 48(4), 1035–1078.

Prescott, J.J. & Rockoff, J. E. (2011). Do Sex Offender Registration and Notification Laws Affect Criminal Behavior? *Journal of Law and Economics*, 54(1), 161–206.

Robbers, M. L. P. (2009). Lifers on the Outside: Sex Offenders and Disintegrative Shaming. *International Journal of Offender Therapy and Comparative Criminology*, 53(1), 5–28. DOI: 10.1177/0306624X07312953.

Salmon, T. M. (2010). Sex Offender Registry: Reliability Could Be Significantly Improved. Report of the Vermont State Auditor. Available at https://auditor.vermont.gov/sites/auditor/files/files/reports/performance-audits/Final_SOR_report.pdf.

Sandler, J. C., Freeman, N. J., & Socia, K. M. (2008). Does a Watched Pot Boil? A Time-Series Analysis of New York State's Sex Offender Registration and Notification Law. *Psychology, Public Policy, & Law*, 14(4), 284–302. DOI: 10.1037/a0013881.

Sandler, J. C., Letourneau, E. J., Vandiver, D. M., Shields, R. T., & Chaffin, M. (2017). Juvenile Sexual Crime Reporting Rates are Not Influenced by Juvenile Sex Offender Registration Policies. *Psychology, Public Policy, and Law*, 23(2), 131–40.

Schram, D. D. & Milloy, C. D. (1995). Community Notification: A Study of Offender Characteristics and Recidivism. *Urban Policy Research*, 1–30. www.wsipp.wa.gov/ReportFile/1208/Wsipp_Community-Notification-A-Study-of-Offender-Characteristics-and-Recidivism_Full-Report.pdf.

Seidler, K. (2010). Community Management of Sex Offenders: Stigma Versus Support. *Sexual Abuse in Australia and New Zealand*, 2(2), 66–76.

Socia, K. M., Levenson, J. S., Ackerman, A. R., & Harris, A. J. (2015). "Brothers under the Bridge": Factors Influencing the Transience of Registered Sex Offenders in Florida. *Sexual Abuse: A Journal of Research and Treatment*, 27(6), 559–586. DOI: 10.1177/1079063214521472.

Shao, L. & Li, J. (2006). The Effect of Sex Offender Registration Laws on Rape Victimization. Unpublished manuscript. University of Alabama, Department of Economics, Tuscaloosa.

Stucky, T. D. & Ottensmann, J. R. (2016). Registered Sex Offenders and Reported Sex Offenses. *Crime & Delinquency*, 62(8), 1026–1045. DOI: 10.1177/0011128714556738.

Terry, K. J. (2015). Sex Offender Laws in the United States: Smart Policy or Disproportionate Sanctions? *International Journal of Comparative and Applied Criminal Justice*, 39(2), 113–127. DOI: 10.1080/01924036.2014.973048.

Tewksbury, R. (2004). Experiences and Attitudes of Registered Female Sex Offenders. *Federal Probation: A Journal of Correctional Philosophy and Practice*, 68(3), 3–4, 9. www.uscourts.gov/sites/default/files/fed_probation_dec_2004.pdf.

Tewksbury, R. (2005). Collateral Consequences of Sex Offender Registration. *Journal of Contemporary Criminal Justice*, 21(1), 67–81. DOI: 10.1177/1043986204271704.

Tewksbury, R. & Jennings, W. G. (2010). Assessing the Impact of Sex Offender Registration and Community Notification on Sex-Offending Trajectories. *Criminal Justice and Behavior*, 37(5), 570–582. DOI: 10.1177/0093854810363570.

Tewksbury, R., Jennings, W. G., & Zgoba, K. M. (2012). A Longitudinal Examination of Sex Offender Recidivism Prior to and Following the Implementation of SORN. *Behavioral Sciences and the Law*, 30(3), 308–328. DOI: 10.1002/bsl.1009.

Tewksbury, R. & Lees, M. B. (2007). Perceptions of Punishment: How Registered Sex Offenders View Registries. *Crime & Delinquency*, 53(3), 380–407. DOI: 10.1177/0011128706286915.

Tewksbury, R., Mustaine, E. E., & Rolfe, S. (2016). Sex Offender Residential Mobility and Relegation: The Collateral Consequences Continue. *American Journal of Criminal Justice*, *41*, 852–866.

Tewksbury, R. & Zgoba, K. M. (2010). Perceptions and Coping with Punishment: How Registered Sex Offenders Respond to Stress, Internet Restrictions, and the Collateral Consequences of Registration. *International Journal of Offender Therapy and Comparative Criminology*, 54(4), 537–551. DOI: 10.1177/0306624X09339180.

Vasquez, B. E., Maddan, S., & Walker, J. T. (2008). The Influence of Sex Offender Registration and Notification Laws in the United States: A Time-Series Analysis. *Crime & Delinquency*, 54(2), 175–192.

Yeh, S. (2015). Revealing the Rapist Next Door: Property Impacts of a Sex Offender Registry. *International Review of Law and Economics*, *44*, 42–60.

Zevitz, R. G. (2006). Sex Offender Community Notification: Its Role in Recidivism and Offender Reintegration. *Criminal Justice Studies*, 19(2), 193–208.

Zevitz, R. G. & Farkas, M. A. (2000). Sex Offender Community Notification: Managing High Risk Criminal or Exacting Further Vengeance? *Behavioral Sciences and the Law*, *18*, 375–391.

Zgoba, K. M., Jennings, W. G., & Salerno, L. M. (2018). Megan's Law 20 Years Later: An Empirical Analysis and Policy Review. *Criminal Justice and Behavior*, 45(7), 1028–1046. DOI: 10.1177/0093854818771409.

Zgoba, K. M. & Levenson, J. S. (2012). Failure to Register as a Predictor of Sex Offense Recidivism: The Big Bad Wolf or a Red Herring? *Sexual Abuse, 24* (4), 328–349. doi:10.1177/1079063211421010.

Zgoba, K., Veysey, B. M., & Dalessandro, M. (2010). An Analysis of the Effectiveness of Community Notification and Registration: Do the Best Intentions Predict the Best Practices? *Justice Quarterly*, 27(5), 667–691. DOI: 10.1080/07418820903357673.

Zgoba, K., Witt, P., Dalessandro, M., & Veysey, B. (2008). Megan's Law: Assessing the Practical and Monetary Efficacy. *National Institute of Justice*, 1–44. www.ncjrs.gov/pdffiles1/nij/grants/225370.pdf.

8

Integrating the Etiology of Sexual Offending into Evidence-Based Policy and Practices

Jill S. Levenson

Chapter 8 examines the disconnect between the etiology of sexual offending and the mechanics of SORN laws. Using what is known about sexual
offending and the psychology of individuals who commit sex crimes, the
chapter argues that registration and notification (as well as residence
restrictions) are destined to be ineffective if not counterproductive. The
discussion begins with an overview of the diverse etiology of sexual offending. A range of biological, psychological, and social factors can account for
the commission of a sexual offense, and the specific set of causes behind an
individual's offending shape the recidivism risk they pose postconviction.
The chapter refutes many common assumptions underlying SORN laws.
First-time offenders who are well-known to their victims account for the
majority of sex offenses. This is out of step with the "stranger danger"
concept motivating SORN laws. Further, research establishes that recidivism risk diminishes over time and can be addressed through treatment.
Finally, the chapter shows how SORN laws may increase recidivism risk.
The stigmatization and isolation they produce, interacting with existing risk
factors, may undermine protective factors and interfere with treatment
gains. It argues that evidence-based, targeted laws would be more efficient
and effective than current SORN laws.

In order to formulate effective solutions to a problem, stakeholders must first recognize
the components of the problem and the factors that contribute to it. Understanding
the etiology of sexual offending can help inform sex offender registration and notification (SORN) laws and community supervision strategies. This chapter will first
summarize the etiological understanding of sexual offending behavior. Then, it will
examine the assumptions underlying SORN laws and why the laws are not effective in
reducing sexual offense recidivism, taking into account what is known about offense
motivations and patterns. Finally, the chapter will review how SORN laws may even
contribute to risk and include some recommendations for SORN policy and management practices based on what we know about offender risks, needs, and patterns, as
they pertain to individuals required to register as sex offenders.

    Pervasive misperceptions about sex offenders have fuelled the enactment of
contemporary criminal justice policies that treat people convicted of sex crimes

differently from other types of criminals. As seen in other chapters of this volume, there is much evidence to contradict common myths of stranger danger, high recidivism rates, and non-amenability to treatment. This chapter will explore our understanding of the etiology of sexually abusive behavior to lend insight into why these strongly held beliefs lead to misguided policies.

8.1 WHY DO PEOPLE COMMIT SEX CRIMES?

People commit sexual crimes for a variety of interacting reasons. Each offender's conduct is influenced by individualized permutations of these factors and their recidivism risk is in turn unique to the factors underlying their behavior. Publicly, however, sexual offenders are frequently regarded as a homogeneous group: motivated by singular forces and presenting monolithic risks. There is an assumption that most, if not all, are extremely dangerous, prone to re-offending, and beyond hope for rehabilitation. These beliefs are entrenched in public perception and thus community members are very much in favor of management policies such as SORN laws and residence restrictions (Anderson & Sample, 2008; A. J. Harris & Socia, 2014; Levenson, Brannon, Fortney, & Baker, 2007; Lieb & Nunlist, 2008; Mears, Mancini, Gertz, & Bratton, 2008).

Over the past twenty-five years, however, research shows that criminal sexual offending is motivated by a range of factors presenting a spectrum of risk (Grady, Levenson, & Bolder, 2016; Levenson, Willis, & Prescott, 2017; Marshall, 2010; Seto, 2008). Some abusers are motivated by sexually deviant interests, while others use sex to achieve power and control, and still others offend based on shockingly misguided efforts to connect intimately with others. There are also individuals who offend due to general criminality or antisocial attitudes, while others describe moments or episodes of poor judgment that led to unlawful sexual behaviors that are otherwise uncharacteristic of their typical conduct. Some sex offenses occur because a person has a paraphilic disorder such as pedophilia, or a problem with hypersexuality manifesting in sexualized coping strategies, sexual preoccupation, and an excessive sexual appetite that compromises judgment and decision-making. Though there is debate about the diagnoses of hebephilia (preferential attraction to pubescent young teens), hypersexuality, and paraphilic interest in coercive sex (Blanchard, 2013; Quinsey, 2010; Reid et al., 2012; Stephens, Seto, Goodwill, & Cantor, 2017), there is a clinical consensus that some individuals have atypical sexual interests that lead them to seek sexual contact in ways that are illegal and victimizing. In the next section, I review the research around these underlying factors influencing sex offender behavior.

8.1.1 *Pedophilia*

Pedophilic disorder is described by the Diagnostic and Statistical Manual of Mental Disorders, 5th Edition (DSM-5) as a sexual attraction to prepubescent (typically under age 13 years) children, manifested by a pattern of fantasies, urges, or behaviors that persists over a period of at least three months and causes clinically significant distress or impairment in social, occupational, or other important areas of functioning (American Psychiatric Association, 2013, p. 4). The attraction can be exclusive (attracted only to children) or not. Though more than 80 percent of registered sex offenders have minor victims, it is estimated that only about 40 percent would meet criteria for pedophilic disorder (Ackerman, Harris, Levenson, & Zgoba, 2011; Kingston, Firestone, Moulden, & Bradford, 2007; Levenson, Grady, & Leibowitz, 2016). Not all child molesters meet DSM criteria for pedophilic disorder, and not all people with pedophilia abuse children (Cantor & McPhail, 2016; Levenson, Grady, & Morin, 2019). Though debated in the literature and not listed in the DSM, there is evidence to suggest that some individuals have a "hebephilic" sexual interest in pubescent teens who are just developing secondary sex characteristics (e.g., emergence of pubic hair, breast buds) (Seto, 2008, p. 4; Stephens et al., 2017).

Scholars continue to speculate about the etiology of pedophilia, pointing to a complex interaction of biological, social, and psychological factors. From a biological point of view, there is evidence that for some people, pedophilia is a type of sexual orientation, biologically predetermined, and not likely to be altered (Cantor & McPhail, 2016; Seto, 2018, 2012). But physiological underpinnings also interact with the social environment in early life, creating an intersecting web of psychological and social influences contributing to the development of sexual interests. Though sexual abuse in childhood does not cause offending, it can be an experience that shapes sexuality as well as ability to have healthy interpersonal relationships (Levenson, Willis, et al., 2017). For example, for some individuals who were molested in childhood, subsequent sexually abusive behavior can provide compensation for feelings of powerlessness. Emotional congruence with children develops in some cases to protect against perceived social rejection by other adults (Finkelhor & Baron, 1986; Konrad, Kuhle, Amelung, & Beier, 2018). Also, social learning by which individuals model their own abuser's behavior and distorted thinking, or association of sexual arousal with adult-child sexual activity, can also impact development of sexually deviant interests and behavior (Seto, 2008).

8.1.2 *Paraphilic Coercion*

For some individuals, hostility toward women is revealed through sexual violence. Rape and sexual assault can be a way of obtaining power or control, usually against adult victims. Paraphilic coercion, though debated among scholars and not listed as a diagnosis in the DSM-5 (Quinsey, 2010), is a construct describing men with established preferences for sexual coercion over consensual sex. Previous editions of the DSM have rejected inclusion of paraphilic rape disorders for a variety of political concerns (Zander, 2008). Clinical and theoretical evidence suggest that a small group of men prefer nonconsensual sex and that this desire represents a pathological and deviant sexual interest (Kingston, 2016).

8.1.3 *Hypersexuality*

Another contributor to sexual behavior problems involves the vast volume, variety, availability, accessibility, and affordability of sexual material on the internet. Many people demonstrate excessive sexual appetite or behavior loosely based on models of "addiction" or "compulsion" in which they engage in sexual acts despite adverse consequences to self or others (Malamuth, 2014). For instance, people with hypersexuality might engage in repetitive infidelity, online pornography consumption, or become preoccupied with sex to a point of interference in their life. Hypersexuality can cross lines into unlawful or victimizing behaviors such as viewing or sharing of child pornography, engaging in sexual interactions with minors online, and exhibitionism or voyeurism using social media or other technology. Though consensus for the hypersexuality construct is controversial, therapists reveal an increase in requests for therapy services related to sexual self-regulation problems and related consequences (Reid et al., 2012). Hypersexual Disorder (HD), proposed in the DSM-5 appendix, provides a starting point for clinicians to be able to refine the conceptualization of harmfully excessive sexual behavior and the parameters by which it deviates from normative sexuality.

8.1.4 *Childhood Trauma*

Trauma-informed perspectives on sexual offending suggest that adverse childhood environments, characterized by various forms of abuse, neglect, and family dysfunction, can be a breeding ground for sexual offending (Levenson, Willis, et al., 2017; Reavis, Looman, Franco, & Rojas, 2013). Child abuse does not cause sex offending, and many abused children are resilient and do not grow up to engage in criminality. However, a lack of nurturing in childhood can lead to mistrust, hostility, and insecure attachment, which then contribute to social rejection, loneliness, negative peer associations, and delinquent behavior (Grady et al., 2016; Hanson & Morton-Bourgon, 2005). "The form of sexuality that develops in the context of pervasive intimacy deficits is likely to be impersonal and selfish, and may even be adversarial ... Attitudes allowing non-consenting sex can develop through the individual's effort to understand their own experiences and adopting the attitudes of their significant others (friends, family, abusers)" (Hanson et al., 2005, pp. 1154–55).

Witnessing violence in the childhood home can be a template for distorted power dynamics in relationships as well as inaccurate ideas about gender roles, male privilege, respect, and consent. For others, sex can become a coping mechanism used to self-medicate negative moods and painful emotions, taking on a compulsive quality and interfering with self-regulation and healthy decision-making. Sexually abusive behavior can be a maladaptive way of soothing distress and/or meeting needs for intimacy, affection, attention, power, or control. Of course, none of these theories should be construed as an excuse for assaultive behavior. It is important, however, to understand how interpersonal violence develops, so that we can inform our sexual abuse prevention and intervention strategies accordingly (Levenson, Willis, et al., 2017).

Research is clear that childhood adversity is more common in the histories of sex offenders than in the general population, and that it increases the risk for delinquent behavior in adolescence and adulthood (Levenson, Baglivio, et al., 2017; Levenson & Socia, 2015). Prospectively collected data from 1,539 children in the Chicago Longitudinal Study identified child maltreatment as a significant predictor of later criminal behavior (Mersky, Topitzes, & Reynolds, 2012). In addition, adverse child-hood experiences (ACEs) were exceedingly common among 64,000 juvenile delin-quents in Florida (Baglivio et al., 2014) and in a subsample of juveniles arrested for sex crimes (Levenson, Baglivio, et al., 2017). Among adult criminals, greater exposure to early trauma is significantly associated with mental health disorders, drug abuse, and serious crime (Harlow, 1999; Henry, 2020; Messina, Grella, Burdon, & Prendergast, 2007). Though some people exhibit resilience following adversity, traumagenic child-hood environments may be the most destructive for those with negative personality traits and limited intellectual or social resources, and impoverished socioeconomic conditions can further exacerbate problems (Patterson, DeBaryshe, & Ramsey, 1990).

Pathogenic parenting and deprived environments reinforce dysfunctional relational styles and maladaptive coping, contributing to psychosocial problems across the life-span (Patterson et al., 1990). Chronic toxic stress in childhood leads to an overproduc-tion of hormones associated with fight or flight responses, obstructing neural connections in the brain and hindering cognitive processing, executive functioning, and self-regulation capacities into adulthood (Alink, Cicchetti, Kim, & Rogosch, 2012; Creeden, 2009; Finkelhor & Kendall-Tackett, 1997; SAMHSA, 2014; Streeck-Fischer & van der Kolk, 2000; van der Kolk, 2006). Research has indicated that the multiplicity, frequency, and chronicity of childhood adversities create what has become known as complex trauma response, manifesting in maladaptive coping strategies, mental health symptoms, personality pathology, and relational problems (Cloitre et al., 2009; Herman, 1992, 1997; van der Kolk, 2014).

Attachment theory suggests a number of long-term negative effects resulting from troubled childhoods, including deficient relational skills, self-regulation problems, and psychopathology (Bowlby, 1977; Jovev & Jackson, 2004; Loper, Mahmoodzadegan, & Warren, 2008). Sexually abusive behaviors may have some roots in early attachment disruptions, and those affected might seek to satisfy unmet emotional needs and connections to others through sexual or aggressive means (Beech & Mitchell, 2005; Bushman, Baumeister, & Phillips, 2001; Grady et al., 2016; Hudson & Ward, 1997; Hudson, Ward, & McCormack, 1999; Levenson, Willis, et al., 2017; Smallbone & Dadds, 1998; Vondra, Shaw, Swearingen, Cohen, & Owens, 2001). Disorganized or disrupted attachments can contribute to aggression, sexualized coping, boundary violations, affect dysregulation, emotional congruence with children, pursuit of non-threatening others, or gender hostility.

These conditions contribute to the dynamic risk factors known to be associated with sex offense recidivism (Levenson, Willis, et al., 2017). These empirically supported criminogenic needs are sometimes known as the "central eight" (Andrews & Bonta, 2010): (1) antisocial attitudes; (2) antisocial behavior; (3) antisocial peers and associates; (4) antisocial personality and temperament; (5) family/marital stressors; (6) substance abuse; (7) lack of education, employment, stability, or achievement; and (8) lack of prosocial activities.

In summary, the etiology of sexual offending is a complex interaction of biological, psychological, and social factors. Motivations and factors facilitating sex offending can include any combination of paraphilic interests, hypersexuality, personality traits, and states like intoxication that lower inhibitions and challenge impulse control when presented with an opportunity for sexual offending (Seto, 2019). For some individuals, the disorder of pedophilia is a biologically predetermined sexual orientation, but in other cases, early experiences can alter sexual development and arousal patterns. Furthermore, early household dysfunction can shape criminal and sexually abusive behavior through lack of appropriate role models, exposure to violent or unhealthy relationships, and internalization of negative cognitive schemas about self and others. The neurobiological impact of trauma can contribute to attachment deficits, impairments in cognitive processing and decision-making, and deficiencies in emotional and behavioral self-regulation skills.

8.2 WHAT SORN LAWS TARGET: FLAWED ETIOLOGICAL PRESUMPTIONS

Research shows that legislators enact punitive laws to assuage the fears of their constituents, responding to commonly held views that sex offenders as a group are perverted, sick, compulsive, untreatable, and inevitably re-offend (Sample & Kadleck, 2008). Sex offender registration and notification laws often apply to all individuals convicted of sex offenses, suggestive of an assumption that sex offenders pose a constant, homogenous risk to public safety. These mistaken assumptions were manifest in a 2003 US Supreme Court decision that declared recidivism rates to be "frightening and high" (Ellman & Ellman, 2015). This phrase is frequently repeated in legislative preambles across the nation to justify the need for community protection policies. Sex offender registration and notification laws, consistent with guidelines contained in the federal Adam Walsh Act ((AWA) 2006), with its expansive net of registerable offenses, are driven by the view that sex offenders have a high and immutable risk to re-offend.

Further contributing to their deviation from empirical understandings of offender behavior, SORN laws are often enacted in reaction to isolated, highly publicized cases that are not necessarily representative of the "typical" sex crime. Therefore, it is not surprising that they do not target the factors reviewed above that contribute to sex offender behavior. SORN laws often have been devised in a "one size fits all" approach, rooted in presumptions of enduring paraphilic interests, predatory patterns, and uncontrollable impulses. Management strategies based on these often-erroneous ideas focus primarily on tracking and monitoring, which fails to address and correct the dynamic criminogenic factors that raise risk for recidivism.

8.2.1 *Stranger Danger*

Many aspects of SORN laws, from associated housing and employment restrictions to registration and notification itself, boil down to an effort to eliminate opportunities for convicted sex offenders to target youths unknown to them. Central to this design is an assumption that sex offenders prey on vulnerable youths at large. In theory, by providing background information on those required to register, parents and guardians can take steps to protect their charges from predatory strangers who may sexually abuse children.

There are indeed some predatory sex offenders who target unsuspecting strangers, but in reality, the vast majority of child sexual abuse victims somehow know their victimizers (Bureau of Justice Statistics, 2000). About 93 percent of the perpetrators of child sexual abuse are well-known to victims and their families (Berliner, Schram, Miller, & Milloy, 1995; Bureau of Justice Statistics, 2002). Sex offender registration and notification laws, and the housing exclusion zones that often exist alongside them, are designed to diminish opportunities for convicted sex offenders to prey upon vulnerable youngsters, but very few offenders encounter child victims in the types of public settings motivating the laws.

For instance, despite the underlying logic of ever-expanding housing restrictions, sex offenders do not sexually offend against children because of their residential proximity to schools, but because they typically groom victims by cultivating relationships with children and families who are familiar to them (Duwe, Donnay, & Tewksbury, 2008; Zandbergen, Levenson, & Hart, 2010). The predatory offense patterns and public locations that such laws seek to address are applicable in only 1–4 percent of cases (Colombino, Mercado, Levenson, & Jeglic, 2011; Mogavero & Kennedy, 2017). Children are most likely to be sexually abused by a trusted person within their own social and family circles (Bureau of Justice Statistics, 2000; Colombino et al., 2011). Residence restriction and registration and notification laws, in short, ostracize and relegate convicted sex offenders to the margins of society in exchange for an unestablished marginal reduction in risk.

8.2.2 *High Recidivism Rates and Longitudinal Risk*

The world's leading researchers on sex offense risk have been studying recidivism for over two decades and accumulated a compelling body of evidence about the longitudinal patterns of post-conviction offending (Hanson, A. J. Harris, Helmus, & Thornton, 2014; Hanson, A. J. R. Harris, Letourneau, Helmus, & Thornton, 2018; A. J. R. Harris &

Hanson, 2012). Across studies, sexual recidivism rates average between 9–18 percent, depending on the sample and the follow-up period, with the majority of re-offenses occurring in the first five years at large (Hanson et al., 2014; Hanson et al., 2018; Zgoba et al., 2015). Some types of sex offenders fall into higher-risk categories, such as pedophiles with male victims, and those who are more antisocial (A. J. R. Harris & Hanson, 2004). Registered sex offenders who are assessed at low risk are actually *less likely* than other types of criminals to be arrested for a subsequent sex crime.

Research also now sheds considerable light on longitudinal risk. The longitudinal recidivism outcomes of sexual offenders have been studied for decades, and it is clear that risk declines in a linear fashion the longer an individual remains in the community offense-free (Hanson et al., 2014; Hanson et al., 2018). After ten years in the community offense-free, risk declines substantially, and moderate-risk sex offenders have recidivism rates that are comparable to general criminal offenders. After sixteen years living offense-free, even high-risk sex offenders are *no more likely* to be arrested for a new sexual crime than a general offender with no prior sex crime arrest (Hanson et al., 2014). Therefore, lifetime registration durations create an inefficient distribution of resources with questionable benefit to community safety (Levenson et al., 2016).

While some sex offenders have victimized many more individuals than those for whom they have been arrested (Abel et al., 1987; Ahlmeyer, Heil, McKee, & English, 2000; English, Jones, Patrick, & Pasini-Hill, 2003; Heil, Ahlmeyer, & Simons, 2003; Hindman, 1988), most have not, and it is a small, readily discernible group of registrants who are high-volume offenders, distorting the true recidivism picture.

8.2.3 Treatment Doesn't Work

By targeting and isolating individuals, SORN laws reduce the emphasis on, or at least trust in, the efficacy of psychological treatment and its goals to increase stability through strengthening factors known to mitigate risk. Lifetime registration reinforces the assumption that convicted sex offenders are irredeemable, and that no amount of treatment permits their safe reintegration. While in most states registrants are required to attend counseling programs as part of probation or parole, common housing and employment restrictions reflect doubts as to these programs' ability to manage the risks they pose.

Psychological interventions for sex offenders focus on changing behavior and thinking rather than "curing" a sexually deviant orientation. Studies show substantial reductions in re-offending behavior for sex offenders who complete specialized psychological treatment programs (Hanson, Bourgon, Helmus, & Hodgson, 2009; Hanson et al., 2002; Losel & Schmucker, 2005; Schmucker & Lösel, 2015). Treatment addresses the risk factors and psychosocial needs of each individual, including self-regulation problems, intimacy deficits, deviant sexual interests, criminality, lack of empathy, and comorbid conditions such as substance abuse, anxiety, depression, or post-traumatic stress disorders (Andrews & Bonta, 2010, 2017;

Levenson, Willis, et al., 2017; Yates, Prescott, & Ward, 2010). A good community adjustment, facilitated by opportunities for building stability and a positive social environment, helps to enable the cognitive transformation and prosocial identity associated with desistance from crime (D. A. Harris, Pedneault, & Willis, 2017; Lussier & Gress, 2014; Maruna, LeBel, Mitchell, & Naples, 2004). Allied professionals such as community corrections officers and treatment providers can collaborate to support an offender with a comprehensive plan of treatment, case management, supervision, and safety planning (Newstrom et al., 2019).

8.2.4 *The Need for Special Monitoring*

Finally, policy over the past two decades has been built upon the premise that sex offenders need special monitoring to track their whereabouts and keep a close eye on them. At last count, according to the National Center for Missing and Exploited Children (NCMEC), there were over 900,000 RSOs in the United States. This number highlights the contradictions of a one-size-fits-all approach: Treating all sex offenders as irredeemable and in need of close monitoring redirects official attention that would otherwise be solely dedicated to those offenders that require it. Overinclusive registries actually interfere with law enforcement's ability to monitor those at great risk to reoffend, and, presuming strangers need to be protected against, it dilutes the public's ability to identify truly dangerous individuals. Sex offender management systems should utilize empirically derived risk protocols and individual assessments of strengths and needs, and deliver services in a client-centered fashion that maximizes the ability of individuals to reintegrate into society and desist from reoffending (Bonta & Andrews, 2017; Hanson et al., 2009). Since many convicted sex offenders have complex psychiatric needs, trauma-related disorders, and addictions (which increase dynamic risk for re-offense), access to services such as mental health and substance abuse treatments should be part of any community management system to reduce risk.

8.3 HOW SORN LAWS LIKELY EXACERBATE, RATHER THAN ADDRESS, THE CHALLENGES OF SEX OFFENDERS

Sociologist Robert Merton warned nearly a century ago that well-intentioned social policies passed in response to a perceived threat can result in unintended negative consequences that outweigh their benefits (Merton, 1936). After conviction, or after release from jail or prison, SORN laws exacerbate the social and practical barriers to reintegration common to anyone with a criminal history. The broader negative effects of SORN for registrants are discussed more fully elsewhere in this volume. In the following section, I focus on how the consequences of SORN interact with the risk factors described previously and heighten recidivism risks.

8.3.1 *SORN and "Sex Offender" Self-Identity*

The unique stigma of the "sex offender" label can foster a profound sense of disempowerment, social isolation, hopelessness, and shame (Fix et al., 2020; Jeglic, Mercado, & Levenson, 2011; Levenson & Cotter, 2005; Levenson, D'Amora, & Hern, 2007; Mercado, Alvarez, & Levenson, 2008; Tewksbury & Mustaine, 2009). Facing significant obstructions to community reentry, many RSOs describe a deep sense of desperation and despair that challenges their often already limited coping skills. In times of crisis and despondence, everyone is more likely to resort to familiar (possibly dysfunctional) coping strategies. Recently, Harris and Levenson (2020) described how post-conviction traumatic stress can contribute to the maladaptive coping that increases dynamic risk. When registrants trying to reintegrate are faced with challenges meeting their basic needs, they are less able to successfully implement self-regulation and prevention strategies.

Labeling theory advises that the identity and behaviors of individuals are shaped by the words used to define or categorize them; the disparaging labels attached to those who deviate from social norms become deeply ingrained in one's self-concept (Goffman, 1963; Maruna et al., 2004). Stereotypes can lead to self-fulfilling prophecies, by which an individual adopts assumptions made by others and then behaves in ways that conform to those notions (Paternoster & Iovanni, 1989). Some crime theorists suggest that exclusionary policies and shaming labels that separate stigmatized groups from mainstream social life can ironically serve to solidify deviant identities and reinforce criminal behavior (Bernburg, Krohn, & Rivera, 2006; Paternoster et al., 1989). In 1902, sociologist Charles Cooley shared his theory of the "Looking-glass self," hypothesizing that we see ourselves reflected in eyes of others which shapes how we perceive our own identity.

A person's interactions with others and societal rhetoric build a social identity that is constructed and maintained over time. Thus, when a society portrays people by the very label we *don't* want them to be, their internalized narrative precludes the cognitive transformation that fosters social conformity and reduced recidivism risk (Maruna et al., 2004; Willis, 2015). This is particularly true of the "registered sex offender" designation, which defines individuals for life, in ways that unequivocally negate any positive aspect of their character and behavior.

8.3.2 *One-Size Does Not Fit All*

Sex offender management policies are often applied broadly to anyone convicted of a sexual crime based on assumptions that most, if not all, have pervasive and enduring paraphilic interests that are unremitting even with treatment, and that these individuals have lifelong recidivism risk. As noted earlier, a broad spectrum of motivations, etiology, and offense patterns characterize sex offenders, and the heterogeneity of the sex offender population raises doubts about the applicability and efficacy of current policies. Dominant strategies fail to incorporate individualized assessment in a way that can identify and address the specific criminogenic risks, protective factors, and psychosocial needs of those who engage in sexually abusive behavior.

Successful intervention always begins with a good assessment. Integrating the realities of sex crime patterns, victimization preferences, paraphilic psychopathology, and the environmental context of offending is useful in developing effective and cost-efficient policies that protect communities while rehabilitating and safely reintegrating offenders. Currently, federal AWA guidelines and most state SORN regimes rest on offense-based scheme that classifies individuals based on the statute of conviction. Unfortunately, statutory nomenclature provides little insight into the clinical and contextual circumstances of a particular crime. As discussed earlier, for instance, not all persons arrested for sexual contact with a minor have a pedophilic disorder. Therefore, it seems inefficient and counterproductive to monitor everyone indefinitely, and to strictly regulate housing and employment options without regard for the ways that those conditions interact with potential risk. Case management plans devised by treatment providers and probation/parole officers based on the risks and needs of a particular offender are more likely to manage risk effectively.

Individualized case management requires an empirically validated risk assessment using tools that exist to classify registrants into relative risk categories. While offense-based schemes classify offenders based on the crime of conviction, actuarial assessment procedures evaluate known risk factors and are more accurate in identifying potential recidivists (Freeman & Sandler, 2010; Zgoba et al., 2015). Offense-based classifications inflate risk in many cases, but they can also underestimate the risk of offenders who plea bargained their cases down to lesser offenses. The result is a registry with so many seemingly high-risk offenders that its very purpose – to help the public identify truly sexually dangerous persons – is undermined (A. J. Harris, 2011; Harris, Lobanov-Rostovsky, & Levenson, 2010). Moreover, overly inclusive registries exacerbate the stigma and other negative consequences of conviction for lower-risk individuals, creating a set of re-entry barriers that may preclude rehabilitation and increase risk for future criminal behavior. Finally, risk management systems not using an empirically supported process fail to provide the best intervention for a given individual, perhaps compromising public safety.

8.3.3 *Isolation of Registrants*

Kelly Socia discusses the status-based consequence of residence restrictions more fully in Chapter 6 of this volume. Not one research study evaluating the effectiveness of residence restrictions has produced evidence that they prevent recidivistic sex crimes (Duwe et al., 2008; Huebner et al., 2014; Socia, 2014; Zandbergen et al., 2010). This is unsurprising, because the laws bear no resemblance to what is known about the causes and etiology of sexual crimes. As discussed, the vast majority of sexual offending against children occurs among familiar parties, not strangers lurking in school zones and such (Colombino et al., 2011; Duwe et al., 2008; Mogavero & Kennedy, 2017). Policies restricting where sex offenders live, rather than where they go and what they do, ignore the empirical realities of sexually abusive behavior and are misguided protection strategies (Colombino et al., 2011).

Research clearly shows that such laws diminish housing availability and increase the likelihood of transience and homelessness, factors that interfere with safe and successful reintegration (Huebner et al., 2013; Levenson, 2016; Levenson, Ackerman, Socia, & Harris, 2015). In densely populated metropolitan areas, extensive exclusion zones leave few compliant residential options, creating a crisis of housing instability that exacerbates psychosocial stressors and contributes to risk for criminal recidivism and registration noncompliance. Testament to their inefficacy, the US Department of Justice has advised against their use (Lobanov-Rostovsky, 2015).

8.3.4 *Explicitly Ignoring Risk Factors*

Because the etiology and motivation of sex offenders differ widely, an effective management system must utilize a risk-needs-responsivity (RNR) framework to maximize the ability of individuals to benefit from treatment and facilitate successful reintegration (Bonta et al., 2017; Hanson et al., 2009). Under such a regime, dynamic risk factors would be assessed and monitored by treatment providers and community corrections officers, so that targeted interventions can be implemented when needed. Specialized sex offender treatment programs can address risk factors within the context of an offender's daily life. Successful completion of these programs significantly reduces recidivism (Hanson et al., 2002; Losel & Schmucker, 2005).

Self-regulation deficits that manifest as dynamic risk factors often stem from the neurobiological consequences of adverse events throughout an individual's life. Thus, trauma-informed treatment does not focus exclusively on offense-related relapse prevention, but rather it also seeks to help clients improve sexual, emotional, and behavioral self-regulation across various domains of functioning (Levenson, Willis, et al., 2017). For example, offenders may associate with peers who also use violence to solve problems because this is familiar and normalized to them. Individuals may be quick to anger, aggression, intimidation, or impulsiveness due to underlying mental disorders including post-traumatic stress (Harris & Levenson, 2020). Or they may use drugs or alcohol to self-medicate, which can exacerbate self-regulation deficits by lowering inhibitions, increasing impulsivity, and interfering with decision-making capacity (Levenson, Willis, et al., 2017). These are dynamic risk factors that are addressed in many treatment programs, but are not often viewed as important or relevant in policy development, ignoring the realities of the etiology of offending behavior.

At present, however, SORN laws do nothing to address these risk factors head-on. Even more concerning, to the extent that the loss of opportunity, stigmatization, and the threat of vigilantism impose additional stressors and traumas upon registrants, SORN laws negatively interact with offender self-regulation deficits in ways that can lead to more offending, not less. De-emphasizing treatment while enforcing isolation and ostracization explicitly omits interventions directed toward risk factors in favor of punitive, potentially self-defeating restrictions.

8.3.5 *Diluting Resources*

Available research raises questions about the use of lifelong registration, the costs and benefits of registries, and the social justice implications for ex-offenders who seek a second chance to pursue a productive and law-abiding life (Levenson et al., 2016). If we want to diminish risk for sexual re-offense, we need to pay attention to decades of psychological and criminological research about desistance from crime. Evidence-based policies would be more aligned with our understanding of basic human needs and motivation (D. A. Harris et al., 2017), and the RNR principles of effective correctional rehabilitation (Bonta et al., 2017). Based on what we know about sexual offending etiology and offense patterns, it is not necessary (or cost-efficient) to apply lifelong registration to everyone. It does not reflect what we know about recidivism risk, as discussed, and can interfere with the ability to meet human needs, which exacerbates risk of re-offense and undermines public safety.

Registered sex offenders who successfully complete treatment and supervision should be considered for early relief from registration. Lifetime registration implies that individuals are beyond redemption, but when individuals demonstrate lifestyle stability and improved ability to manage their own behavior, their risk is reduced. Consistent with static risk research, lifetime registration should be reserved for repeat offenders who have documented pedophilic disorders, predatory patterns, or multiple victims, and those who used force or physical violence when committing their crimes (Levenson et al., 2016).

8.4 SUMMARY

With hundreds of thousands of individuals populating an ever-growing registry system, law enforcement resources have been overextended and the ability of the public to distinguish high-risk individuals has been undermined. Sex offender registration and notification policies ignore knowledge about basic human needs and psychological motivation, undercutting prospects for successful reintegration and risk management. In the absence of clear evidence demonstrating effectiveness of SORN laws protecting children, preventing sexual violence, or reducing recidivism, such laws may hinder rather than advance efforts toward community safety goals. Evidence-based recommendations for reform should include registration durations, requirements, and restrictions that are guided by empirically derived risk assessment research, and residence restrictions that legislate individuals into homelessness should be abolished. Current policies fail to use empirical research to guide their implementation, resulting in an inefficient allocation of fiscal resources.

REFERENCES

Abel, G. G., Becker, J. V., Cunningham-Rathner, J., Mittelman, M. S., Murphy, M. S., & Rouleau, J. L. (1987). Self-Reported Crimes of Nonincarcerated Paraphiliacs. *Journal of Interpersonal Violence, 2,* 3–25.

Ackerman, A. R., Harris, A. J., Levenson, J. S., & Zgoba, K. (2011). Who Are the People in Your Neighborhood? A Descriptive Analysis of Individuals on Public Sex Offender Registries. *International Journal of Psychiatry and Law, 34,* 149–159. DOI: 10.1016/j.ijlp.2011.04.001

Ahlmeyer, S., Heil, P., McKee, B., & English, K. (2000). The Impact of Polygraphy on Admissions of Victims and Offenses in Adult Sexual Offenders. *Sexual Abuse: Journal of Research & Treatment, 12*(2), 123–138.

Alink, L. R., Cicchetti, D., Kim, J., & Rogosch, F. A. (2012). Longitudinal Associations among Child Maltreatment, Social Functioning, and Cortisol Regulation. *Developmental psychology, 48*(1), 224–236.

American Psychiatric Association. (2013). *Diagnostic and Statistical Manual of Mental Disorders* (5th ed.). Washington, DC: American Psychiatric Association.

Anderson, A. L., & Sample, L. (2008). Public Awareness and Action Resulting from Sex Offender Community Notification Laws. *Criminal Justice Policy Review, 19*(4), 371–396.

Andrews, D. A., & Bonta, J. (2010). Rehabilitating Criminal Justice Policy and Practice. *Psychology, Public Policy, and Law, 16*(1), 39–55.

Andrews, D. A., & Bonta, J. (2017). *The Psychology of Criminal Conduct* (4th ed.). Cincinnati, OH: Anderson Publishing.

Baglivio, M. T., Epps, N., Swartz, K., Huq, M. S., Sheer, A., & Hardt, N. S. (2014). The Prevalence of Adverse Childhood Experiences (ACE) in the Lives of Juvenile Offenders. *Journal of Juvenile Justice, 3*(2), 1–23.

Beech, A. R., & Mitchell, I. J. (2005). A Neurobiological Perspective on Attachment Problems in Sexual Offenders and The Role of Selective Serotonin Re-Uptake Inhibitors in the Treatment of such Problems. *Clinical Psychology Review, 25*(2), 153–182.

Berliner, L., Schram, D., Miller, L., & Milloy, C. D. (1995). A Sentencing Alternative for Sex Offenders: A Study of Decision Making and Recidivism. *Journal of Interpersonal Violence, 10*(4), 487–502.

Bernburg, J. G., Krohn, M. D., & Rivera, C. J. (2006). Official Labeling, Criminal Embeddedness, and Subsequent Delinquency a Longitudinal Test of Labeling Theory. *Journal of Research in Crime and Delinquency, 43*(1), 67–88.

Blanchard, R. (2013). A Dissenting Opinion on DSM-5 Pedophilic Disorder. *Archives of Sexual Behavior, 42*(5), 675–678.

Bonta, J., & Andrews, D. A. (2017). *The Psychology of Criminal Conduct* (6th ed.). New York, NY: Routledge.

Bowlby, J. (1977). The Making and Breaking of Affectional Bonds. I. Aetiology and Psychopathology in the Light of Attachment Theory. An Expanded Version of the Fiftieth Maudsley Lecture, Delivered before the Royal College of Psychiatrists, 19 November 1976. *The British Journal of Psychiatry, 130*(3), 201–210.

Broward County Commission. (2009). *Final Report: Sexual Offender & Sexual Predator Residence Task Force.* Fort Lauderdale, FL: www.floridaatsa.com/Final_Report_-_Sexual_Offender_Sexual_Residence_Task_Force.pdf.

Bureau of Justice Statistics. (2000). *Sexual Assault of Young Children as Reported to Law Enforcement: Victim, Incident, and Offender Characteristics* (NCJ 182990). Retrieved from Washington, DC: www.bjs.gov/content/pub/pdf/saycrle.pdf.

Bureau of Justice Statistics. (2002). *Criminal Victimization* (NCJ 199994). Retrieved from Washington, DC: www.ojp.usdoj.gov/bjs/cvictgen.htm.

Bushman, B. J., Baumeister, R. F., & Phillips, C. M. (2001). Do People Aggress to Improve their Mood? Catharsis Beliefs, Affect Regulation Opportunity, and Aggressive Responding. *Journal of Personality and Social Psychology*, 81(1), 17–32.

Cantor, J. M., & McPhail, I. V. (2016). Non-offending Pedophiles. *Current Sexual Health Reports*, 8(3), 121–128. DOI: 10.1007/s11930-016-0076-z.

Cloitre, M., Stolbach, B. C., Herman, J. L., van der Kolk, B., Pynoos, R., Wang, J., & Petkova, E. (2009). A Developmental Approach to Complex PTSD: Childhood and Adult Cumulative Trauma as Predictors of Symptom Complexity. *Journal of Traumatic Stress*, 22(5), 399–408.

Colombino, N., Mercado, C. C., Levenson, J. S., & Jeglic, E. L. (2011). Preventing Sexual Violence: Can Examination of Offense Location Inform Sex Crime Policy? *International Journal of Psychiatry and Law*, 34(3), 160–167. DOI: 10.1016/j.ijlp.2011.04.002.

Creeden, K. (2009). How Trauma and Attachment can Impact Neurodevelopment: Informing Our Understanding and Treatment of Sexual Behaviour Problems. *Journal of Sexual Aggression*, 15(3), 261–273.

Duwe, G., Donnay, W., & Tewksbury, R. (2008). Does Residential Proximity Matter? A Geographic Analysis of Sex Offense Recidivism. *Criminal Justice and Behavior*, 35(4), 484–504. DOI: 10.1177/0093854807313690.

Ellman, I. M., & Ellman, T. (2015). "Frightening and High": The Supreme Court's Crucial Mistake About Sex Crime Statistics. *Constitutional Commentary*, 30, 495–667.

English, K., Jones, L., Patrick, D., & Pasini-Hill, D. (2003). Sexual Offender Containment: Use of the Postconviction Polygraph. *Annals of the New York Academy of Sciences*, 989, 411–427.

Finkelhor, D., & Baron, L. (1986). Risk Factors for Child Sexual Abuse. *Journal of Interpersonal Violence*, 1(1), 43–71.

Finkelhor, D., & Kendall-Tackett, K. (1997). A Developmental Perspective on the Childhood Impact of Crime, Abuse, and Violent Victimization. In D. Cicchetti & S. Toth (eds.), *Rochester Symposium on Developmental Psychopathology: Developmental Perspectives on Trauma: Theory, Research, and Intervention* (Vol. 8, pp. 1–32). Rochester, NY: University of Rochester Press.

Fix, R., Thompson, K., Letourneau, E., & Burkhart, B. (2020). Development and Psychometric Properties of the Concerns about Juvenile Sex Offender Registration and Notification Questionnaire (C-JSORNQ). *Sexuality Research & Social Policy*. https://doi .org/10.1007/s13178-020-00468-4.

Freeman, N. J., & Sandler, J. C. (2010). The Adam Walsh Act: A False Sense of Security or an Effective Public Policy Initiative? *Criminal Justice Policy Review*, 21(1), 31–49.

Goffman, E. (1963). *Stigma: Notes on a Spoiled Identity*. New York, NY: Simon & Schuster.

Grady, M. D., Levenson, J. S., & Bolder, T. (2016). Linking Adverse Childhood Effects and Attachment: A Theory of Etiology for Sexual Offending. *Trauma, Violence, & Abuse*, 18(4), 433–444. DOI: 1524838015627147.

Hanson, R. K., Bourgon, G., Helmus, L., & Hodgson, S. (2009). The Principles of Effective Correctional Treatment also Apply to Sexual Offenders: A Meta-Analysis. *Criminal Justice and Behavior*, 36(9), 865–891.

Hanson, R. K., Gordon, A., Harris, A. J. R., Marques, J. K., Murphy, W., Quinsey, V. L., & Seto, M. C. (2002). First Report of the Collaborative Outcome Data Project on the Effectiveness of Treatment for Sex Offenders. *Sexual Abuse: A Journal of Research and Treatment*, 14(2), 169–194.

Hanson, R. K., Harris, A. J., Helmus, L., & Thornton, D. (2014). High-Risk Sex Offenders May Not be High Risk Forever. *Journal of Interpersonal Violence*, 29(15), 2792–2813. DOI: 0886260514526062.

Hanson, R. K., Harris, A. J. R., Letourneau, E., Helmus, L., & Thornton, D. (2018). Reductions in Risk Based on Time Offense Free in the Community: Once a Sexual Offender, Not Always a Sexual Offender. *Psychology, Public Policy, and Law*, 24(1), 48–63.

Hanson, R. K., & Morton-Bourgon, K. (2005). The Characteristics of Persistent Sexual Offenders: A Meta-analysis of Recidivism Studies. *Journal of Consulting and Clinical Psychology*, 73(6), 1154–1163. http://dx.doi.org/10.1037/0022-006X.73.6.1154.

Harlow, C. W. (1999). *Prior Abuse Reported by Inmates and Probationers*. Retrieved from Rockville, MD: US Department of Justice.

Harris, A. J. (2011). SORNA in the Post-Deadline Era: What's the Next Move? *Sex Offender Law Report*, 12(6), 81–86.

Harris, A. J., Lobanov-Rostovsky, C., & Levenson, J. S. (2010). Widening the Net: The Effects of Transitioning to the Adam Walsh Act Classification System. *Criminal Justice and Behavior*, 37(5), 503–519.

Harris, A. J., & Socia, K. M. (2014). What's in a Name? Evaluating the Effects of the "Sex Offender" Label on Public Opinions and Beliefs. *Sexual Abuse: A Journal of Research and Treatment*, 28(7), 660–678. DOI: 1079063214564391.

Harris, A. J. R., & Hanson, R. K. (2004). *Sex Offender Recidivism: A Simple Question* (2004–03). Retrieved from Ottawa: www.static99.org/pdfdocs/harrisandhanson2004simpleq.pdf.

Harris, A. J. R., & Hanson, R. K. (2012, October 19). *When Is a Sex Offender No Longer a Sex Offender?* Paper presented at the 31st Annual Research and Treatment Conference of the Association for the Treatment of Sexual Abusers, Denver, CO.

Harris, D. A., & Levenson, J. (2020). Life on "The List" is a Life Lived in Fear: Post-Conviction Traumatic Stress in Men Convicted of Sexual Offenses. *International Journal of Offender Therapy and Comparative Criminology*. https://doi.org/10.1177/0306624X20952397.

Harris, D. A., Pedneault, A., & Willis, G. (2017). The Pursuit of Primary Human Goods in Men Desisting From Sexual Offending. *Sexual Abuse*, 31(2), 197–219. DOI: 10.1177/1079063217729155.

Heil, P., Ahlmeyer, S., & Simons, D. (2003). Crossover Sexual Offenses. *Sexual Abuse: A Journal of Research and Treatment*, 15(4), 221–236.

Henry, B. F. (2020). Typologies of Adversity in Childhood & Adulthood as Determinants of Mental Health & Substance Use Disorders of Adults Incarcerated in US Prisons. *Child Abuse & Neglect*, 99, 104251. https://doi.org/https://doi.org/10.1016/j.chiabu.2019.104251.

Herman, J. L. (1992). Complex PTSD: A Syndrome in Survivors of Prolonged and Repeated Trauma. *Journal of Traumatic Stress*, 5(3), 377–391.

Herman, J. L. (1997). *Trauma and Recovery*. New York: Basic Books.

Hindman, J. (1988). Research Disputes Assumptions about Child Molesters. *National District Attorney's Association Bulletin*, 7(4), 1, 3.

Hudson, S. M., & Ward, T. (1997). Rape: Psychopathology and Theory. In D. R. Laws & W. O'donohue (eds.), *Sexual Deviance*. New York: Guilford Press.

Hudson, S. M., Ward, T., & McCormack, J. C. (1999). Offense Pathways in Sexual Offenders. *Journal of Interpersonal Violence*, 14(8), 779–798.

Huebner, B. M., Bynum, T. S., Rydberg, J., Kras, K., Grommon, E., & Pleggenkuhle, B. (2013). An Evaluation of Sex Offender Residency Restrictions in Michigan and Missouri. www.ncjrs.gov/pdffiles1/nij/grants/242952.pdf.

Huebner, B. M., Kras, K. R., Rydberg, J., Bynum, T. S., Grommon, E., & Pleggenkuhle, B. (2014). The Effect and Implications of Sex Offender Residence Restrictions. *Criminology & Public Policy*, 13(1), 139–168. DOI: 10.1111/1745-9133.12066.

Jeglic, E., Mercado, C. C., & Levenson, J. S. (2011). The Prevalence and Correlates of Depression and Hopelessness among Sex Offenders Subject to Community Notification and Residence Restriction Legislation. *Journal of Criminal Justice*, 37 (1), 46–59.

Jovev, M., & Jackson, H. J. (2004). Early Maladaptive Schemas in Personality Disordered Individuals. *Journal of Personality Disorders*, 18(5), 467–478.

Kingston, D. A. (2016). *The Assessment of Paraphilic and Non-Paraphilic Rapists*. In the Wiley Handbook on the Theories, Assessment and Treatment of Sexual Offending, 877–902. John Wiley & Sons. https://doi.org/10.1002/9781118574003.watts0041.

Kingston, D. A., Firestone, P., Moulden, H., & Bradford, J. M. (2007). The Utility of the Diagnosis of Pedophilia: A Comparison of Various Classification Procedures. *Archives of Sexual Behavior*, 36(3), 423–436. DOI: 10.1007/s10508-006-9091-x.

Konrad, A., Kuhle, L. F., Amelung, T., & Beier, K. M. (2018). Is Emotional Congruence with Children Associated with Sexual Offending in Pedophiles and Hebephiles from the Community? *Sexual Abuse*, 30(1), 3–22. DOI: 10.1177/1079063215620397.

Levenson, J. S. (2016). Hidden Challenges: Sex Offenders Legislated into Homelessness. *Journal of Social Work*, 18(3), 348–363. DOI: 1468017316654811.

Levenson, J. S., Ackerman, A. R., Socia, K. M., & Harris, A. J. (2015). Where for Art Thou? Transient Sex Offenders and Residence Restrictions. *Criminal Justice Policy Review*, 26(4), 319–344. DOI: 10.1177/0887403413512326.

Levenson, J. S., Baglivio, M. T., Wolff, K. T., Epps, N., Royall, W. C., Gomez, K. C., & Kaplan, D. (2017). You Learn What You Live: Prevalence of Childhood Adversity in the Lives of Juveniles Arrested for Sexual Offenses. *Advances in Social Work*, 18(1), 1–18.

Levenson, J. S., Brannon, Y., Fortney, T., & Baker, J. (2007). Public Perceptions About Sex Offenders and Community Protection Policies. *Analyses of Social Issues and Public Policy*, 7(1), 137–161. DOI: 10.1111/j.1530-2415.2007.00119.x.

Levenson, J. S., & Cotter, L. P. (2005). The Effect of Megan's Law on Sex Offender Reintegration. *Journal of Contemporary Criminal Justice*, 21(1), 49–66.

Levenson, J. S., D'Amora, D. A., & Hern, A. (2007). Megan's Law and Its Impact on Community Re-entry for Sex Offenders. *Behavioral Sciences & the Law*, 25, 587–602.

Levenson, J. S., Grady, M. D., & Morin, J. W. (2019). Beyond the "Ick Factor": Counseling Non-offending Persons with Pedophilia. *Clinical Social Work Journal*, 48, 330–338. https://doi.org/10.1007/s10615-019-00712-4.

Levenson, J. S., Grady, M. D., & Leibowitz, G. (2016). Grand Challenges: Social Justice and the Need for Evidence-Based Sex Offender Registry Reform. *Journal of Sociology & Social Welfare*, 43(2), 3–38.

Levenson, J. S., & Socia, K. M. (2015). Adverse Childhood Experiences and Arrest Patterns in a Sample of Sexual Offenders. *Journal of Interpersonal Violence*, 31, 1883–1911. DOI: 10.1177/0886260515570751.

Levenson, J. S., Willis, G., & Prescott, D. (2017). *Trauma-Informed Care: Transforming Treatment of People Who Sexually Abuse*. Brandon, VT: Safer Society Press.

Lieb, R., & Nunlist, C. (2008). *Community Notification as Viewed by Washington's Citizens: A Ten-Year Follow-Up*. (08–03-1101). www.wsipp.wa.gov/ReportFile/1010/Wsipp_Community-Notification-as-Viewed-by-Washingtons-Citizens-A-10-Year-Follow-Up_Full-Report.pdf.

Lobanov-Rostovsky, C. (2015). *Adult Sex Offender Management*. Retrieved from www.smart.gov/pdfs/AdultSexOffenderManagement.pdf.

Loper, A. B., Mahmoodzadegan, N., & Warren, J. I. (2008). Childhood Maltreatment and Cluster B Personality Pathology in Female Serious Offenders. *Sexual Abuse: A Journal of Research and Treatment*, 20(2), 139–160.

Losel, F., & Schmucker, M. (2005). The Effectiveness of Treatment for Sexual Offenders: A Comprehensive Meta-analysis. *Journal of Experimental Criminology*, 1, 117–146.

Lussier, P., & Gress, C. L. Z. (2014). Community Re-entry and the Path Toward Desistance: A Quasi-experimental Longitudinal Study of Dynamic Factors and Community Risk Management of Adult Sex Offenders. *Journal of Criminal Justice*, 42(2), 111–122. http://dx .doi.org/10.1016/j.jcrimjus.2013.09.006.

Malamuth, N. M. (2014). *Pornography and Sexual Aggression*. Academic Press.

Marshall, W. L. (2010). The Role of Attachments, Intimacy, and Loneliness in the Etiology and Maintenance of Sexual Offending. *Sexual and Relationship Therapy*, 25(1), 73–85.

Maruna, S., LeBel, T. P., Mitchell, N., & Naples, M. (2004). Pygmalion in the Reintegration Process: Desistance from Crime through the Looking Glass. *Psychology, Crime & Law*, 10 (3), 271–281. DOI: 10.1080/10683160410001662762.

Mears, D. P., Mancini, C., Gertz, M., & Bratton, J. (2008). Sex Crimes, Children, and Pornography: Public Views and Public Policy. *Crime & Delinquency*, 54, 532–650.

Mercado, C. C., Alvarez, S., & Levenson, J. S. (2008). The Impact of Specialized Sex Offender Legislation on Community Re-entry. *Sexual Abuse: A Journal of Research & Treatment*, 20(2), 188–205. DOI: 10.1177/1079063208317540.

Mersky, J. P., Topitzes, J., & Reynolds, A. J. (2012). Unsafe at Any Age: Linking Childhood and Adolescent Maltreatment to Delinquency and Crime. *Journal of Research in Crime and Delinquency*, 49(2), 295–318.

Merton, R. K. (1936). The Unanticipated Consequences of Purposive Social Action. *American Sociological Review*, 1(6), 894–904. www.jstor.org/stable/2084615.

Messina, N., Grella, C., Burdon, W., & Prendergast, M. (2007). Childhood Adverse Events and Current Traumatic Distress A Comparison of Men and Women Drug-Dependent Prisoners. *Criminal Justice and Behavior*, 34(11), 1385–1401.

Mogavero, M. C., & Kennedy, L. W. (2017). The Social and Geographic Patterns of Sexual Offending: Is Sex Offender Residence Restriction Legislation Practical? *Victims & Offenders*, 12(3), 401–433. DOI: 10.1080/15564886.2015.1084962.

Newstrom, N., Miner, M., Hoefer, C., Hanson, R. K., & Robinson, B. E. (2019). Sex Offender Supervision: Communication, Training, and Mutual Respect Are Necessary for Effective Collaboration Between Probation Officers and Therapists. *Sexual Abuse*, 31(5), 607–631. DOI: 10.1177/1079063218775970.

Paternoster, R., & Iovanni, L. (1989). The Labeling Perspective and Delinquency: An Elaboration of the Theory and Assessment of the Evidence. *Justice Quarterly*, 6, 359–394.

Patterson, G. R., DeBaryshe, B. D., & Ramsey, E. (1990). A Developmental Perspective on Antisocial Behavior. *American Psychologist*, 44(2), 329–335.

Quinsey, V. L. (2010). Coercive Paraphilic Disorder. *Archives of Sexual Behavior*, 39(2), 405–410. DOI: 10.1007/s10508-009-9547-x.

Reavis, J., Looman, J., Franco, K., & Rojas, B. (2013). Adverse Childhood Experiences and Adult Criminality: How Long Must We Live Before We Possess Our Own Lives? *The Permanente Journal*, 17(2), 44–48.

Reid, R.C., Carpenter, B. N., Hook, J. N., Garos, S., Manning, J. C., Gilliland, R., Cooper, E. B., McKittrick, H., Davtian, M., & Fong, T. (2012). Report of Findings in a DSM 5 Field Trial for Hypersexual Disorder. *Journal of Sexual Medicine*, 9(11), 2868–2877.

SAMHSA. (2014). *SAMHSA's Concept of Trauma and Guidance for a Trauma-informed Approach.* http://store.samhsa.gov/shin/content//SMA14-4884/SMA14-4884.pdf: Substance Abuse and Mental Health Services Administration.

Sample, L. L., & Kadleck, C. (2008). Sex Offender Laws: Legislators' Accounts of the Need for Policy. *Criminal Justice Policy Review, 19*(1), 40–62. DOI: 10.1177/0887403407308292

Schmucker, M., & Lösel, F. (2015). The Effects of Sexual Offender Treatment on Recidivism: An International Meta-analysis of Sound Quality Evaluations. *Journal of Experimental Criminology, 11,* 597–630. DOI: 10.1007/s11292-015-9241-z.

Seto, M. C. (2019). The Motivation-Facilitation Model of Sexual Offending. *Sexual Abuse, 31* (1), 3–24. https://doi.org/10.1177/1079063217720919.

Seto, M. C. (2018). *Pedophilia and Sexual Offending Against Children: Theory, Assessment, and Intervention* (2nd ed.). Washington, DC: American Psychological Association.

Seto, M. C. (2008). *Pedophilia and Sexual Offending Against Children: Theory, Assessment, and Intervention.* Washington, DC: American Psychological Association.

Seto, M. C. (2012). Is Pedophilia a Sexual Orientation? *Archives of Sexual Behavior, 41*(1), 231–236.

Smallbone, S. W., & Dadds, M. R. (1998). Childhood Attachment and Adult Attachment in Incarcerated Adult Male Sex Offenders. *Journal of Interpersonal Violence, 13*(5), 555–573.

Socia, K. M. (2014). Residence Restrictions Are Ineffective, Inefficient, and Inadequate: So Now What? *Criminology & Public Policy, 13*(1), 179–188.

Stephens, S., Seto, M. C., Goodwill, A. M., & Cantor, J. M. (2017). Evidence of Construct Validity in the Assessment of Hebephilia. *Archives of Sexual Behavior, 46*(1), 301–309.

Streeck-Fischer, A., & van der Kolk, B. A. (2000). Down Will Come Baby, Cradle and All: Diagnostic and Therapeutic Implications of Chronic Trauma on Child Development. *Australian and New Zealand Journal of Psychiatry, 34*(6), 903–918.

Tewksbury, R., & Mustaine, E. (2009). Stress and Collateral Consequences for Registered Sex Offenders. *Journal of Public Management and Social Policy, 15*(2), 215–239.

van der Kolk, B. (2006). Clinical Implications of Neuroscience Research in PTSD. *Annals of the New York Academy of Sciences, 1071*(1), 277–293.

van der Kolk, B. (2014). *The Body Keeps the Score: Brain, Mind, and Body in the Healing of Trauma.* New York, NY: Penguin.

Vondra, J. I., Shaw, D. S., Swearingen, L., Cohen, M., & Owens, E. B. (2001). Attachment Stability and Emotional and Behavioral Regulation from Infancy to Preschool Age. *Development and Psychopathology, 13*(01), 13–33.

Willis, G. M. (2015). *Changing the Dialogue, Changing Lives: How Strengths-based Approaches Can Move Us Ahead (keynote presentation).* Paper presented at the Innovative Strategies in Criminal Justice: From Policy to Practice, Edmonton, Canada.

Yates, P. M., Prescott, D. F., & Ward, T. (2010). *Applying the Good Lives and Self-Regulation Models to Sex Offender Treatment: A Practical Guide for Clinicians.* Brandon, VT: Safer Society Press.

Zandbergen, P., Levenson, J. S., & Hart, T. (2010). Residential Proximity to Schools and Daycares: An Empirical Analysis of Sex Offense Recidivism. *Criminal Justice and Behavior, 37*(5), 482–502. DOI: 10.1177/0093854810363549.

Zander, T. K. (2008). Commentary: Inventing Diagnosis for Civil Commitment of Rapists. *Journal of the American Academy of Psychiatry and the Law Online, 36*(4), 459–469.

Zgoba, K., Miner, M., Levenson, J., Knight, R., Letourneau, E., & Thornton, D. (2015). The Adam Walsh Act. *Sexual Abuse, 28*(8), 722–740. DOI: 10.1177/1079063215569543.

9

Juvenile Registration and Notification Are Failed Policies That Must End

Elizabeth J. Letourneau

Chapter 9 examines the consequences of subjecting children to SORN laws. It argues that registration and notification laws are uniquely ineffective and harmful when applied to children. The chapter begins with a history of how SORN laws came to regulate juvenile sexual misconduct. In response to moral panics around "sexual predators" and "juvenile super-predators," policymakers explicitly expanded the scope of SORN laws to cover children adjudicated delinquent of sex offenses. The chapter next evaluates the effects of these laws on juvenile offending, particularly recidivism. Contrary to the myths underlying their enactment, children found to have engaged in sexual misconduct very rarely reoffend. Further, the evidence is unanimous that SORN laws do not reduce recidivism. The chapter then compiles evidence on the many deleterious effects SORN laws produce when they are applied to children. Studies of providers and children who are registrants demonstrate that SORN laws increase substantially the risk of suicide and sexual victimization. Furthermore, SORN laws are associated with high rates of plea bargaining among children. In light of these failures and dangerous effects, the application of SORN to children should be abandoned.

9.1 INTRODUCTION

Most of the research on sex offender registration and notification (SORN) laws, including that contained in this volume, concerns adults convicted in criminal court. In this chapter, I examine what we know about the controversial but widespread practice of subjecting children adjudicated in juvenile, family, or criminal court to SORN. By "child" or "children," I mean individuals under the age of 18 years, as per the Convention on the Rights of the Child (The United Nations, 1989). In what follows, I focus on the effects of SORN laws on children. While there are fewer publications on the effects of juvenile-focused SORN, there is enough rigorous research to allow us to draw a number of policy-relevant conclusions.

That children engage in harmful and/or illegal sexual behavior is indisputable. Indeed, crime statistics indicate that one-third of sexual offenses committed against children are committed by other children (Finkelhor, Ormrod, & Chaffin, 2009); victim surveys suggest that this incidence level may be closer to one-half (Finkelhor,

Shattuck, Turner, & Hamby, 2014). However, compared to sexual offenses committed against children by adults, offenses committed by children tend to be less serious and occur in contexts of convenience, such as when babysitting, versus contexts overtly manipulated to facilitate the offense (Finkelhor & Ormrod, 2001; Miranda & Corcoran, 2000; Vandiver, 2006). Children who engage in harmful or illegal sexual behavior do so for many reasons, including several reasons that do not typically apply to adult behavior, such as ignorance, impulsivity, and inadequate adult supervision (Letourneau, Schaeffer, Bradshaw, & Feder, 2017). This is not to suggest that sexual offenses committed by children do not cause harm – they certainly can and do, in significant ways. However, effective interventions to address this potential for harm must consider the developmental and psychosocial context in which the offending occurs, and how and why these contexts differ from that associated with adult offending.

Despite reasonable unanimity concerning the need to effectively respond to this problem, agreement on the nature of the response has proven elusive. As reviewed in the next section, contemporary policy trends include harsher punishment and expanded social controls efforts directed at children who commit sexual offenses, trends that many experts believe are harmful, overly punitive, contrary to the *parens patriae* principles of juvenile justice, and counterproductive (Chaffin, 2008; Federal Advisory Committee on Juvenile Justice, 2007). Thereafter, the chapter will review the history of subjecting children to SORN, along with a survey of its impact. The chapter concludes with several recommendations for positive change going forward.

9.2 US HISTORY OF REGULATING THE SEXUAL BEHAVIOR OF CHILDREN

Subjecting children to sex crime laws, including SORN, represents something of a conundrum. Children have limited capacity to make sexual decisions and many countries, including the United States, have laws that prohibit children from consenting to sexual behavior. Yet when children do engage in illegal sexual behavior, they are held legally liable for their actions, as if they did have the legal capacity to make sexual decisions. Children do, of course, engage in consensual sexual behavior, which becomes increasingly common as they progress through adolescence. Surveys of US high school-aged children (typically 14–18 years) indicate that one-third of ninth graders to two-thirds of twelfth graders report having engaged in sexual intercourse (Centers for Disease Control and Prevention, 2012).

Traditionally, adolescent sexual activity has been seen as undesirable and several legal strategies discourage child sexuality, including establishing the legal age of consent, criminalization via statutory rape, and other laws (Chaffin, Chenoweth, & Letourneau, 2016; Pearlstein, 2010). In the United States, the legal age of consent varies between 16–18 years of age depending upon the state (Cocca, 2004). As summarized by

Chaffin et al. (2016), "[s]tatutory rape laws criminalize non-forcible, consenting sexual contact that would be legal except for the age(s) of the individuals involved."

While long present in US legal codes, statutory rape laws fell into disuse until the 1990s when they were revived due to a confluence of an ascendant conservative social movement and increased awareness of child sexual abuse (Chaffin et al., 2016). In particular, there was an emphasis on deterring adolescent boys and young adult men from impregnating underage girls (Donovan, 1996; Oberman, 2000), with a main motivation being the desire to keep young women and their children off social welfare rolls. Thus, statutory rape cases were brought with increased frequency against (typically) teenage boys who engaged in consensual sex with (typically) similarly aged girls. Yet Chaffin and colleagues found that the consequences of statutory rape allegations were even more severe in cases where boys engaged in sex with other boys and in the rare cases of girls engaged in sex with other girls (Chaffin et al., 2016).

While statutory rape laws were being reinvigorated, the United States in the 1990s was entering the throes of two moral panics, one pertaining to so-called sexual predators (Lieb, Quinsey, & Berliner, 1998; Zimring, 2004) and a second pertaining to so-called juvenile super-predators (Howell, 2003). The panic concerning sexual predators presaged a torrent of sex crime policies that continues to this day, described in Chapters 1 and 6. The panic concerning juvenile criminal offending stemmed in significant part from inflammatory and wildly inaccurate rhetoric forecasting a wave of juvenile offenders who would rape, murder, and rob without constraint (Howell, 2003).

One result of this panic was the increased prosecution of children as adults, based upon state laws allowing for the waiver or transfer of juveniles to adult court (Kupchik, 2006; Myers, 2005; Torbet, et al., 1996). Children charged with sex crimes appear to have disproportionately been the subject of such waivers (DiCataldo, 2009; Rinehart, Armstrong, Shields, & Letourneau, 2016). Combined, panic over sexual offending and juveniles inspired the widely shared yet inaccurate belief that regardless of age, sex offenders are "compulsive, progressive, and incurable," and require specialized legal interventions (Chaffin, Letourneau, & Silovsky, 2002, p. 205).

Michael Miner and I identified three myths that we believe underlie and bind these panics and motivated legal interventions for children who engage in harmful or illegal sexual behavior (Letourneau & Miner, 2005). These include the beliefs that (1) there is an epidemic of juvenile offending, including sexual offending; (2) children who engage in harmful or illegal sexual behavior have more in common with adult sex offenders than with other juvenile delinquents; and (3) in the absence of intensive interventions, children who engage in harmful or illegal sexual behavior remain at exceptionally high risk of re-offending. Each of these beliefs has been convincingly rebutted in the literature yet they persist in driving juvenile sex crime policy and practice (Chaffin, 2008; Letourneau & Caldwell, 2013; Letourneau & Miner, 2005; Zimring, 2004). In light of the criminalization of sexual behavior even among consenting teens, and the prevailing inaccurate beliefs about children who engage in harmful or illegal sexual behavior, it was perhaps inevitable that state and federal policies would eventually subject children to registration and notification requirements.

9.3 HISTORY OF JUVENILE REGISTRATION AND NOTIFICATION POLICIES

As noted elsewhere in this volume, the reach of SORN policies is broad yet also highly variable among jurisdictions. Nowhere is this variability more evident than in the application of SORN to children. While all states subject children convicted in adult court to SORN, states vary markedly on the extent to which they target children adjudicated delinquent as minors (i.e., prosecuted in juvenile or family court, not adult court) for sexual crimes. The federal Jacob Wetterling Act in 1994 and Megan Kanka Act in 1996 imposed a broad array of SORN requirements on states and other jurisdictions, but were silent regarding children adjudicated as minors for sexual offenses.

9.3.1 *State Approaches*

In this vacuum, states adopted SORN policies that varied along a number of dimensions, including the extent to which children are subjected to registration requirements, the eligibility criteria for registration, the duration of registration, and the extent to which notification is employed. Some states crafted SORN policies that explicitly excluded children adjudicated as minors. For example, in 1995, Maryland enacted a law that pertained only to criminal court convictions (Jasani, 2002). Other states, however, explicitly included children adjudicated as minors. For example, the original and the current (2019) South Carolina code reads in part: "Any person, *regardless of age*, residing in the State of South Carolina who in this state has been convicted of, adjudicated delinquent for ... an offense described below ... shall be required to register pursuant to the provisions of this article" (South Carolina Code sec. 23-3-430 (2019)), emphasis added).

Among states that do register children, policy and implementation can vary widely. For example, the initial SORN policies of Texas and Oklahoma targeted children adjudicated as minors, who can be subjected to registration following a separate hearing. Yet, in the first 10 years of implementation, approximately 2,000 Texas children were subjected to registration whereas just 10 Oklahoma children were registered (Morgan, 2002; Vandiver & Teske, 2006). This difference is due to steps Oklahoma took to first require evidence-based treatment of children adjudicated for sexual offenses and subjecting to registration only those who failed to successfully complete treatment.

9.3.2 *Federal Response*

The federal Adam Walsh Act (AWA) was enacted in 2006 in significant part to reduce state variations in SORN policies. Title 1 of the AWA is the first federal policy that specifically targeted for coverage children adjudicated delinquent as minors. Initially, Title 1 required all states and other jurisdictions (e.g., tribes) to register some children age 14 and over who were adjudicated delinquent as minors, subjecting several subgroups (depending on offense) to registration periods lasting from 25 years to life. Title 1 also required that registered children be subjected to online community notification. These policies represented a marked departure from traditional policy separating juvenile and adult offenders and prompted concern from several sectors (Chaffin, 2008; DiCataldo, 2009).

Indeed, following release of the preliminary AWA implementation guidelines in 2008, concern over the guidelines' child registration and notification provisions accounted for a majority of the hundreds of public comments received by the US Department of Justice (Harris & Lobanov-Rostovsky, 2010; McPherson, 2016). State officials identified the juvenile provisions as one of the primary barriers to AWA implementation (Harris & Lobanov-Rostovsky, 2010). Reflecting these concerns, juvenile registration emerged as a prominent theme in Congressional hearings held in 2009 to examine barriers to state implementation of Title 1 (*Sex Offender Registration and Notification Act (SORNA): Barriers to Timely Compliance by States*, 111th Congress, March 10, 2009). Ultimately, the Department of Justice modified Title 1 by eliminating all notification requirements for children adjudicated as minors and by limiting the offenses triggering their registration (see Docket No. OAG 134; AG Order No. 3150–2010, p. 6).

It is important to note that Title 1 of the AWA represents a "floor" – states lose earmarked federal funds if they do not meet these requirements, but they can and often do exceed these requirements. For example, South Carolina subjects children of any age adjudicated as minors to registration for a wider variety of sexual offenses than the AWA, mandates that registration last for life in all cases, and discloses juvenile registrant information to the public. Indeed, there likely is no such thing as a truly "private" sex offender registry where a child's registration status is known only to law enforcement. While some states maintain offline registries for children, public notification can still occur to an extent by alerting schools and other child-oriented businesses and organizations about a child's registration status (Beitsch, 2015).

The US Department of Justice extended the deadline by which states and other jurisdictions had to comply with the refined Title 1 requirements for several years but eventually imposed financial penalties for noncompliance. Several states enacted or expanded child registration requirements, apparently to avoid these penalties. For example, Maryland revised its SORN policy to include the registration of children (Md. Criminal Procedure Code § 11–704.1 (2014)). Nevertheless, while 38 states require child registration and 8 states subject child registrants to online notification

(Pittman & Nguyen, 2011), as of the end of September 2019 only 18 states were deemed to have substantially implemented Title 1 of the AWA (SMART, 2019). This failure among states to substantially implement Title 1 is due in large part to opposition to child registration (Harris & Lobanov-Rostovsky, 2016; McPherson, 2016). In response to this ongoing opposition, the Department of Justice issued supplemental guidelines that provide jurisdictions even "greater flexibility in their efforts to substantially implement SORNA's juvenile registration requirement" (Docket No. OAG 151; AG Order No. 3659–2016).

In addition to the foregoing, some states – including those deemed to have substantially implemented Title 1 of the AWA – chose to roll back their child registration requirements. Legislators in Delaware and Oregon enacted revisions that restrict the registration of children relative to their earlier policies (DE House Bill 182; OR House Bill 2320). In other states, legal challenges resulted in changes to child registration policies. The Supreme Courts of Ohio and Pennsylvania, for instance, found elements of their state child registration policies to be unconstitutional (*In re* C.P., (2012); In the Interest of J.B., 2014).

Organizations opposing child registration altogether or in part include the Federal Advisory Commission on Juvenile Justice (FACJJ), which in 2016 issued a formal recommendation that federal law be amended "to exempt juveniles from sex offender registration, community notification, and residency restriction laws" (FACJJ, 2016). Of note, in their recommendation, the FACJJ focused on the age of the child at the time of the offense (i.e., below the age of 18 years) and not on the court (i.e., juvenile or criminal) in which the child's case was processed. A host of additional organizations are now on record opposing child registration. These include advocacy organizations (e.g., Stop It Now!), professional membership organizations (e.g., American Bar Association), foundations (e.g., Annie E. Casey Foundation), policy institutes (e.g., Justice Policy Institute), and a libertarian organization (e.g., R Street Institute). Virtually all national experts who have published in peer-reviewed journals on the effects of child registration advocate against these policies (e.g., Letourneau et al., 2016). The concerns of these and other organizations and individuals focus on the punitive effects of subjecting children to registration, the failure of registration policies to consider developmental differences between children and adults, and the fact that the policies are misaligned with the rehabilitative focus of juvenile justice. These concerns are bolstered by the lack of empirical evidence showing any positive effects of registering juveniles, as discussed later in this chapter.

Despite the foregoing, proponents of the registration of children certainly remain. Missouri Governor Jeremiah Nixon, for instance, vetoed a bill that would remove children from his state's public registry and provide them with the opportunity to petition for relief from registration after 5 years, stating that "the bill would reverse the significant steps … taken to protect the rights of victims and undermine the important public safety functions provided by the sex offender registry and public notification websites" (Nixon, 2013).

9.4 NO POLICY EFFECTS ON INTENDED OUTCOMES

Despite its appeal in some quarters, juvenile SORN lacks support in the social science literature. Proponents maintain that SORN deters sexual recidivism among children (Letourneau & Caldwell, 2013; Najdowski, Cleary, & Stevenson, 2016). To date, however, no study supports this contention. In an early evaluation, my colleagues and I compared the recidivism rates of 111 matched pairs of registered and nonregistered boys, all of whom had been adjudicated delinquent for a registerable sexual offense in South Carolina (Letourneau & Armstrong, 2008). There were no differences in recidivism rates. In fact, of the 222 boys in this study, just 2 were adjudicated for a subsequent sexual offense across the average 4.5 years of follow-up.

In a later, larger evaluation, we examined the impact of registration status on sexual recidivism in a sample of 1,275 boys with sexual offense adjudications in South Carolina (Letourneau, Bandyopadhyay, Sinha, & Armstrong, 2009b). Again, registration status had no impact on new sexual offense adjudications. On the contrary, we found registered boys were marginally *more* likely to sustain new sexual offense charges, a finding we attributed to surveillance effects (i.e., they were the subject of police monitoring).

Caldwell and Dickinson (2009) compared the recidivism rates of 106 registered and 66 unregistered boys and found that registration status did not predict new sexual charges. Two additional exploratory studies examined whether registration tier designations, created in Title 1 of the AWA, correctly predicted future sexual offending in boys (higher tiers are supposed to indicate higher recidivism risk). Based on a sample of 91 boys adjudicated for sexual offenses, Caldwell and colleagues found that tiers were unrelated to subsequent sexual offense charges (Caldwell, Ziemke, & Vitacco, 2008). Likewise, based on a sample of 112 boys adjudicated for sexual offenses, Batastini and colleagues found that boys who met criteria for registration and boys who did not had similar sexual recidivism rates (Batastini, Hunt, Present-Koller, & DeMatteo, 2011).

In short, studies examining the policies of several states and the federal government have all concluded that subjecting children to SORN has no impact on sexual recidivism.

9.4.1 *Why Juvenile SORN Policies Fall Short of Their Aims*

As noted previously, SORN policies are based on an inaccurate understanding of children who commit sex offenses. Perhaps most importantly, the policies assume that children are at an especially high risk of recidivating. This is simply not true. In the most definitive study to date, Caldwell completed a meta-analysis combining data from 106 studies involving nearly 34,000 cases of children adjudicated as minors for sexual offenses (Caldwell, 2016). The weighted mean 5-year average sexual recidivism rate was just under 5 percent. However, this rate declined by 73 percent, to just 2.75 percent, when studies were limited to those published more recently (between 2000 and 2015). It would be difficult for any policy – even one based on sound theory and facts – to reduce an already very low sexual recidivism rate. Yet, as described more fully in the conclusion of this chapter, such reductions have been achieved, by evidence-based clinical interventions that address the actual needs of children and their families.

In my view, the only other way that registration and notification policies targeting juveniles could achieve a public or community safety effect is via general (as opposed to specific) deterrence – that is, by reducing the likelihood of children as a whole from engaging in an initial sexual offense. This theory of general deterrence posits that consequences perceived as sufficiently certain, severe, and/or swift will dissuade some people from engaging in the undesired behavior in the first place (Kleck, Sever, Li, & Gertz, 2005; Zimring & Hawkins, 1973).

My colleagues and I conducted three evaluations of the possible general deterrent effects of juvenile registration policies, none of which found evidence of such an effect. In the first study of its kind, we examined the impact of South Carolina's original registration policy as well as an updated policy that included online notification focusing on first-time sexual offense charges levied against children in family court between 1991 and 2004 (N = 3,148 cases) (Letourneau, Bandyopadhyay, Armstrong, & Sinha, 2010). Results indicated no significant change in the likelihood of first-time sexual offense charges for children between the pre-policy, initial registration policy, and registration plus online notification policy time periods. In a later similar study, we examined the effects of juvenile registration policies on first-time sexual offense charges in Maryland (N = 5,657) and Oregon (N = 13,279) and also first-time sexual offense adjudications in Maryland (N = 1,631) and Oregon (N = 5,451). Again, we found no impact of either state's juvenile registration policy on first-time charges or adjudications (Letourneau et al., 2019). In a third study, we examined the impact of four states' juvenile registration policies on reports (which precede formal charges) of first-time sexual offenses (Sandler, Letourneau, Vandiver, Shields, & Chaffin, 2017). Utilizing National Incident Based Reporting System data, we found no support for a general deterrent effect of juvenile registration policies in Idaho, South Carolina, Utah, or Virginia.

Thus, across three different outcomes (reports, charges, and adjudications) and six different states with widely varying juvenile SORN policies (Idaho, Maryland, South Carolina, Oregon, Utah, and Virginia), there is no evidence of a general deterrent effect of juvenile registration policies on the behavior of children. Why might these policies fail in this respect? As noted previously, registration and notification policies are based on flawed understandings of children who engage in harmful or illegal sexual behavior. More generally, uncertainty exists over how general deterrence is achieved. Some research indicates that adults' perceptions of criminal sanctions are almost completely unrelated to the reality of those sanctions, throwing into question the basis of achieving general deterrence (Kleck, Sever, Li, & Gertz, 2005). Even in cases where a general deterrent effect might be expected (e.g., highly specific messaging aimed at people most likely to engage in a specific criminal behavior), the signals might be wasted on children, whose capacities to form accurate perceptions of criminal sanctions are even more limited than those of adults (Steinberg & Scott, 2003). Indeed, according to one recent study (Cleary & Najdowski, 2019), very often children are unaware that their behavior could result in application of SORN, and if even aware, are not deterred. In short, the likelihood of an adolescent satisfying the series of complex cognitive steps hypothesized as underlying general deterrence is limited by many barriers (Najdowski et al., 2016; Sandler et al., 2017; Stevenson, Najdowski, & Wiley, 2013).

9.5 UNINTENDED IMPACT ON JUVENILE CASE PROCESSING

While research fails to support the intended effects of juvenile registration on sexual offending, studies have identified unintended, though possibly predictable, consequences of these policies. I first became interested in studying juvenile registration policies as a result of one of these unintended consequences. I was recruiting children for a randomized controlled trial testing the effectiveness of a family-based intervention for problem sexual behaviors (see Letourneau et al., 2009). Although the county from which we were recruiting typically adjudicated hundreds of children each year for sexual offenses, we were having difficulty locating any such children to participate in our study. The reason came into focus when local prosecutors explained that, in order to avoid their new onerous juvenile registration policy, they were charging kids with physical assault rather than (registerable) sexual assault offenses.

In our eventual study of the cases, my colleagues and I found evidence that South Carolina's registration policy impacted juvenile sexual offense case processing in two ways. First, following policy implementation, there was a dramatic increase in these cases being dismissed by prosecutors outright (Letourneau, Bandyopadhyay, Sinha, & Armstrong, 2009a). Second, for cases that were not dismissed, there was a dramatic increase in the likelihood of an initial sexual offense charge being changed to another type of charge, typically physical assault, after the policy was implemented (Letourneau, Armstrong, Bandyopadhyay, & Sinha, 2013). We did not see similar results for robbery or physical assault charges, supporting our hypothesis that the changes in rates of dismissal and plea bargains were in response to South Carolina's juvenile registration policy. Moreover, several prosecutors confirmed that the strategy of pleading guilty to physical assault was primarily to avoid South Carolina's lifetime juvenile registration policy.

Why would prosecutors (and judges and defense attorneys) alter the way in which they respond to juvenile sexual offense cases following the implementation of registration policy? As suggested, we believe this is because they perceived the registration of children as inappropriate, at least for some children in some circumstances. We are in the process of trying to replicate these findings using data from other states. In particular, it would be important to determine whether findings differ when examining the policies of states that allow for judicial discretion or otherwise limit the registration of children.

9.6 HARMFUL CONSEQUENCES FOR CHILDREN

From the outset, subjecting children to SORN generated concerns that it would cause them harm (e.g., see Trivits & Reppucci, 2002). These concerns grew, as anecdotal evidence of harm accrued. A small qualitative study of four families documented the adverse psychological and social consequences, including isolation, stigma, and fear associated with juvenile registration (Comartin, Kernsmith, & Miles, 2010). A report by Human Rights Watch (2013) detailed the experiences of hundreds of families affected by juvenile registration and documented harrowing accounts of registered children being shot at and attempting or committing suicide.

Seeking a more empirical understanding of possible adverse effects, my colleagues and I conducted two surveys. The first survey was completed by 256 US-based therapists and counselors ("providers") who work directly with children who have engaged in harmful and/or illegal sexual behavior (Harris, Walfield, Shields, & Letourneau, 2016). Providers were asked to indicate the degree to which, relative to non-registered children, registered children were likely to experience harmful consequences in five domains: mental health, harassment and unfair treatment, school problems, living instability, and risk of re-offending.

The majority of providers believed that SORN had deleterious effects on most of the items assessing each of the first four domains (see Harris et al., 2016, Table 1). For example, under the mental health domain, providers almost uniformly believed that SORN caused children to experience more shame and embarrassment. More than half of providers believed that public notification was associated with increased suicidal ideation (37 percent believed that registration was associated with increased suicidal ideation). Under the harassment and unfair treatment domain, most providers believed that registration and notification made children afraid for their own safety (65 percent and 82 percent for registration and notification, respectively). Under the school problems domain, the majority of providers reported that registration and notification were likely to impede children from attending school (58 percent and 69 percent, respectively). And under the living instability domain, the majority of providers believed that registration and notification required children to change caregivers (51 percent and 66 percent for registration and notification respectively). However, only a minority of providers believed that registration or notification increased the risk of children engaging in future nonsexual offenses (21 percent and 37 percent, respectively) or sexual offenses (18 percent and 35 percent, respectively). This high degree of provider agreement about the harmful effects of registration and notification across major life domains of children is even more remarkable given that neither provider characteristics (e.g., gender, age) nor client characteristics (e.g., age, criminal history) influenced the results, suggesting that our findings are robust and generalizable. In short, professionals with experience working directly with children believe juvenile SORN policies cause harm to these children.

To more directly assess the effects of juvenile SORN, we conducted a second survey, of 256 children ages 12–17 years who were in treatment for having engaged in harmful and/or illegal sexual behavior. Our findings from this survey (Letourneau et al., 2017) exclude the 5 girls who participated and pertain only to the 251 boys. Among these boys, 29 percent ($n = 73$) were subjected to some form of sex offender registration and/or notification requirements. After controlling for between group differences in age and adjudication status (registered children tended to be older and more likely to have a formal sexual offense adjudication), we compared registered and non-registered children on six domains: mental health, social support, personal conduct, peer relationships, peer conduct, and safety and violence.

The results were quite troubling. Relative to non-registered children, registered children reported worse mental health outcomes, more problems with their peers, a lower sense of safety, and a higher rate of victimization. In particular, relative to non-registered children, registered children were four times as likely to report having attempted suicide in the past thirty days, five times as likely to report having been approached by an adult for sex in the past year, and nearly twice as likely to have been sexually assaulted in the past year. The findings suggest that juvenile registration and notification are associated with increased risk of the very type of harm the strategies were meant to prevent. In a separate study, children facing the specter of registration and notification expressed significant concern about the impact of the requirements on relationships with friends, dating partners, and the broader community (Fix, Thompson, Letourneau, & Burkhart, 2020).

Why might juvenile SORN have these untoward effects? I believe that the policies create a context in which adults and peers – including those who might not otherwise harm a child – are at increased risk for doing so. Sex offender registration and notification, in short, makes the world more dangerous for those children subject to it, perhaps even more so that it does with adults. There are few labels as toxic as "sex offender," yet recent research suggests that "juvenile sex offender" is even worse. In their study, Harris and Socia (2016) found that adults who read about "juvenile sex offenders" were more likely to endorse harsh consequences and to believe that the children will become adult offenders, compared to adults who read about "minor youth who have committed crimes of a sexual nature." Sex offender registration and notification overtly labels children as sex offenders. This labeling marks these children as "others" and likely increases the fear and loathing they experience, including from law enforcement agents, probation and parole officers, educators, other parents, peers, and the general public. A robust literature shows that children labeled as qualitatively different from the rest of us or from our own children are at increased risk for iatrogenic effects that have long lasting consequences (e.g., see Bernburg & Krohn, 2003), just as our survey suggests.

9.7 CONCLUSIONS AND RECOMMENDATIONS

Juvenile SORN laws are ineffective and harmful. To my knowledge, there is not a single indicator suggesting that these policies improve community safety or child wellbeing in any way. Sex offender registration and notification not only fails to achieve its fundamental promise of reducing sexual offending, it appears to *increase* the risk of child sexual abuse and the incidence of other serious short- and long-term negative consequences for children.

Nevertheless, proponents make several arguments in support of subjecting children to SORN. First, there is the argument that "we don't want to remove an effective tool from prosecutors." Registration and notification are effective at encouraging plea bargains, to non-registerable offenses, as we have demonstrated in our research. But do prosecutors really need (or even want) to rely on a strategy associated with increased risk of childhood suicide and assault? And should policy makers be willing to make that trade-off even if they are? We believe not and, indeed, prosecutors and judges are beginning to speak out against juvenile SORN. For example, Paul Stern, a prosecutor for 35 years, contributed an article to the Association of Prosecuting Attorney's Child Abuse Prosecution Project in which he describes the many problems with subjecting children to registration and strongly urges fellow prosecutors to take a more evidence-based and individualized approach (Stern, n.d.). Even more striking, as mentioned earlier, the Federal Advisory Council on Juvenile Justice, chaired by a respected former trial court and chief judge, recently advised the US Department of Justice to exempt children from registration and notification laws (Timberlake & Ague, 2016, July 15). And recently, the American Bar Association's (ABA) Juvenile Justice Committee empaneled a group to "work on language that would create a presumption of no registration unless the State proves that registration is necessary to protect public safety" (ABA Juvenile Justice Committee Meeting Minutes, 2017, May 6).

The second argument made in support of juvenile SORN relates to concern for victims. For example, upon hearing a summary of our research findings, a congressional staff member explained to me that she has to look out for the interests of victims. Indeed, each of us is charged with looking out for the best interests of children. My argument is that this concern rightly pertains to *all* children, including children who have made mistakes, even mistakes that harmed others. Moreover, victims are not served by failed policy. As of this writing, some of the largest US-based victims' advocacy organizations, including the American Professional Society on the Abuse of Children, are developing consensus statements against juvenile registration. Mrs. Patty Wetterling – whose advocacy following her son's kidnapping, sexual assault, and murder helped launch modern SORN – has advocated against juvenile registration (Stillman, 2016).

A final argument advanced in support is that SORN provides another way to punish offenders. But the US Supreme Court has held that SORN laws are constitutional precisely because they were intended to and actually serve a nonpunitive goal, that of improving public safety (Smith v. Doe, 2003). If harm also accrues to registered individuals, that harm may be considered incidental. But what if harm is the *only* outcome? And, in particular, what if this harm accrues to children or to people who were children when they committed their crimes? When we recognize that juvenile SORN serves no purpose other than to further punish children, we should recognize these policies as unconstitutional.

What can be done instead of subjecting children to SORN? A small but empirically strong body of research indicates that children who have engaged in harmful or illegal sexual behavior can be effectively treated (Dopp, Borduin, Rothman, & Letourneau, 2017) and that children who might engage in such behaviors can be effectively prevented from doing so (Letourneau et al., 2017). More research is needed to develop additional strategies, as are broader research dissemination efforts. Government funding for juvenile SORN is estimated to run between $10 million and $100 million annually (Belzer, 2015). These funds should be diverted away from ineffective SORN strategies to the development, validation, and dissemination of effective child sexual abuse prevention and intervention strategies.

In conclusion, given the available data that SORN fails to prevent sexual abuse, interferes with juvenile case processing, and is linked to suicide attempts by and sexual assault victimization of children, there is no apparent justification for its continued use. In response to a request for public feedback on proposed changes to the implementation of federal juvenile SORN requirements, more than a dozen colleagues – including nearly every expert who has published research on juvenile registration – joined me in urging an end to juvenile SORN (Letourneau et al., 2016). As we agreed, there are few areas of US policy where the evidence of failure is clearer or where there is stronger consensus regarding what we should be doing differently. Juvenile SORN is a policy that fails to protect communities and inflicts harm upon those it targets without justification. Therefore, it should be discontinued.

REFERENCES

American Bar Association, Juvenile Justice Committee (2017, May 6). Minutes of the Meeting on May 6, 2017. Available under "Resources" tab at http://apps.americanbar.org/dch/com mittee.cfm?com=cr200000.

Batastini, A. B., Hunt, E., Present-Koller, J., & DeMatteo, D. (2011). Federal standards for community registration of juvenile sex offenders: An evaluation of risk prediction and future implications. *Psychology, Public Policy, and Law*, 17(3), 451–474.

Beitsch, R. (November. 24, 2015). States slowly scale back juvenile sex offender registries. Available at: www.theatlantic.com/politics/archive/2015/11/states-slowly-scale-back-juvenile -sex-offender-registries/433473/.

Belzer, R. B. (2015, September). The costs and benefits of subjecting juveniles to sex-offender registration and notification. *R Street Policy Studio No. 41*. Available at www.rstreet.org /policy-study/the-costs-and-benefits-of-subjecting-juveniles-to-sex-offender-registration-and -notification/.

Bernburg, J. G., & Krohn, M. D. (2003). Labeling, Life Changes, and Adult Crime: The Direct and Indirect Effects of Official Intervention in Adolescence on Crime in Early Adulthood. *Criminology*, 41, 1287–1318.

Caldwell, M. F., & Dickinson, C. (2009). Sex Offender Registration and Recidivism Risk in Juvenile Sexual Offenders. *Behavioral Sciences and the Law*, 27, 941–956.

Caldwell, M. F. (2016). Quantifying the Decline in Juvenile Sexual Recidivism Rates. *Psychology, Public Policy, and Law*, 22(4), 414–426.

Caldwell, M., Ziemke, M., & Vitacco, M. (2008). An Examination of the Sex Offender Registration and Notification Act as Applied to Juveniles: Evaluating the Ability to Predict Sexual Recidivism. *Psychology, Public Policy, and Law*, 14(2), 89–114.

Centers for Disease Control and Prevention. (2012). Youth risk behavior surveillance – United States, 2011 (see Table 64, Page No. 111). Morbidity and Mortality Weekly Report, 61. Retrieved from www.cdc.gov/mmwr/pdf/ss/ss6104.pdf.

Chaffin, M. (2008). Our Minds are Made Up – Don't Confuse us with the Facts: Commentary on Policies Concerning Children with Sexual Behavior Problems and Juvenile Sex Offenders. *Child Maltreatment*, 13, 110–121.

Chaffin, M., Chenoweth, S. A., & Letourneau, E. J. (2016). Same-sex and Race-based Disparities in Statutory Rape Arrests. *Journal of Interpersonal Violence*, 31, 26–48.

Chaffin, M., Letourneau, E. J., & Silovsky, J. F. (2002). Adults, adolescents and children who sexually abuse children: A developmental perspective. In J. Briere, L. Berliner & T. Reid (eds.), *The APSAC Handbook on Child Maltreatment* (2nd ed., 205–232). Thousand Oaks, CA: Sage.

Cleary, H., & Najdowski, C.J. (2019). Awareness of Sex Offender Registration Policies and Self-Reported Sexual Offending in a Community Sample of Adolescents. *Sexuality Research and Social Policy*, 18 (November 18, 2019)

Cocca, C.E. (2004). *Jailbait: The Politics of Statutory Rape Laws in the United States*. Albany: State University of New York Press.

Comartin, E. B., Kernsmith, P. D., & Miles, B. W. (2010). Family Experiences of Young Adult Sex Offender Registration. *Journal of Child Sexual Abuse*, 19, 204–225.

DiCataldo, F. C. (2009). The perversion of youth. New York: New York University Press.

Donovan, P. (1996). Can Statutory Rape Laws be Effective in Preventing Adolescent Pregnancy? *Family Planning Perspectives*, 29, 30–40.

Dopp, A., Borduin, C., M., Rothman, D., & Letourneau, E. J. (2017). Evidence-Based Treatments for Youths Who Engage in Illegal Sexual Behaviors. *Journal of Clinical Child and Adolescent Psychology*, 46(5), 631–645.

Federal Advisory Committee on Juvenile Justice (2007, August). *Annual recommendations report to the president and congress of the United States*. Accessed at www.facjj.org/annual reports/ccFACJJ%20Report%20508.pdf.

Federal Advisory Committee on Juvenile Justice (2016, July). Recommendations of the Federal Advisory Committee on Juvenile Justice. Available at https://facjj.ojp.gov/ojpas set/Documents/FACJJ_Recommendation_OJJDP_July_2016.pdf.

Finkelhor, D., & Ormrod, R. (2001, September). Crimes against children by babysitters. *OJJDP Juvenile Justice Bulletin, NCJ* 189102.

Finkelhor, D., Ormrod, R., & Chaffin, M. (2009, December). Juveniles who commit sexual offenses against minors. *Juvenile Justice Bulletin* (1–12). U.S. Department of Justice, Office of Justice Programs, Office of Juvenile Justice and Delinquency Prevention. Available at www.ncjrs.gov/pdffiles1/ojjdp/227763.pdf.

Finkelhor, D., Shattuck, A., Turner, H. A., & Hamby, S. L. (2014). The Lifetime Prevalence of Child Sexual Abuse and Sexual Assault Assessed in Late Adolescence. *Journal of Adolescent Health*, 55(3), 329–333.

Fix, R. L., Thompson, K. R., Letourneau, E. J., & Burkhart, B. R. (2020). Development and Psychometric Properties of the Concerns about Juvenile Sex Offender Registration and Notification Questionnaire (C-JSORNQ). *Sexuality Research and Social Policy*. https://doi .org/10.1007/s13178-020-00468-4.

Garfinkle, E. (2003). Coming of Age in America: The Misapplication of Sex-Offender Registration and Community-Notification Laws to Juveniles. *California L. Rev.*, 91, 163–208.

Harris, A. J., & Lobanov-Rostovsky, C. (2010). Implementing the Adam Walsh Act's Sex Offender Registration and Notification Provisions: A Survey of the States. *Criminal Justice Policy Review*, 21(2), 202–222.

Harris, A. J., & Socia, K. M. (2016). What's in a Name? Evaluating the Effects of the "Sex Offender" Label on Public Opinions and Beliefs. *Sexual Abuse: A Journal of Research and Treatment*, 28, 660–678.

Harris, A. J., Walfield, S., Shields, R., & Letourneau, E. J. (2016). Collateral Consequences of Juvenile Sex Offender Registration and Notification: Results from a Survey of Treatment Providers. *Sexual Abuse: A Journal of Research and Treatment*, 28, 770–790.

Howell, J. C. (2003). *Preventing & Reducing Juvenile Delinquency: A Comprehensive Framework*. Thousand Oaks, CA: Sage.

Human Rights Watch (2013, May). *Raised on the Registry: The Irreparable Harm of Placing Children on Sex Offender Registries in the U.S.* Washington, D.C.: Human Rights Watch.

Jasani, R. K. (2002). Graves v. State: Undermining Legislative Intent: Allowing Sexually Violent Repeat Offenders to Avoid Enhanced Registration Requirements Under Maryland's Registration of Offenders Statute. *Maryland Law Review*, 61, 739–760.

Kleck, G., Sever, B., Li, S., & Gertz, M. (2005). The Missing Link in General Deterrence Research. *Criminology*, 43, 623–660.

Kupchik, A. (2006). *Judging Juveniles: Prosecuting Adolescents in Adult and Juvenile Court.* New York: New York University.

Letourneau, E. J., & Armstrong, K. S. (2008). Recidivism Rates for Registered and Nonregistered Juvenile Sexual Offenders. *Sexual Abuse: A Journal of Research and Treatment*, 20, 393–408.

Letourneau, E. J., Armstrong, K. S., Bandyopadhyay, D., & Sinha, D. (2013). Sex Offender Registration and Notification Policy Increases Juvenile Plea Bargains. *Sexual Abuse: A Journal of Research and Treatment*, 25, 189–207.

Letourneau, E. J., Bandyopadhyay, D., Sinha, D., & Armstrong, K. S. (2009a). The Effects of Sex Offender Registration Policies on Juvenile Justice Decision Making. *Sexual Abuse: A Journal of Research and Treatment*, 21, 149–165.

Letourneau, E. J., Bandyopadhyay, D., Armstrong, K. S., & Sinha, D. (2010). Do Sex Offender Registration and Notification Requirements Deter Juvenile Sex Crimes? *Criminal Justice and Behavior*, 37, 553–569.

Letourneau, E. J., Bandyopadhyay, D., Sinha, D., & Armstrong, K. S. (2009b). The Influence of Sex Offender Registration on Juvenile Sexual Recidivism. *Criminal Justice Policy Review*, 20, 136–153.

Letourneau, E. J., & Caldwell, M. F. (2013). Expensive, Harmful Policies that Don't Work or How Juvenile Sexual Offending is Addressed in the U.S. *International Journal of Behavioral Consultation and Therapy*, 8, 25–31.

Letourneau, E. J., Caldwell, M. F., Shields, R., Bonner, B., Borduin, C. M., DiCataldo, F., Dopp, A. R., Zimring, F. (2016) Comments on The Supplemental Guidelines for Juvenile Registration Under the Sex Offender Registration and Notification Act; Docket no. OAG 151; AG Order No. 3659-2016 www.njjn.org/uploads/digital-library/Experts%20Respond% 20to%20SORNA%20Proposed%20Guidelines_Final%5B8%5D.pdf.

Letourneau, E. J., Henggeler, S. W., Borduin, C. M., Schewe, P. A., McCart, M. R., Chapman, J. E., & Saldana, L. (2009). Multisystemic Therapy for Juvenile Sexual Offenders: 1-Year Results from a Randomized Effectiveness Trial. *Journal of Family Psychology*, 23, 89–102. PMCID: PMC2710607.

Letourneau, E. J., & Miner, M. H. (2005). Juvenile Sex Offenders: A Case Against the Legal and Clinical Status Quo. *Sexual Abuse: A Journal of Research and Treatment*, 17, 313–331.

Letourneau, E. J., Schaeffer, C. M., Bradshaw, C. P., & Feder, K. A. (2017). Preventing the Onset of Child Sexual Abuse by Targeting Young Adolescents with Universal Prevention Programming. *Child Maltreatment*, 22, 100–111.

Letourneau, E. J., Shields, R. T., Nair, R., Kahn, G., Sandler, J. C., & Vandiver, D. M. (2019). Juvenile Registration and Notification Policies Fail to Prevent First-time Sexual Offenses: An Extension of Findings to Two New States. *Criminal Justice Policy Review*, 30(7), 109–123.

Lieb, R., Quinsey, V., & Berliner, L. (1998). Sexual Predators and Social Policy. *Crime and Justice*, 23, 43–114.

McPherson, L. (2016). The Sex Offender Registration and Notification Act (SORNA) at 10 years: History, implementation, and the future. *Drake Law Review*, 64, 741–796.

Miranda, A. O., & Corcoran, C. L. (2000). Comparison of Perpetration Characteristics between Male Juvenile and Adult Sexual Offenders: Preliminary Results. *Sexual Abuse: A Journal of Research and Treatment*, 12, 179–188.

Morgan, R. (2002). Juvenile justice: Sex-offender registry has complex legal hurdles. *Tulsa World*, February 26, 2002. Available at www.tulsaworld.com/archives/juvenile-justice-sex-offender-registry-has-complex-legal-hurdles/article_f745c52c-8e57-5e34-b51c-5011805e7ac3.html.

Myers, D. L. (2005). *Boys among Men: Trying and Sentencing Juveniles as Adults*. Westport, CT: Praeger.

Najdowski, C. J., Cleary, H. M. D., & Stevenson, M. C. (2016). Adolescent Sex Offender Registration Policy: Perspectives on General Deterrence Potential from Criminology and Development Psychology. *Psychology, Public Policy, and Law*, 22, 114–125.

Nixon, J. W. (2013, July 3). To the Secretary of State of the State of Missouri: Herewith I return to you Senate Committee Substitute for House Bill No. 301. Retrieved on June 19, 2018 from www.house.mo.gov/billtracking/bills131/rpt/HB301vl.pdf.

Oberman, M. (2000). Regulating Consensual Sex with Minors: Defining a Role for Statutory Rape. *Buffalo Law Review*, 48, 703–784.

Pearlstein, L. (2010). Walking the Tightrope of Statutory Rape Law: Using International Legal Standards to Serve the Best Interests of Juvenile Offenders and Victims. *American Criminal Law Review*, 47, 109–128.

Pittman, N., & Nguyen, Q. (2011). *A Snapshot of Juvenile Sex Offender Registration Laws: A Survey of the United States*. Philadelphia, PA: Defender Association of Philadelphia. Available at: https://stoneleighfoundation.org/wp-content/uploads/2018/02/Snapshot-of-Juvenile-Sex-Offender-Registration-Notification-Laws-2011.pdf.

Rinehart, J. K., Armstrong, K. S., Shields, R. T., & Letourneau, E. J. (2016). The Effects of Transfer Laws on Youth with Violent Offenses. *Criminal Justice and Behavior*, 43, 1619–1638.

Roldan, C. (2015, May 25). Columbia lawmaker pushes for juvenile sex offender registry reform. *The Post and Courier*. Retrieved on June 19, 2018 from www.postandcourier.com/article/20150525/PC1603/150529760&ref=email.

Sandler, J. C., Letourneau, E., Vandiver, D. M., Shields, R. T., & Chaffin, M. (2017). Juvenile Sexual Crime Reporting Rates Are Not Influenced by Juvenile Sex Offender.

SMART, Newsroom, www.smart.gov/newsroom.htm (last visited September 30, 2019).

Steinberg, L., & Scott, E. S. (2003). Not guilty by reason of adolescence: Developmental immaturity, diminished responsibility, and the juvenile death penalty. *American Psychologist*, 58(12), 1009–1018.

Stern, P. (n.d.). *An empirically-based approach for prosecuting juvenile sex crimes*. Child Abuse Prosecution Project: Association of Prosecuting Attorneys. Available at www .childabuseprosecution.apainc.org/monographs.

Stevenson, M. C., Najdowski, C. J., & Wiley, T. R. (2013). Knowledge of Juvenile Sex Offender Registration Laws Predicts Adolescent Sexual Behavior. *Journal of Child Sexual Abuse: Research, Treatment, & Program Innovations for Victims, Survivors, & Offenders*, 22, 103–118.

Stillman, S. (2016). The list: When juveniles are found guilty of sexual misconduct, the sex-offender registry can be a life sentence. *The New Yorker, Annals of Justice, March 14, 2016*. Available at www.newyorker.com/magazine/2016/03/14/when-kids-are-accused-of-sex-crimes.

The United Nations. (1989). Convention on the Rights of the Child. *Treaty Series*, 1577, 3.

Timberlake, G. W., & Ague, S. (2016, July 15). Recommendations of the Federal Advisory Committee on Juvenile Justice. Letter to Mr. Robert Listenbee, Administrator, Office of Juvenile Justice and Delinquency Prevention. Available at https://facjj.ojp.gov/ojpasset/ Documents/FACJJ_Recommendation_OJJDP_July_2016.pdf.

Torbet, P., Gable, R., Hurst, H., IV, Montgomery, I., Szymanski, L., & Thomas, D. (1996). *State Responses to Serious and Violent Juvenile Crime*. Washington, DC: Office of Juvenile Justice and Delinquency Prevention.

Trivits, L. C., & Reppucci, N. D. (2002). Application of Megan's Law to Juveniles. *American Psychologist*, 57(9), 690.

Vandiver, D. M. (2006). A Prospective Analysis of Juvenile Male Sex Offenders: Characteristics and Recidivism Rates as Adults. *Journal of Interpersonal Violence*, 21, 673–688.

Vandiver, D. M., & Teske, R. (2006). Juvenile Female and Male Sex Offenders: A Comparison of Offender, Victim, and Judicial Processing Characteristics. *International Journal of Offender Therapy and Comparative Criminology*, 50, 148–165.

Yee, G. (2017, May 8). Should minors convicted of certain sex offenses be required to register as offenders for life? S.C. Supreme Court rules yes as attorneys, researchers cast doubts. *The Post and Courier*. Accessed on September 5, 2017 at www.postandcourier.com/news/should-minors-convicted-of-certain-sex-crimes-be-required-to/article_ee9c39b4-30ef-11e7-b160-176003785d08.html.

Zimring, F. E. (2004). *An American Travesty: Legal Responses to Adolescent Sexual Offending*. Chicago, IL: The University of Chicago Press.

Zimring, F. E., & Hawkins, G. J. (1973). *Deterrence: The Legal Threat in Crime Control*. Chicago, IL: The University of Chicago Press.

CASELAW

In re C.P., 967 N.E.2d 729 (Ohio 2012)
In the Interest of J.B.,107 A.3d 1 (Pa. 2014)
Smith v. *Doe*, 538 U.S. 84 (2003)

STATUTE

South Carolina Code sec. 23-3-430 (2019)

Conclusion

Sex offender registration and notification (SORN) laws were motivated by several basic empirical assumptions: (1) that individuals convicted of sex offenses recidivate at far higher rates than other subpopulations convicted of crimes (they do not) and (2) that to effectively combat sexual offending, especially concerning children, communities need identifying and locational information regarding individuals convicted of sex offenses so that they can take protective precautions (when in reality most sexual offending is committed by persons known to victims and first-time offenders, who by definition are not registrants).

Although the foregoing realities are now widely recognized, several fundamental questions regarding SORN have loomed since its genesis. In particular, does SORN succeed in its avowed goal of reducing sexual offending, in particular among those previously convicted of sexual offenses? If not, or even to the extent that SORN is effective, are there collateral negative effects, on registrants and others (especially family members), that raise concern that it actually has a net crime-increasing impact? Even more practically, is there evidence that community members actually use registry information to protect themselves or others? And what of the financial and other resource costs associated with the operation of SORN laws? Do they warrant continued use of SORN, which can preclude other potentially more useful interventions, as registry populations expand by many thousands of individuals each year (both as a result of adding new registrants and retaining those who, once registered, remain on registries for decades and often their lifetimes)?

Until recently, such basic questions went unanswered, as political leaders, and the communities they represent, eagerly supported the continued operation and growth of SORN systems. As the chapters in this volume demonstrate, however, this knowledge vacuum no longer exists.

Enlightened policy making obliges that we heed findings concerning the impact of governmental programs. In modern America, however, no politician relishes being perceived as "soft" on crime, especially when it comes to individuals convicted of sex crimes – arguably the nation's most reviled and feared subpopulation. Moreover, SORN laws are often named after particular victims, usually children, heightening the political risks for anyone advocating change. Finally, there are the realities that SORN satisfies a common visceral desire to publicly shame and isolate individuals convicted of sex offenses, and that private companies now have a significant financial stake in the implementation of SORN.

Despite these barriers, of late there have been signs that a shift might be underway. Recently, for instance, California, which enacted the nation's first statewide sex offender registry (in 1947), and today boasts the nation's largest registry, overhauled its SORN system. Responding to studies critical of the registry's offense-based, blanket lifetime duration approach, the state adopted a tier-based regime that is based in part on individual risk assessments, requiring ten and twenty years – as well as lifetime – registration, and enhanced the wherewithal of registrants to seek removal from the registry. Meanwhile, several courts recently addressing constitutional challenges to SORN have granted relief, and state government-affiliated entities charged with re-evaluating SORN have recommended changes, signaling an increased willingness to question the status quo.

Sex offender registration and notification, in some shape or form, will not likely disappear in its entirety anytime soon. However, it is hoped that the research provided and discussed in these pages will provide the basis for achieving much-needed evidence-based, constructive change in SORN laws and policies, in the name of reducing the incidence of sexual offending.

Index